THE RUINS OF TIME

THE RUINS OF TIME

*Four and a half centuries of conquest
and discovery among the Maya*

DAVID GRANT ADAMSON

PRAEGER PUBLISHERS
NEW YORK

Published in the United States of America in 1975
by Praeger Publishers, Inc.
111 Fourth Avenue, New York, N.Y. 10003

Library of Congress Cataloging in Publication Data

Adamson, David Grant, 1927–
   The ruins of time.

   Bibliography:
   Includes index.
   1. Mayas--Antiquities. 2. Mexico--Antiquities. 3. Central
America--Antiquities. 4. Archaeology--History. I. Title.
F1435.A54   970.4'2   74-30024
ISBN 0-275-46720-1

Printed in Great Britain

For Isobel Johnston

ACKNOWLEDGEMENTS

I should like to express my gratitude to Ian Graham, Director of the Maya Hieroglyphic Inscription Study, to whose broad knowledge of the Maya and the archaeology of the region this book owes a great deal. Many of my other debts are acknowledged in the form of the bibliography at the back of the book. My thanks are also due to the Peabody Museum, Harvard, and the librarians of the British Honduras Archives for having given me permission to examine their files. Finally, I would like to express my thanks to *The Daily Telegraph Magazine* for their assistance.

CONTENTS

ILLUSTRATIONS

(All photographs by the author, unless otherwise stated.)

Eat, eat, thou hast bread;
Drink, drink, thou hast water;
On that day, dust possesses the earth,
On that day, a blight is on the face of the earth,
On that day, a cloud rises,
On that day, a mountain rises,
On that day, a strong man seizes the land,
On that day, things fall to ruin,
On that day, the tender leaf is destroyed,
On that day, the dying eyes are closed,
On that day, three signs are on the tree,
On that day, three generations hang there,
On that day, the battle flag is raised,
And they are scattered afar in the forest.

The Seventh Prophecy of Chilam Balam,
translated by D. G. Brinton

AUTHOR'S PREFACE

Over two million Maya Indians still live more or less where
they have lived for the past 2,000 years in Central America: on
a large tract of volcanic mountains, tropical rain forest and dry
scrublands that stretches from close to Guatemala's Pacific
coast in the south to the end of the Yucatán peninsula, in
Mexico, to the north. Its eastern extension takes in British
Honduras and the fringe of Honduras and, on the other side,
the Mexican states of Chiapas and Tabasco. To the ordinary
traveller the unity of the area is not obvious. The glum Indians
of the Guatemala highlands in their brightly woven costumes
seem to have little in common with their marginally more
cheerful cousins in the Yucatán, where the men wear Western
clothes and the women sparkling white *huipíls*, thigh-length
smocks brocaded at the hems and necks, with lace-edged petti-
coats covering the rest of them down to the knees. In between
these northern and southern regions lies the central one of the
rain forests, which, although it is perhaps the most important of
all to the Mayanists (the collective term for those who study
the Maya and their works), seems to have very few Indians at
all. However, it does have the Lacandónes, the last unbaptized
Maya, who live in the Chiapas forests surrounded by an air of
mystery considerably more dense than their numbers, which
amount to about 150.

The southern region contributed very little to the civilization
that began to grow in the third and fourth centuries A.D. The
first hieroglyphs may have been cut there, but after that the
altitude or earthquakes and volcanoes, or possibly even a too
benign climate, seems to have deadened the sensitivities and
responses of the people, despite their linguistic and cultural
affinities with the rest of the Maya. It will not concern this book
very much, although, curiously, it is the only part of the Maya

world where the traditions of the ancient ritual year of 260 days are maintained. And anyone who wishes to glimpse the intense inwardness of the Indians can hardly do better than visit some of the small highland towns of Guatemala and watch them at prayer, lightly veiled by the smoke of copal incense that drifts in through the blackened, broken door-windows of the churches, muttering their pleas or confessions from within a few inches of the flickering candles that carpet the aisles. They pray, it seems, to the candles rather than whatever it is they symbolize. They are oblivious even to the cameras and tourists that nowadays form part of their daily lives in the towns. Perhaps an intellectual chasm between the animism of the peasants and the increasingly abstract interests and artistic tastes of the native aristocracy was the prime cause of the collapse of the Classic period of Maya civilization in the ninth century, a disruption followed by a decline which had not ended when the Spaniards arrived in the early sixteenth century. Whatever the cause (or, probably, causes), the Mayanists have been left a wealth of mysteries to speculate with, notably the decipherment of the hieroglyphic writing found on stones and in the four surviving Maya codices, or books.

Writing about the Maya presents peculiar problems. Having reached the end of the seventeenth century in the company of historians and holy fathers, one is suddenly transferred into the hands of eccentrics, antiquarians' and scholars who determinedly march back deep into the past, beyond where one started with legend and history. At the same time, archaeologists and anthropologists rely on technologies, and those are always developing, so one is nevertheless moving with the main impulses of the nineteenth and twentieth centuries. The nearest parallel I can think of is with astronomy, where the creations of thousands of millions of years ago move outwards at near the speed of light while the astronomers pursue them to the edge of the known universe with ever bigger and better telescopes.

X = *sh*
C = *K*, always hard
A = hard *a*, as in bat
AY = like *eye*
U (before a, e, i, o) = *W*, i.e. *uo*, the second month of the
Maya year, is pronounced like *woe*
I = *ee*
Those who are not acquainted with Spanish should note that
the 'acute' accent in many Maya and Spanish names indicates
where the stress is placed, not phonetic value.

GLOSSARY

Anahte	Maya hieroglyphic book
Cacique	local chief
Ceiba	sacred tree, tree of life
Cenote	pool caused by collapse of roof of limestone cave
Chiclero	chewing gum collector
Creoles	white ruling class
Encomienda	feudal estate
Estelero	robber of sites, particularly of stelae
Glyph	a carved hieroglyph, usually contained within square
Ladinos	people of mixed-blood, non-Indians
Milpas	temporary fields created by slash-and-burn methods
Posole	a maize gruel
Sapote	chewing gum tree
Stela	large, upright stone usually, but not always, carved with figures and hieroglyphs
Tamale	maize dough flavoured with chili and herbs, sometimes containing meats, steamed in maize husk
Tortilla	pancake of maize dough, eaten as bread

UNITED STATES

GULF OF MEXICO

MEXICO

PACIFIC

OCEAN

YUCATÁN
PENINSULA

CUBA

BRITISH
HONDURAS

GUATEMALA HONDURAS

NICARAGUA

EL SALVADOR

MAYA AREA

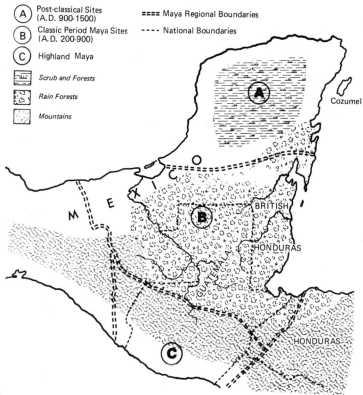

(A) Post-classical Sites
(A.D. 900-1500)

(B) Classic Period Maya Sites
(A.D. 200-900)

(C) Highland Maya

Scrub and Forests

Rain Forests

Mountains

==== Maya Regional Boundaries

---- National Boundaries

Cozumel

M E X I C O

BRITISH
HONDURAS

GUATEMALA

HONDURAS

The Maya world, its region and its context

Towns and archaeological sites

PART I

CONQUEST

The Strength of Darkness

There are no rivers in the northern Yucatán, no gold or other metals, the land is not particularly fertile and the landscape never makes the heart leap. In places it is so flat – and the roads so straight – that the lights of an oncoming car can be seen ten or fifteen miles away. The terrain is a shelf of tertiary and quaternary limestone, with the only notable elevation the long cicatrice of the 300-feet high Puuc hills. From their summits, the folds and crinkles of the land are unseen, houses, churches and temples are lost in a low, scraggy forest with the colour and apparent consistency of Spanish moss. It is a warm, silent vacuum into which nothing, not even the sea, seems anxious to rush. Yet it has always been contested ground, the site of high civilizations. One has only to walk around the great ruins of Chichén Itzá and Uxmal to see that. It was in the Yucatán that the Spaniards encountered a great Indian civilization for the first time, and for thirty years, from the second decade to the fourth decade of the sixteenth century, they struggled to conquer it. At times it was a fairly desultory struggle: the Spaniards were first drawn on, past Yucatán, by the far greater riches of Mexico; later, it was Peru which enticed them away. 'There have come from Castile and the islands,' wrote Bernal Díaz, the robust and humane chronicler of Cortés' conquest of Mexico, 'many Spaniards poor and greedy and with a dog's hunger for wealth and slaves.' The Yucatán was not a good place for satisfying either appetite. It was a bare-bones country, a place where no one made his fortune. Even its conquistadors,

Francisco de Montejo and his bastard son, El Mozo, were the least fortunate of those who subjected the three major civilizations, the Aztecs, the Peruvians and the Maya. The northern Yucatán was the heart of Maya civilization for 500 years before the Spanish arrived. The rainfall is seasonal and fairly good, but the water drops through the limestone surface to gather on the rockbeds beneath. It was not easy to get at without iron tools and as a result settlements gathered around natural wells and cenotes, the deep pools where the limestone had collapsed over the water table. Often the Maya oases were caves that led to underground streams twisting below the limestone, sometimes so deep that the Indians had to descend broad, scaffolded stairways, like those described by John Lloyd Stephens, the nineteenth-century American writer, at Bolonchén; occasionally so shallow that the roots of trees intertwine with the stalactites in the chambers where the water god was worshipped. In these places the water level barely changes between dry season and rainy season, and small blind fish live as mysteriously as elves, swarming through tunnels and waterways that have never been mapped and probably never will be.

The Maya may have been pessimistic and dour, but their world had a depth and complexity for which imagination is not quite the right word. It was too real for that; at times their animistic belief in the magic existence of animals seems almost prosaic. The macaw, with his brilliant plumage, was an agent of the sun god, the jaguar's spotted coat represented the night sky and he was a god of the underworld, which was also dark. Gods existed in all living things, and the Maya had a primitive, hair-raising awe at the wildness around them and its secret ability to communicate with another, higher level of the supernatural. It was the ancestor of the excited shock we sometimes get when a fox runs through a hedge at dawn and stares at us, or a plover twists in flight like a key in the sky. The stars, too, had their associations with the divine world. Polaris, the North Star, was worshipped as Shaman-Ek, god of merchants and travellers. The light of newly risen Venus was particularly unlucky and brought sickness, and its god, Lahun-Chan, was a drunken, ribald gossip associated by some meso-American train of thought with the rabbit, also lecherous and incontinent. Their days, each one a god and his burden, jolt our own instinctive association of days with light and thus a basic sunrise to sunset reckoning. Maya days began with sunset, perhaps because they believed in the ultimate supremacy of darkness where all things began; perhaps, quite simply and logically, a day had departed and a new one was on its way through the night.

Diego de Landa, the sixteenth-century Bishop who can claim to be the first historian and student of the Maya (however inadvertently and disastrously he reached that position) described the physical and social structure of their society:

> 'The natives lived together in towns, well arranged, and they kept the land clean, free of weeds and planted with good trees. The houses were arranged in this way: in the middle of the town were the temples with handsome plazas, and around the temples were the houses of the rulers and priests, and after these came those of the principal people. In this way, the richest and most highly esteemed lived nearest to the temples, and towards the edge of the town, were the houses of the lower classes. And the wells, if there were not many, were near the houses of the lords. They planted their best lands with trees and they sowed cotton, pepper and maize, and they lived thus close together for fear of their enemies, who took them captive. It was because of the wars of the Spaniards that they scattered in the woods.'

In control of this rather geometric society was a theocracy in which the ruler, or Halach Uinic, was subject to the influence of the Head Priest, the Ah-Kin-May, whose power rested on prophets and priests and a retinue of musicians, artists and lowlier functionaries. On the secular side, authority was passed down from the ruler through his military commander to local chiefs (termed caciques by the Spaniards) and councils of elders. At the base of this structure were the common people, the *mazehualob*, and the slaves. It was a rigid, puritanical society, with adultery, rape and the seduction of virgins regarded as among the most serious crimes. Men of rank were sacrificed for their delinquencies; the less exalted of both sexes were shot to death with arrows; and the lower order enslaved.

Their obsession with blood was raw and devoid of any desire for euphemisms of the sort that led to communion wine and the unique sacrifice and resurrection of Christ. Blood for personal offerings was drawn from the genitals (the number of scars on a warrior's penis was equated with his valour; some were so badly mutilated that for a time the Spaniards thought the Maya practised circumcision and therefore must have come from the Middle East), from the tongue (by pulling a cord through it or with a longer fingernail kept specially for snagging a vein at its root), the ears and elbows.

Diego García Palacio, a sixteenth-century official, and others described the ceremony of public sacrifice, which when new year days were being celebrated often involved the slaughter of illegitimate boys between six and twelve. For a day and a night before the sacrifice, conch-shells and drums were sounded and the people assembled. Four priests burnt copal (which smells like a rather sweeter version of the incense used in Roman Catholic churches) and rubber in four braziers and prayed in the direction of the four cardinal points. The Maya, like some orientals, associated the cardinal points with colours; white for the north, red for the east, where the sun rises, yellow, no doubt for the hot sun of the south, and black for the west, where the night begins. At the corners of the earth were four gods, known as *bacabs*, and to complicate things even more for anyone trying to understand the Maya pantheon, many gods seem to have had four versions corresponding with the cardinal points. After the initial ceremonies were completed, the priests retired for private ceremonies and then went to the High Priest's house and brought out the victim, who was paraded four times round the temple plaza. The High Priest and those responsible for the actual business of the sacrifice climbed the steps of the pyramid to the temple while the boy and the secular ruler and leading citizens followed. Only the priests and the boy entered the

Scene of human sacrifice, Temple of the Warriors, Chichén Itzá (from *The Book of Chilam Balam of Chumayel*, trans. by Ralph L. Roys. New edition copyright 1967 by the University of Oklahoma Press)

temple where four priests seized the arms and legs of the victim and stretched him over a convex stone. With the body arched and taut, a priest made an incision in the left breast with a flint knife and tore out the heart and gave it to the High Priest who placed it in an embroidered bag. The blood was collected in four calabashes and sprinkled in four directions. Sometimes, it seems, the heart and any remaining blood were put back in the body, which was then buried in the temple. In other cases, the corpse was flung down the temple steps where it was flayed so that a priest could dance in the skin. Sometimes the flesh was eaten. Military prisoners had a more decorative ending, decked in feathers and ornaments, with strings of cacao beads around their necks and bells on their wrists and ankles. The victorious soldiers practised sexual continence for five to fifteen days before the sacrifices.

Aesthetics and a fierce desire for uniformity dictated the curious practice of deforming children's skulls by pressing them, while the bones and the brains were pliable, between boards, so that the forehead would slope back to a point where it met the flattened back of the head. To judge by Maya art and the intellectual effort that went into the creation of the calendrical system and the hieroglyphic writing, intelligence was not affected. In essence, perhaps, head deformation was no more strange than Spanish friars' tonsures, and possibly both customs had their roots in the connection between mind and spirit. The Maya head, with plumes nodding on its pinnacle, had a sculptural resemblance to the pyramids of the rain forests, with their straight backs and sharply inclined front stairways crowned by temples and carved roof combs. Another deformation, exclusive to girls, was the squint induced by hanging a small ball in front of a baby's eyes. Cross eyes were regarded as a mark of beauty.

Like their heads, the intellectual development of the Maya was also lopsided. Government was an under-nourished science in which they did not approach the achievements of the Aztecs and the Peruvians. The great markets which amazed the Spaniards in Mexico were not to be found in the Yucatán, and despite the *sacbeob*, the 'white roads' built of limestone surfaced with cement, communications were not developed methodically as they were in Peru. Most of the roads were short and seem to have been used mainly for ceremonial purposes. The longest, which led from Yaxuna, near Chichén Itzá, to Cobá, in the eastern Yucatán, ran for sixty miles. It may be symptomatic of the decline of the Maya, that the construction of the roads was explained by myth rather than by history. The roads were built by a magician-king, Ez, who worked only at night. The dawn caught him one day and he was turned to stone. Another story has a familiar ring to it: the devout King Ucan unrolled the roads like a ribbon from a stone on his shoulders until a beautiful princess appeared and beckoned. The chaste king tried to avoid her but, however he turned, she blocked his way, and at last he dropped his stone to make love to her. His magic power vanished and he was unable to pick up his stone again.

The strength of darkness and the power of abstinence, which is a form of sacrifice, make it easy for us to be deceived by civilizations like that of the Maya. The cunning of their art, the volutes that suggest a freeing of the imagination, the intimations of humanism, the delicate hint of compassion in a drawing of a dead prisoner, all distract us from the governing reality of cruel propitiations to appease a malevolent world. Beneath the plumes and the arabesques, there is seen the half-bestial glare of neolithic man, uncertain and fearful. The slaughtered deer had to be asked for forgiveness, wars were often fought not for land or booty but for prisoners to be sacrificed; the word for love was also the word for pain. The only known sport, the ballgame, had associations with violent death. In the forbidding ballcourt at Chichén Itzá, there are carvings showing the captain of the losing team being decapitated, while in games played in lowlier leagues players were often injured and sometimes killed by the solid rubber ball. One feels that psychologically they have not changed very much. All accounts of them speak of their indifference to suffering and their emotional detachment. A nineteenth-century Mexican wrote that their love of spouses, children and parents was barely lukewarm. They contemplated with dry eyes the suffering and even the deaths of those closest to them. Violent robberies and thefts were not crimes they indulged in much. Their faults were a failure to honour contracts, drunkenness and lasciviousness (which presumably had been kept well buttoned up by the hefty punishments of the pre-Conquest era). Folk beliefs tend to be threatening or have a pursed-lips quality about them. The beautiful Xtabay allows men to catch her and then, in allegorical fashion, turns into a bundle of thorns with legs as thin as a turkey's, giving her would-be lover such a shock that he has fainting spells and a high delirious fever. Giants wait astride streets at midnight to throttle passers-by with their knees. 'It is notorious', wrote Diego Lopez de Cogolludo, the seventeenth-century historian of the Yucatán, 'that there are Indian witches who with certain words open roses before their season for blowing, and give them to others to compel women to their wicked purposes: these offer the roses to smell or place them under the pillow, and if the person to whom they are given inhales the scent, she loses her reason for a length of time and calls for him who gave it her and for whom the rose was opened.' Thus roses symbolized not romantic love but lechery, as perhaps they did with us too once upon a time.

2

The Land of Maiam

Between Cuba and the Yucatán peninsula the equatorial currents of the north and south Atlantics reach their destination, surging seven inches above their previous level as they enter the swirling basin of the Gulf of Mexico. This great westward flow, backed by the trade winds, brought Columbus and other explorers to the Americas. Dugout canoes manned by lost Caribs from Jamaica occasionally washed up on the eastern shores of Yucatán bringing news of other lands, and possibly an advance warning of the Spanish arrival, but in the islands there seem to have been no reciprocal stories of the 'Land of Gold' in Mexico. Unaware of the riches close at hand, the Spaniards and Portuguese for a quarter of a century after Columbus landed in the Bahamas in 1492 directed their explorations south, along the coast of Brazil, and towards the isthmus of Panama, where they searched for a route across the great southern ocean to Cathay.

In that period it was Columbus who came closest to discovering the Maya and Mexican civilizations. On his fourth and last voyage in 1502, mentally and physically exhausted and within a few years of death, he sailed his storm-battered flotilla of four ships among the Bay Islands, off Honduras. Shortly after they anchored near the island of Gunaja, a canoe, probably hewn from mahogany or cedar, was seen approaching from the west. It was as long as a Spanish galley, eight feet wide in the middle and it was paddled by a crew of twenty-five Indians. In the middle, under a palm-thatched awning that gave the craft something of the appearance of an outsized Venetian gondola, sat a merchant and his wives and children. All were so stupefied with fear that they did not oppose being brought aboard Columbus' flagship, the *Gallego*. Perhaps what they were seeing was so outside the dimensions of their imaginations and culture that, like the Australian aborigines when Captain Cook's ship sailed into Botany Bay, they felt that neither the ship nor its sailors had any real existence. However, when an attempt was made to examine the material they were wearing, the Indians drew back modestly and rearranged their clothing. Modesty was then, as it is now, a marked characteristic of the Maya. After the naked savagery of the Caribs, such decorum pleased Columbus. What should have been even more impressive was the merchandise, which included copper axes and bells, a crude foundry, cocoa beans (the currency of the land), wooden swords edged with sharp flints, pottery and dyed cloths. For sustenance, there was maize bread and roots and posole, a maize gruel. The canoe had come from the west and there, the merchant explained as well as he could, was the land of Maiam, a place of great wealth. Unlike the Mexicans, the Maya had little gold, but even if there had been gold among the cargo it is doubtful whether Columbus would have done as the trader urged and turned west. He was obsessed with his original mission, the discovery of the sea route to China and the Spice Islands. Columbus sailed east along the Honduras coast to the Gulf of Darien and after a disastrous voyage was finally marooned on Jamaica.

In the end it was neither explorers nor conquistadores who became the first Europeans to land in the Maya realms. Sailing from Darién to Santo Domingo in 1511 a caravel commanded by Captain Hernández de Córdova Valdivia (who was on his way to lay a complaint against a rival in Darién) struck the Vibora shallows near Jamaica and broke up, taking with her 10,000 crowns of gold. Eighteen survivors, including two women, clambered into the ship's boat and attempted to reach Cuba or Jamaica, but without sails and with an inadequate number of oars, the boat drifted west on the equatorial current towards Yucatán. Thirst and exposure killed seven before the remainder were stranded on the island of Cozumel, shrine of Ixchel, the moon goddess, patron of medicine, and famous as a place of pilgrimage among the Maya, many of whom annually made the short journey from the mainland. Narrow white beaches, swamps, lagoons and in places low limestone cliffs constitute the coasts of Cozumel and the Yucatán. Beyond the shores is a thick mat of jungle and bush, in those days broken only by milpas, fields created by slash-and-burn cultivation, and here and there the stuccoed white pyramids and walls of temples. These last so entranced the first discoverers six years later with illusions of the Orient that they named the town of Ecab, close to their first landfall at Cape Catoche, 'El gran Cairo'. The sea is pale green inshore and very clear. At night under a vertical moon the sharks nose across the reefs into the sandy shallows.

Castaways in the literature inspired by wrecks in tropical seas encountered benevolent magicians, helpful spirits and a sustaining nature. Caliban was kept in his place. But in the pagan starkness of Cozumel the moon goddess was a wanton (according to some accounts) who betrayed her husband, the sun, god of music and poetry. The custodian of her shrine, Ah Naum Pat, accepted the survivors as bounty from the sea and sacrificed Captain Valdivia and four others, probably by tearing out their hearts on temples similar to those of 'El gran Cairo'. The bodies were eaten. The remainder were kept in a coop to be fattened for a later festival, but an improved diet may have given them the strength to escape, which they did. One had his head split open with an axe and lived for three years tolerated as a clown. The others were enslaved by a more merciful lord on the mainland. The relentlessly hard work of grinding maize into flour soon disposed of the two women and disease killed all but two of the men. These two were Geronimo de Aguilar, a simple lay brother who held on to his breviary and marked the passage of time, and Gonzalo Guerrero, a tough, crafty soul, whose later history as a renegade who fought against the Spaniards led to him being vilified by the chroniclers as an 'evil person', one who had been brought up among 'low and vile people' and was probably not a Christian.

The story of Aguilar and Guerrero twines through the early years of exploration and conquest like a moral tale designed to exemplify the dual nature of man. Aguilar, long hair tied with a red leather thong, humble and squatting like a slave, was hardly able to speak Spanish when he first encountered his countrymen again after eight years of hewing wood and drawing water. According to legend, he was forced by his Indian master to spend a night alone with a fourteen-year-old temptress equipped with a hammock made for two. 'He determined to conquer his sensuality,' wrote a chronicler, and hold to his promise to God, which was not to sleep with an infidel woman. God's part of the bargain was that chastity would bring freedom. Aguilar's master was so impressed by his slave's restraint that thereafter he entrusted his wife and family to him, which showed, said the chronicler, that even savages recognized virtue. Applied to the Maya, that was an unfair remark since they practised continence with more determination than did the Spaniards. Before an important festival the Maya *élite* would fast and sleep apart from their women for as long as 100 days. Guerrero obtained his freedom on an entirely opposite course. He married a Maya woman of high rank after being accepted as a warrior, gave himself up completely to the native way of life, tattooed his body and drew blood from his tongue in sacrifice. Even allowing for exaggeration in the Spanish accounts, he played a large part in devising strategies which delayed the conquest of the Yucatán Maya until after the two other principal civilizations, the Peruvian and the Aztec, had succumbed. Cortés, who heard of the castaways shortly after he arrived in Cozumel in 1519, sent Aguilar to Guerrero with a message intended to woo him back to the Spanish fold. But Guerrero, who seems at that time to have been in the service of the Lord of Zama, or Tulum, the walled city on the mainland coast which later explorers in a mood of colonialist propaganda compared with Seville, declined to return. Bernal Díaz describes how Guerrero's angry wife berated Aguilar as a slave. Finally Guerrero replied in these terms: 'Brother Aguilar, I am married. I have three sons and am a cacique and a captain in the wars. Go you in God's name. My face is marked and my ears bored. What would those Spaniards think if I went among them? Look at these three beautiful boys. I beg you, give me some of these green beads for them and say that my brother sent them as a present to me from our country.'

After the defeat in 1535 of the first serious attempt by the Spaniards to conquer the Yucatán, the Maya of Chetumal, which is on the borders of what are now Mexico and British Honduras, dispatched Guerrero in command of a fleet of fifty canoes to Honduras to fight the Spaniards there. He was killed by an arquebus shot and his tattooed and almost naked body was found on the battlefield.

Aguilar went on to play a small but important part in the conquest of Mexico. Since he spoke Maya fluently he provided a reliable link between Cortés and his Maya mistress, Malinche, who came to him among a much-appreciated gift to the conquistadores of twenty women donated by the chiefs of Tabasco. 'She was of fine figure, frank manners, prompt genius and intrepid spirit,' wrote Díaz. She spoke Nahuatl, the language of the Aztecs, as well as Maya, and thus, with Aguilar, Cortés had a complete means of communication as he advanced into Mexico.

Unlike the Aztecs, there was among the Maya little or no tendency to confuse white men with the return of Quetzalcoatl, or Kukulcán as he was called by the Maya (the name means 'plumed serpent' in both languages, Nahuatl and Maya); and that may help to explain why Captain Valdivia and his men were not treated as gods or even as the messengers of gods. What Prescott in *The Conquest of Mexico* called 'the low prophetic murmurs with which Nature, in the moral as in the physical world, announced the march of the hurricane' were disregarded by the Maya, addicted though they were to prophesies. According to the Aztecs, Quetzalcoatl, a Mexican god, was tall, fair-skinned, bearded and renowned as an instructor in benevolent pursuits. He lived a bachelor existence in a rather precious house of jadeite, silver, feathers and white and red shells. The jealousy of his rival, the war god, led to him being ousted from Tula, the Toltec capital fifty miles north of the present Mexico City, and he departed for the Gulf of Mexico, where he put to sea on a raft of serpents (the serpent plumed with the feathers of the sacred quetzal bird of the Guatemala highlands was his emblem) for the land of Tlapallan. Quetzalcoatl was also a ruler and the expulsion probably occurred at the end of the tenth century and no doubt reflects the overthrow of a priestly dynasty by the increasingly important Toltec military orders. The arrival of the Spaniards in the Caribbean islands possibly started the 'low prophetic murmurs' of his return to Mexico and they grew steadily in volume until, when Cortés and his army of adventurers finally arrived in Mexico, Montezuma was fatally uncertain whether he had to deal with a god and his followers or men.

The Maya legend of Quetzalcoatl–Kukulcán was significantly different. Kukulcán arrived in the Yucatán in the same year as his expulsion from Tula, and, since Tlapallan means 'Red Land', and as red has religious significance as the symbolic colour of the east, it looks as if Tlapallan and the Yucatán were the same place. Among the Maya, Kukulcán was regarded both as a god and a just statesman. He was never, however, accorded the profound devotion directed to the members of the ancient Maya pantheon. In fact he was blamed for introducing a new and harsher religion which laid strong emphasis on idolatry and sacrifice. The Maya histories had him returning to Mexico several centuries before the Spaniards arrived, and thus they were not nervously awaiting the inauguration of a new era.

The prophetic books of Chilam Balam suggest that there was a prophecy of a new religion and the arrival of strangers among the Maya, but it is difficult to be certain that this is not hind-sight or a self-serving clerical elaboration written in after the conquest. The priests played very skilfully on the Maya belief that everything was ordained. Chilam Balam, which means Jaguar Priest, is believed to have lived at the end of the fifteenth and beginning of the sixteenth centuries, but the documents from which Ralph Roys, the American scholar, made a supremely difficult and often poetic translation, were all com-piled much later, often from the original Maya books written in the hieroglyphic script. These ancient books, or anahtes, were made of fig-bark beaten and rubbed into coarse papers with blocks of chalky limestone shaped like the top of a scrubbing brush, except twice as thick, and grooved on both sides, one fine, the other broader. The stones are found fairly often, so bookmaking must have been a comparatively common occupation. The books were eight inches or more high and as much as eleven feet in length, and the surface was coated with lime so that it could be painted on with clear outlines. The hieroglyphs covered both sides and the book was folded like a screen. One imagines that it was not a system of writing that allowed much in the way of flexibility or literary flourishes. The renderings frequently have the sound of someone ploddingly reading off the square glyphic blocks, each with a self-con-tained message, before setting down the interpretation in Maya written in European script. The most famous of the books is that of Chilam Balam of Chumayel, in which village a Don Juan Josef Hoil made a compilation of local documents in 1782. The book was lost from a library in Mérida, the capital of Yucatán province, in the second decade of this century, and that anything at all of the prophecies has survived is a tribute to nineteenth- and twentieth-century scholars who took care to photograph and copy documents when they happened on them.

As history the books of Chilam Balam occupy much the same position as *Finnegan's Wake* does among novels. They are muddled and obscure and yet at times magnificent. Odd phrases stick in the mind. 'I die,' he said, 'because of the town festival,' which carries an echo, poignant and fatalistic, of an ancient sacrifice. Often, laments over the introduction of a new religion by the Itzá and the Toltecs are inextricably mixed with similar regrets about Christianity. The prophecy of the coming of Christianity (which Chilam Balam delivered stretched out flat on the floor in a trance) is mixed up with the story of a Spaniard called Don Antonio Martinez. Although Roys conjectures he might have lived in the latter half of the seventeenth century, it seems more likely that he was Antonio Martín, a Spanish pirate who went over to the English privateers in the 1590s and apparently became a Protestant. At any rate, he prayed with the English, to the disgust of Spanish prisoners. Like Antonio Martinez in the book, Martín was imprisoned in Havana and escaped. 'Let nine chairs be raised up for us to sit on [said Antonio Martinez]. The sea shall burn. I shall be raised up. There was fire in his eye. Sand and spray shall be raised aloft. The face of the sun shall be darkened by the great tempest.' Nine, incidentally, is the number of departments in the Maya underworld and is a sacred number.

Although the Maya of the classic period had a starting date in time that is equivalent to 3113 B.C. in our chronology, by the time of the conquest they had abandoned the long count and used what is known as the 'short count' which put history and prophecy in recurring cycles of time, with confusing results for everyone, including the Maya. The cycle consisted of thirteen katuns, each katun containing twenty 'short years' of 360 days (very confusingly the Maya had three types of year: the ritual one of 260 days; the tun or 360-day year; and the true solar year which they achieved by adding five unlucky days to the tun). The complete cycle was the equivalent of $256\frac{1}{2}$ of our years. Each supposedly contained an identical sequence of events; so, for example, events in katun 12 would be repeated when the same katun came round again $256\frac{1}{2}$ years later, and so on *ad infinitum*. It was this belief, rather than any addiction to Quetzalcoatl and his legend, which played an important part in determining the history of the Itzás, a Maya people with a

Lord of the Katun (from *The Book of Chilam Balam of Chumayel*, trans. by Ralph L. Roys. New edition copyright 1967 by the University of Oklahoma Press)

messianic instinct as strong as that of the Jews, whom in some ways they resembled. When the Spaniards finally conquered the Yucatán, the Itzás shut themselves off in the rain forests, having decided on the basis of their prophesies that their conversion to Christianity was not due until the end of the current thirteen katun cycle, which gave them another 150 years of paganism and freedom.

One has an immediate problem in attempting to outline the pre-conquest history of the Maya and their achievements. It is that there is no tradition or even legend of what occurred during the Classic Period from the third century A.D. to the ninth. The great cities with their temples and magnificent sculpture are there, deep in the jungles, but they are mute. The populations that sustained them have gone; the inscriptions, apart from those parts with calendrical information, are undeciphered. Chichén Itzá, in the Yucatán, appears to have been part of this cultural flowering when Maya civilization was at its height, but on the whole the Classic Period belongs to the rain forests. All we do know is that it ended during a period of great change and turbulence in Central America in which the

39

enormous ceremonial centre and city of Teotihuacán, in the Valley of Mexico, as well as the temple sites and cities of the rain forests were abandoned. The very conjectural explanations of what happened will have to be left until later, but clearly a ruling *élite* was destroyed and with it vanished the spiritual dynamism of the Classic Period. Such abandonments are by no means unique, but what is strange about the central area of the Maya is the depopulation of a huge region which must once have supported a large number of people. But of all this – the forested temples and the mystery of the departed population – the Spaniards were to know almost nothing for three centuries.

The civilization which they discovered in the Yucatán had been torn apart, repaired, and then torn apart again. It was militaristic, feuding and showed no sign of cultural renovation. In all this it is that extraordinary race the Itzá who were (so far as the Yucatán is concerned) the catalysts. Their histories claim that in the fifth and sixth centuries they founded Chichén Itzá, the largest ceremonial centre in the north, where the so-called Castillo, a temple dedicated to the worship of Quetzal-coatl–Kukulcán, still looms above the sisal plantations and the grey-green plain. For a thousand years the Itzá were victims of what the great American Mayanist Sylvanus Morley has called 'chronological coercion'. Each time a cycle of thirteen katuns (256 years) ended they 'went beneath the trees, beneath the bushes, beneath the vines, to their misfortune', as the books of Chilam Balam put it. Accordingly, in the seventh century they were driven out of, or for some reason forced to leave, Chichén Itzá. Their new home was Chakanputun, which may have been on the west coast at the present site of Champoton, a small town where an equally small river enters the sea. Between it and the Bahia de la Ascención, almost 500 miles away by sea, on the east coast, there are no other rivers in the Yucatán.

After 256 years at Chakanputun, the Itzá returned to Chichén Itzá, bringing with them Kukulcán and perhaps the Toltecs. Whether there was a separate and later Toltec invasion of the Yucatán is to me at least very unclear, although several authorities say there was. On the whole, though, it seems more likely that the Itzá had mixed allegiances; they were Maya, probably Chontal-speaking traders (as Eric Thompson suggests) who came in close touch with the Toltec civilization and may even have been tributaries. Like the Toltecs, they wore the down-flying bird (descents from the sky were rarely accomplished feet first in Meso-American mythology: birds, gods, dogs bringing drought, even Ah Muzencab, the Maya bee god, arrived head first at a sharp angle) on their hats and they worshipped Kukulcán and the plumed serpent.

The Itzá were hated by the old Maya as 'foreigners', 'those who speak our language brokenly', 'tricksters', 'people without fathers and mothers' and 'two-day occupants of the mat', which meant that as upstart holders of authority they had little staying power. 'There was no great teacher, no great speaker, no supreme priest when the change of rulers occurred at their arrival,' say the books of Chilam Balam. 'Lewd were the

Itzá priest (from *The Book of Chilam Balam of Chumayel*, trans. by Ralph L. Roys. New edition copyright 1967 by the University of Oklahoma Press)

priests, when they came to be established here by the foreigners.'
The last is a reference to the sexual aspects of Toltec religion
and the introduction of stone phalluses, such as those which
can be seen superimposed on a building of the Classic Maya
Period at Chichén Itzá. Such practices shocked the puritanical
orthodox Maya, with whom religious eroticism seems to have
been limited to the sexual symbolism of the frangipani flower
(still used as church decorations) and blood sacrifices drawn
from the penis.

Whatever the links, Chichén Itzá became a Toltec shrine
erected on an earlier Maya one. The art that decorates its
buildings is harsh and vigorous. Jaguars and eagles devour

Eagle devouring heart,
Toltec art, Chichén Itzá

hearts; warriors decorate innumerable square pillars and the
atmosphere is stark, military and cruel. The plumed serpent of
Kukulcán, who here seems to have given up his earlier benevolent pursuits, is found on stairways, walls and hovering over a
sacrificial victim, waiting to accept his heart.

Tatiana Proskouriakoff, of Harvard's Peabody Museum, has
compared the Classic Period with the rise of light and reason in

classical Greece, and the later post-Classic Period in the Yucatán to the supremacy of Rome, followed by the barbarian invasion. But whether the developments in the north were all downwards is hard to say. Perhaps militarism and the organization and technology it requires is as necessary to human evolution as religion and astrology. The Itzá, in the last phase of their domination, founded a league composed of three cities: Mayapán, Chichén Itzá and Uxmal, the impressive Maya city ruled by the Xiu, a family of Toltec-Itzá nobles. Mayapan, which became the leader of the trinity, is nowadays little more than a melancholy heap of rubble, but it is evidence that the Maya had advanced socially in that they were able to build fortified towns in which people gathered together for secular instead of religious reasons. At the time of its destruction in the middle of the fifteenth century, Mayapan covered more than two and a half square miles and had a population estimated at over 12,000.

Anyone who reads two standard works on the Maya, Thompson's *The Rise and Fall of Maya Civilization* and *The Maya* by Michael Coe, will find that their dating of one important event in what passes for Maya history differs by a quarter of a millennium. The confusion is caused primarily by the recurrence of similar dates within different katun cycles. It is impossible to say with any pretence of accuracy when or even what happened in the last 500 years before the Spaniards arrived. Because it sounds logical, I have taken the chronology worked out by Roys (with slight alterations to allow for a different, more precise correlation of Maya dates with Christian ones) who, in turn, based his reckoning on the First Chronicle of Chilam Balam.

The date on which the Mayanists differ is that on which Hunac Ceel, a strongman who came from Mayapan, threw the Itzá out of Chichén Itzá. It is a fairly pedantic issue and without going into rival arguments, I shall assume that this occurred around 1205 A.D. Ceel had made his way to the top in the first place by an extraordinary bit of opportunism during a pilgrimage to the Well of Sacrifice, the deep, gloomy cenote at Chichén Itzá. The victims had been thrown in from the temple platform seventy feet above the surface but none had returned to give the god's message to the priests. Usually at least one survived the fall and swam to the side to cling on until he or she was hauled up. So firm was the belief in these subaqueous exchanges that a girl who threatened to ask the gods to send drought and crop failures, instead of the reverse, was rejected as a sacrifice. For no one to reappear was a bad omen, and Hunac Ceel leaned over the southern rim of the cenote and determined that only he could receive the message. Thereupon he plunged in. The gist of what the gods were waiting to tell him was that he should rule Mayapan. Once in power Ceel appears to have instigated a civil war which began with the seizure of the wife of the ruler of Izamal by the ruler of Chichén Itzá. Aided by Toltec mercenaries (who probably introduced the bow and arrow as well as the spear-thrower to Maya warfare), Ceel cleared Chichén Itzá and then turned his attention to Izamal, which was also crushed. After almost half a century 'beneath the vines' the dispossessed Itzá seized Mayapan which, under the rule of a family called the Cocoms, established suzerainty over the whole of the Yucatán and held on to its power for more than 200 years. The Xius of Uxmal (also Itzás) and other nobles were forced to live in Mayapan, their lives guarantees that their subjects would deliver tribute to the Cocoms. In 1461 or thereabouts, when in England the Wars of the Roses were in full bloom, the hostage Xius gathered together a secret conspiracy of Maya nobles who overthrew the Cocoms and sacked Mayapan. Only one Cocom survived: he was on a trading visit to Honduras. A blood feud had been started that was to provide the Spaniards with incidental but important assistance.

The various lords who had been obliged to live in Mayapan picked up their sacred anahtes and departed to build townships and temples of their own. 'The whole country appeared to be but one town,' wrote Bishop Diego de Landa one hundred years later in *Relacion de las Cosas de Yucatan* (*Account of Events in Yucatán*). But while this suburbanization was in full swing, an appalling hurricane of 'four winds', which means that it swirled from all quarters, struck the Yucatán, levelling houses and trees, killing the game, so that the peninsula no longer deserved its old name of 'The Land of Deer and Turkey'. In 1500 there came a plague described as 'the blood vomit', and that too was an omen of the disaster moving towards the Maya on the equatorial current.

3

The Conquest Begins

A world beyond their comprehension overwhelmed the Maya. In the books of Chilam Balam one can hear the voice of paganism and the old society speaking out of the twilight. All was lost; the inevitable had happened as it always did, but this time it was not the Toltecs (who after all lived on much the same intellectual, emotional and technological level as themselves and therefore could be assimilated) or some other race of Indian conquerors who arrived. It was a force which seemed to demand simultaneously their slavery and their elevation to a more abstract level of spirituality.

'Then with the true God, the true Dios', said the books of Chilam Balam, 'came the beginning of our misery. It was the beginning of tribute, the beginning of strife with blow-guns, the beginning of strife by trampling on people, the beginning of robbery with violence, the beginning of forced debts, the beginning of debts enforced by false testimony, the beginning of individual strife, a beginning of vexation, a beginning of robbery with violence . . .'

The Maya had no doubt it was the true God who had arrived but, like their own gods, he brought misery more often than happiness. A legal system as ambiguous in its aims as the Church that extended God's mercy forced them to work to pay off debts, to fulfil obligations that were the inventions of a greedy, violent and yet immensely superior civilization. Nothing was stable. They were trampled into their stony land by the conquerors' horse and they were shot down by 'blow-guns', which since Maya blow-guns are lethal only to small birds is surely a mistranslation for fire-arms.

The conquistadors arrived like waves from ships passing on to more important destinations. For three years in succession, from 1517 to 1519, they landed in north-eastern Yucatán and then brushed along the shore as they moved westwards towards Mexico. The first discoverers set forth from Cuba in three ships in February 1517 under a rich hidalgo, or nobleman, Francisco Hernández de Córdoba, and sailed towards the setting sun in search of new lands. Bruised by a great storm, they arrived after twenty-one days at Cape Cotoche, a name derived from the Indians replying to Spanish requests for information about where they were with the phrase '*cones cotoche*', come to our houses. The origin of the name Yucatán may have more symbolism than this initial misunderstanding. It appears to be a corruption of '*Ci-u-than*', we don't understand you.

With the white temples of 'Gran Cairo', or Ecab, beckoning them, Córdoba and his men landed and were soon ambushed in a thicket. Aguilar, the enslaved castaway, said later that Guerrero had organized the attack, but this seems unlikely. The ambush was fought off and the Spaniards retreated to their ships impressed by the temples, the idols and some golden birds and fish they had found. Sailing close to the shore, they travelled slowly westward until need for water forced them to land at what is now the pleasant sea-port of Campeche. There, Father Alonso Gonsalez had sufficient time while the casks were being filled to celebrate the first mass on Central American soil. At the same time, the Spaniards had an opportunity to note that sacrifices were part of the native religion. The newly spilled blood they saw in the temples filled them, said Bernal Díaz, who took part in all three of the first voyages, with 'surprise and horror'. Priests, their hair clotted and stiff with human blood, fumigated the Spaniards with incense and gave them a clear warning to go, which they did. That the Maya knew who had arrived was obvious from the fact that they pointed to the east and said 'Castilian'. Farther down the coast at Champoton, the traditional landing place of Quetzalcoatl, the plumed serpent, disaster overtook the expedition. A rapidly summoned army attacked and killed fifty-seven Spaniards, forcing the survivors to flee in sinking boats. Perhaps it was on that occasion that the Indians dressed in the clothes of dead Spaniards and danced on the sands, mimicking them as in a masque. The little fleet turned towards Cuba, where Córdóba, who had twelve wounds, died shortly after a voyage made more terrible by thirst. The idols the discoverers had taken from 'El Gran Cairo' were examined by the sagest minds in Havana and it was agreed that they must have been carried to the new land by Jewish colonists fleeing after the destruction of Jerusalem by Titus and Vespasian.

The expedition under the command of Juan de Grijalva in the following year, 1518, was larger and better organized. Driven south by the currents, it missed Cape Catoche and made landfall on Cozumel, where the inhabitants of the settlements fled. Despite the presence of two Spanish-speaking Maya captured on Córdoba's voyage, little contact was made with the Indians (and no rumour reached Grijalva of the existence of the castaways, Aguilar and Guerrero) and the fleet sailed peacefully around the peninsula until it reached Champoton, where, in a battle fought amid a swarm of locusts, Córdoba and the other victims of the earlier landing were avenged with the aid of the falconets (small artillery pieces) the Spaniards brought ashore. A greyhound was left behind by accident and not recovered until a year later when Cortés' expedition found him fat and contented on a diet of rabbits and deer. Grijalva sailed on into the Gulf of Mexico to richer lands where the beckoning name 'Mexico' began to be heard and the explorers received small presents of gold from the Indians. Fast messengers had carried news of the Spanish arrival to Montezuma, at his capital Tenochtitlán, within twenty-four hours, and his local governor was ordered to exchange gold for green glass beads and make general inquiries about the strangers who might or might not be gods. The recipient of this first instalment of Mexico's treasures was Francisco de Montejo who, as the conqueror of the Yucatán, never again came quite so close to vast riches.

The 1519 expedition under Cortés brought with it 500 soldiers in eleven ships, ten brass cannons as well as falconets, sixteen horses (all of which Bernal Díaz was able to describe, and give the names of their owners, when he wrote his history fifty-three years later) and a Negro slave, who was as valuable as the horses. Cortés' mission was not to seek land; it had no purpose other than to obtain gold. Cortés, after landing at Cozumel in February 1519 (the significance of February as the month of arrival for expeditions is that it is the coolest and driest time of the year in much of the Caribbean), held a parade of his troops and reassured the Indians by paying for food and articles taken from them. Pedro de Alvarado, the brutal conqueror of the Maya in the highlands of Guatemala, was severely rebuked for his thefts. After a month, during which Aguilar was recovered from his Indian master, the fleet set sail for the Land of Gold, landing in the Maya province of Tabasco on the way. It was there, at Centla, that Cortés fought his first important battle on the new continent. Unimpressed by the presence of King Charles the Fifth's notary and the conquistador's explanation that His Majesty had been given the land by Pope Alexander VI, the Indians prepared for battle, summoning their forces with conch-shells and drums. The Maya were slaughtered by the hundreds and Cortés claimed the country for the king by making three cuts with his sword in a ceiba, the Maya sacred tree, and announcing he would fight anyone who challenged his possession. The king's notary stood by to make sure that no legal requirement was left out. Desperate in the face of such a curious foe, the Indians attacked again, throwing up dust to hide the losses caused by cannons and crossbow bolts, and Cortés was obliged to bring his cavalry into action to decide the day. Three horsemen and five horses were killed but the infantry casualties were light, despite the wounds inflicted on most of the men. As was their custom, the Spaniards dressed their injuries and those of the horses with unguents of fat taken from Indian corpses. Cortés, still intent on practising conciliation, persuaded the Indians to send an embassy of chiefs to surrender the country. A demonstration of the conquerors' weaponry was mounted for their benefit. Both the cannons and the horses were still angry, it was explained. A shot was fired, alarming the chiefs with the explosion and the sound of the ball landing in the woods. Shortly afterwards a stallion, inflamed by the scent of a nearby mare, was led up, terrifying the chiefs still further with his rearing and neighing.

It was not until almost ten years after Córdoba made the first voyage to the Yucatán that its conquest was given serious consideration. In 1526 Francisco Montejo obtained permission from King Charles V, whose court he was visiting as Cortés' emissary, to undertake the conquest. A *capitulación*, or contract, was drawn up under which Montejo contributed the money for the venture and the monarch gave his blessing. From the start there was recognition that the peninsula was poor. Accordingly, only a tenth instead of the normal fifth of precious metals recovered there was to be paid to the court. Montejo was granted the title of Adelantado, civil and military Lord of the Province, to be held by him and his heirs in perpetuity, numerous salaried posts including the command of two fortresses he was to build, a holding in perpetuity of ten square leagues of land which were to be neither the best nor the worst in the province, exemption from all import and export taxes, and four per cent of all income originating within the province for himself and his heirs. As the outlay and the risks involved in such an expedition were enormous, the potential profits and the honours were not quite as unreasonable as they might seem at first sight. Montejo, who had married a rich widow of Salamanca during his visit to the court, sold his wife's jewels and gathered together a fleet of four ships with 380 soldiers (some of whom paid their own way in return for a share in the profits; others were given credit by Montejo), priests, a surgeon, two pharmacists, a silversmith and that essential member of all Spanish expeditions, a lawyer.

Montejo was in his forties when he launched on the central episode of his life. I have seen no portrait of him, and, as there were no chroniclers with his expeditions, there are no first-hand descriptions. He remains a rather vague figure, brave, physically strong and a skilled courtier, but not terribly clever or skilful as a soldier. Although he had overall responsibility for the conquest, he did not complete it. That was left to his son, El Mozo (meaning 'The Younger'; he was also Francisco), born out of wedlock to the daughter of a rich Sevillian and legitimized. El Mozo, as tough and brave as his father, was not yet twenty when he first landed in the Yucatán.

As with all colonial conquests, there were some high motives and a very heavy accretion of base ones. King Charles, Emperor of the Holy Roman Empire, stressed the religious purpose of the conquest in the capitulación. The conquistadors usually put things more ambiguously: 'We came here to serve God and the King and to make ourselves rich.' The Spanish Empire was full of contradictions. Slavery had been formally prohibited in 1500 but in practice the encomienda system, which granted individuals feudal landlordship over the Indians (who provided labour in return for religious instruction) was little different from slavery. It was an issue which occupied decades of argument. Private enterprise carried out the conquests but monarchical absolutism prevailed. The Church sanctioned the conquests for the sake of gaining souls yet took a long time to decide whether Indians had quite the same sort of souls as Spaniards. Brutality and solicitousness, contempt and affection, scholarship and a desire to erase all pre-Conquest beliefs travelled side by side. Northern Europeans and Americans are inclined to think of the conquests as unparalleled examples of greedy hypocrisy, but the truth that emerges from their histories is that while few races could have outdone the Spaniards in avarice, they were also considerably more intellectual, imaginative and adventurous than other nationalities of that time.

The Spaniards who came to America as soldiers were a new breed of men, reasonably literate for the most part, often gullible and superstitious, and imbued with a Renaissance conviction that the individual could effect his own destiny. Their faith and their militarism was the product of 250 years of warfare against the Moors in Spain. Like Don Quixote they often confused romantic nonsense with reality, so that even Cortés was inclined to believe tales of an 'Island of California' where Amazonians conceived from the wind and slaughtered their male offspring. His kinsman, Francisco Cortés, was sent on an expedition to discover these unnatural ladies. Columbus is said to have been inspired by the prophecy in Seneca's *Medea* that a new Thypis, Jason's guide, would exploit the ocean's loosening of its shackles and end Ultima Thule's position as the last of the lands. Among the conquistadors, a favourite book was Montalvo's *Amadis the Gaul*, first printed in 1508, although the story had been popular for some time before that. Amadis was tailored to fit the secret dreams of the new Spanish adventurer. He was the child of a covert affair between Perion, King of Gaul, and the Princess Elisena, who floated the new-born child out to sea in an ark to conceal the birth. Rescued by a Scottish knight, he was raised in the Scottish court. At the precociously early age of twelve he fell in love with the Princess Oriana, daughter of Lisuarte, King of Great Britain, but his obscure origin made him unworthy of her hand. So he was obliged to set out on a round of the traditional adventures of romantic chivalry until he had slaughtered monsters, escaped from bewitched islands and overcome other knights in combat in sufficient quantity to satisfy King Lisuarte that he was *de facto* noble and eligible to marry Oriana. The conquistadors' first sight of Tenochtitlán drew this reflection from Bernal Díaz: '. . . we were amazed and we said it was like the enchanted things related in the books of Amadis because of the huge towers, temples and buildings rising from the water and all of the masonry. And some of the soldiers even asked whether the things we saw were not a dream.'

At a more sophisticated level, the document which perhaps best indicates the Spanish approach to conquest and its ethical problems is the Requerimiento, a sort of Holy Roman Riot Act, which had to be read to the natives three times by the leader of the expedition or his representative, with translations into the local language, before hostilities could be opened. It is in most respects a thoroughly ludicrous document, drawn up before the American conquests and delicately blending the requirements of Roman Law with those of the Church. The about-to-be-conquered were informed that they were vassals of the Crown and that if they accepted their situation without bloodshed they would not be enslaved, since slavery was a condition that could only be imposed on them after a 'just, legal and necessary war'. How they had suddenly become vassals was explained by outlining the Book of Genesis and its account of how the races multiplied and scattered. The fact that some had apparently moved as far as the Yucatán and other places did not exclude them from the authority of St Peter, whom God had appointed head of the entire human race, and his successors in Rome. As a result, the Pope was legally entitled to confer sovereignty over 'the islands and mainland of the ocean sea' on the kings and queens of Spain. The Requerimiento pointed out that other peoples had accepted this situation without resistance and had become Christians. As long as they acceded without warfare, they would be left 'free and unmolested' and in possession of their wives, children and property. The bleak alternative was left until the end.

'If you do not do this, however, or resort maliciously to delay, we warn you that, with the aid of God, we will enter your land against you with force and will make war in every place and by every means we can and are able to employ, and we will then subject you to the yoke and authority of the Church and of their Highnesses. We will take you and your wives and children and make them slaves, and as such we will sell you and them, and will dispose of you and them as their

Highnesses order. And we will take your property and will do you all the harm and evil we can, as is done to vassals who will not obey their lord, or who do not wish to accept him, or who resist and defy him. We avow that the deaths or harm which you will receive thereby will be your own blame and not that of their Highnesses, nor ours, nor of the gentlemen who come with us'*

Armed with his capitulación and the Requerimiento, the Yucatán's new ruler sailed in 1527 to that traditional landing place, Cozumel, where, with lawyer and priests in attendance, he was given a friendly welcome. The island was not his objective, however, and after a few days the expedition moved on Xelhá, on the east coast. A base was established close to a rocky basin into which the sea rushes and is calmed and where, now as then, fish as brilliant as the Lady Montejo's squandered jewels hang between the surface and the sand.

---

* Translation from *The Conquest and Colonisation of Yucatan, 1517–1550*, by Robert Chamberlain (N.Y.: Octagon Books).

4
The Maya Crushed

The conquest of the Yucatán brought Montejo little wealth, a great deal of disgrace and not enough fame. The first two invasions were failures, and by the time his son, El Mozo, had completed the third, twenty years later, the system under which he had been granted the capitulación was obsolescent. The power of the conquistadors waned as royal and ecclesiastical control grew. For both Montejo and El Mozo the grant of titles and concessions in perpetuity proved a mockery. Alvarado the Cruel, in Guatemala, outmanoeuvred and threw Montejo out of Honduras, which he had conquered; ecclesiastical opposition lost him the rich province of Tabasco and the Rio Dolce area, where present-day British Honduras, Guatemala and Honduras meet on the Caribbean; and finally he was stripped of the governship of the Yucatán.

The east coast of Yucatán is perhaps the last place from which anyone should try to launch a conquest. The rains are heavy enough to make the trees and undergrowth dense, and there are large areas of swamps infested with snakes and mosquitoes. Numerous rather undistinguished ruins show that there was once a well-established population in the area, but only two towns, Tulum and Chetumal, were of much importance, and even they were provincial by comparison with those of the north and north-west. The Indians of Xelhá (renamed Salamanca de Xelhá in honour of Montejo's home town) became gradually more disenchanted as Spanish demands for food and supplies continued. At the same time, the diseases bred in the swamps began to take their toll. Montejo, following the precedent set by Cortés in New Spain, burnt the two remaining ships of his fleet so that there was no way of escape for mutineers, and moved north on an exploratory tour. Thanks to the good offices of Naum Pat (possibly but not certainly the same one who sacrificed Captain Valdivia and his men), the cacique of Cozumel, who happened to be on the mainland for a sister's wedding, Montejo's march along the coast was peaceful during its first stages. The Adelantado, who still maintained a brave belief that there must be some gold in the Yucatán, was offered gold ornaments as gifts but feigned a lack of interest for fear the Maya would perceive his and his men's passion for it and hide their treasures away. The Indians, who showed an early tendency to worship horses, as they did tapirs and other creatures, turned dugout canoes into water troughs and spread out heaps of fodder as the little army moved along the trails. It was not until the town of Chauaca that there was a hostile reaction to the reading of the Requerimiento and the Spaniards were forced to do battle. The townspeople fled secretly during the night while the soldiers were asleep and then returned under arms the next morning as the Spaniards struggled to prepare defences. Montejo saved the day by charging into the mass of the enemy on his horse and holding them at bay until his men were ready. The Indians were defeated but ten or twelve Spaniards were killed, some because, lulled by the tranquil atmosphere of the march, they had slept apart from the main party. With the chastened Indians of Chauaca pressed into service as porters, the army moved inland towards Ake, slaughtering several hundred of the inhabitants who came out in red war paint and whirling rattles in an attempt to intimidate the new enemy. No Spaniards were lost on this occasion but several horses and dogs were killed, demonstrating that any mixed feelings about their divinity did not amount to a safeguard.

The Battle of Ake ended Maya resistance in the north-east of the peninsula, but it also marked the point at which the

Adelantado was forced to beat a retreat to his base at Xelhá. Disease, injuries, exhaustion and shortage of supplies had taken their toll. After receiving the submission of the cacique of Loche, who addressed Montejo disdainfully through a thin cloth held in front of him by attendants as he sat in his litter (an insult the Adelantado accepted with good-humoured resignation, possibly because he did not want to risk another battle), the Spaniards turned back. As many as two-thirds of those who set out may have been lost. Spanish armies were small, and the attrition rate through disease and battle so high that few lived to enjoy the riches they sought. Bernal Díaz, for example, estimates that in the disastrous five days of fighting in and around Tenochtitlán in June 1520, during the conquest of Mexico, 870 of the 1,300 Spaniards engaged were 'killed and sacrificed'.

But despite occasionally heavy losses in battle, it was disease that caused the most Spanish deaths. If the Indians were vulnerable to the European ailments their conquerors imported (smallpox is believed to have descended on the Central American mainland with the first expeditions and malaria may have arrived at the same time), so to an equal extent were the Spaniards open to indigenous diseases. These last must have included various forms of dysentery and very probably yellow fever, which may have been one of the plagues mentioned in the Maya chronicles. It is not endemic now, but as recently as the late 1950s it almost decimated the howler monkey population in the Petén.

Disease, though, was never quite powerful enough as an ally to swing the fortunes of war. Armed with stone age weapons, the Maya faced gunpowder, powerful crossbows, cavalry and above all steel. No weapon they possessed was capable of hewing off limbs in the way the Spanish swords did. Never before, wrote a Spanish historian, had they received such 'fierce wounds'. Their attempts to block the Spanish advance with half-moon shaped palisades woven from branches, called *albarradas*, failed pathetically as the weight of the horses pushed them over and swords, used like machetes, sliced through the wood. Even the thickness of the forest did not always save the Indians, since the Spaniards had brought with them dogs, like the modern Great Dane, which could scent and attack them in the bush. The spears, the clubs and the wooden swords edged with obsidian and flint were unpleasant but not very formidable; in fact, the only weapons the Spaniards feared were the flint arrow heads, since these shattered against bone and caused gangrenous wounds. Other unpleasantnesses were the traps left in the path of the oncoming army. One of these was made of thorns poisoned by being left in the body of a fox; death or permanent lameness often followed a long and agonizing illness. The Spaniards soon found that the heat and the agility needed to fight in the forests made steel body armour undesirable. They adopted the quilted cotton worn by the Indians for protection. This was wound round the body in twisted strips and was effective against stone weapons; horses and cavalrymen wore it as long skirts. The Maya of the Yucatán were strongly muscled but slight, usually about five feet three inches in height. The Spaniards were generally heavier and taller than their adversaries; many were large, red-bearded men from Castile and the north. Above all they were audacious in battle. The Maya possessed the soldierly virtues of fatalism and a high threshold of pain, but they were not very imaginative. By tradition, they fought to capture prisoners for sacrifice, since the gods demanded hearts and it was clearly better to obtain them from an enemy than from one's own people. Moreover, the braver the warrior, the more acceptable the sacrifice. The tactics of capture were entirely unsuited to battle against the Spaniards, but the Indians were slow learners. The only guile demonstrated during the first stage of the conquest came from Guerrero when, after the retreat to Xelhá, Montejo the elder split his forces (which had been reinforced by the arrival of a ship with fresh men) for an advance southwards in search of a better port. A letter from Montejo requesting the renegade to aid the king's representative was returned with a reply written on the back in charcoal. He had no freedom but he was 'a good friend' of the Spaniards, and in a sense he may have been, since the Adelantado's men escaped from a potentially dangerous situation without much loss of life. Montejo had gone by sea, while his lieutenant, Alonso Davila, marched on an inland route with a small force of forty men. There was no communication between the two groups and when Montejo, embroiled in warfare on the coast, received a message from an Indian saying that the inland expedition had perished, he accepted it as true and retired. Davila was given a similar message about Montejo and his forces, and he began a slow withdrawal which the Indians did not impede.

For a surprising number of years Montejo was able to convince the Court that all was going well despite a lack of gold and other evidence of success. He garnered offices elsewhere and began to concentrate on more profitable parts of Central America, leaving the subjugation of the Yucatán to El Mozo, still hardly more than a boy but nevertheless evidently a person of character with considerable powers of leadership. The stories of Spanish forays tend on the whole to be rather similar: names, places, dates and events run into a confusing blur, so that in the end it is rather like driving at high speed through the northern Yucatán bush. Very little stands out. One has an impression of anguish, terrible suffering, a nightmarish sense of men lost in a totally hostile and alien forest. One major expedition sent off to conquer Chetumal (on the borders of the Yucatán and British Honduras) ended up by fleeing in canoes to Honduras. Almost incredibly, they took with them their five remaining horses. The immense importance attached to horses is demonstrated by the fact that when one died at sea, the body was immediately thrown overboard so that there would be no temptation to the hungry survivors to slaughter the others for food. As horses often meant the difference between victory and defeat in war with the Indians, perhaps such care is not surprising. The expedition's Indian paddlers, who were kept in stocks like galley slaves, were all lost when a storm swept the canoes out to sea while the Spaniards (presumably with the paddles in their safe-keeping) and the horses were on shore. Eventually, the expedition reached safety in Honduras on foot.

But it was at Chichén Itzá that the most remarkable episode of the conquest took place. There, in 1532 or 1533, El Mozo established the new city of Ciudad Real on the advice of a Maya ally elsewhere who obviously wanted him out of his territory. The massive ruins were suitable for fortification and although there was no longer any city there, the famous Well of Sacrifice made it a place of pilgrimage, a macabre Lourdes, for the whole of the north. There was, moreover, a large population in the vicinity to provide labour for the encomiendas El Mozo and his advisers hoped to create. El Mozo established his offices in one of the plazas and impressed Indians to put up wood and thatch buildings. The associations of the Well of Sacrifice hardly made it inviting as a source of drinking water, but nearby, in the centre of the ruins, there was another excellent source of supply, the cenote of Xtoloc. Anyone who walks around the ruins will find it easy to imagine that the Spaniards centred their defences close to the nunnery (so called because of a tradition that it housed Maya nuns), which with its galleries and steep walls would have made an excellent barracks. Alternatively, they may have used the castillo, the temple pyramid which dominates the heart of the ruins. The Spaniards would hardly have noted the subtleties of this building: a total of 365 steps to the top register the days in the solar year; fifty-two panels on the terraces symbolize the number of years it takes for the solar and ritual years to complete the cycle known as the Calendar Round; and on each of the four sides the nine terraces are divided by a stairway to make eighteen sections, representing the number of months in the Maya year.

The passivity with which the Maya accepted the encomienda system introduced by El Mozo did not go very deep. He was in his office one day when Nacun Cupul, the cacique of Chichén Itzá, seized his sword and attempted to kill him. A Spanish guard sliced off the assailant's arm and Cupul was killed. The

Annex to the House of the Nuns as drawn by Catherwood. The façade is the richest example of classic Maya ornamentation in Chichén Itzá (from Volume II of *Incidents of Travel in Yucatán*).

revolt that followed was put down, but that was only a short respite. The Maya forces gained strength steadily until the one military asset they had, their overwhelming numbers, was concentrated against the Spanish garrison. They made no attempt to rush the fortification; an attempt by the Spaniards to break out was a bloody failure.

It was during this siege among the ruins that a curiously chivalrous combat, a sixteenth-century High Noon, took place. A Spanish crossbowman and a Maya archer, both excellent shots, had for some time tried to kill the other, but neither would allow himself to be caught off guard. One day, however, the Spaniard pretended that he was unaware of the Indian and knelt down. The Indian's arrow hit him in the hand and, according to Bishop Landa, separated his arm bones. At the moment he was hit, the Spaniard released his crossbow bolt and hit the Indian in the breast. Knowing that he was dying but determined that it should not be said a Spaniard killed him, the archer cut a long, flexible vine and then hanged himself 'within sight of all'.

Desperately short of food and with the number of men dwindling daily, the Spaniards sought for a gap in the Indian perimeter through which they could slip away secretly at night. They found one and, according to one account, made their escape by lulling the usually watchful Indians with the tolling of their chapel bell which was rung, presumably rather erratically, by a hungry dog. The dog was attached to the bell by a rope which kept it just out of reach of food which, of course, it continually tried to obtain.

Attempts were made to mount a reconquest from Campeche, the first Spanish town in the Yucatán to survive, but the settlers had little stomach for it. News of Pizarro's conquests in Peru and the riches to be won there had reached them. Men began to trickle away. In the late summer of 1534 Montejo the Elder wrote a letter to the King which was a far cry from the prospectus he must have issued when he first applied for the capitulación. There were no rivers and no gold, he complained; the land was so rocky and covered with bush that there was not a square foot of soil. The natives were almost beyond his powers of description. 'The inhabitants are the most abandoned and treacherous in all the lands discovered to this time, being a people who never yet killed a Christian except by foul means and who never made war except by artifice. Not once have I questioned them in any matter that they have not answered "yes" with the purpose of causing me to leave them and go elsewhere. In them I have failed to find truth touching anything.'

Poor Montejo! His debts mounting and without any prospect of a financial return from the hostile land which was to have been the foundation of a fame equal to that of Cortés and Pizarro, he was forced to ask His Majesty for support and the chance of restoring his fortunes in Honduras. Attempts to hold the Yucatán colony together had failed. The remaining settlers voted for evacuation and by early 1535 the peninsula was once again free of Spaniards, except for a small but significant (because it represented the Church's attempt to prove that love could succeed where the sword had failed) mission of four Franciscan friars at Champoton, now a friendlier place than in the early days of the Spanish invasion.

The respite from conquest was not to last for very long. A drought, the disruption of the Maya economy caused by the Spaniards and a disastrous quarrel between the two rival families, the Xius and the Cocoms, provided conditions for the Spanish return. The Xius, Lords of Mani, a town some twenty-five miles from Uxmal as the crow flies, decided that the drought and failure of crops made it necessary to offer a sacrifice to the rain god at Chichén Itzá's Well of Sacrifice. It was a risky pilgrimage since their route would take them through the territory of Nachi Cocom, of Sotuta, and he had not forgiven the sack of Mayapan and the slaughter of his family in the rebellion instigated by the Xiu almost a century earlier. Nevertheless, the Xiu accepted as sincere a message saying they would be given safe passage. Accordingly, the pilgrims, with slaves of both sexes for sacrifice, set out and were welcomed to the village of Otzmal, where Nachi Cocom had ordered a large house to be put at their disposal. Once the Xiu and their retainers were inside, the thatch was set on fire and the pilgrims were killed as they tried to escape. The Xius were allies of the Spaniards and there may be some truth in another account which has it that they were persuaded to send an embassy to the Cocoms, who after three days of feasting, ordered slaughter of their guests. Only one, Ah Kinchi, was saved, and he was blinded with an arrow and sent back to tell the Spaniards' allies what happened to traitors. The unfortunate Xiu were to be massacred again in the rebellion of 1546, but like so many opportunists, they survived long after the patriots and their families had vanished. Montejo the Elder chose Mani for the ten square leagues of land granted him by the King, and there, adjoining the church and facing a grand ceremonial plaza, not unlike those in front of Maya temples, one can see the massively walled stone house built for the newly converted Francisco de Montejo Xiu. Such patronage gave the family a lease of existence that has lasted into this century. There are still Xiu in the Yucatán, but the last who could truly be regarded as in the royal line died in the nineteenth century. In the 1930s or 1940s, the Mayanist Sylvanus Morley found a descendant called Dioniso, an impoverished peasant, and with true American respect for lineage traced his ancestry back to the year 1000 A.D., when the family are presumed to have been living at Uxmal.

The objective in the third and final stage of the Spanish conquest which began in earnest in 1540 was another ruined city, Tihoo, where the Spaniards were to give the new capital they established the name of Merida because the Maya ruins reminded them of the Roman ones in the Estremaduran city of the same name. In Tihoo, as the Spaniards took stock of their situation, they were alarmed to see a large, armed procession approaching, with a feather-bedecked litter in its midst. The conquerors ranged themselves in battle order, but the preparations were needless. The oncoming host threw down its

Temple of the Inscriptions, Palenque

General view of Palenque, overlooking the plain

Stela H, dedicated in 787 A.D., in the Ceremonial Plaza, Copán. Some authorities believe the figure is that of a woman

Copán (face)

weapons and the reigning Xiu Lord of Mani emerged from the litter to examine 'the bearded sons of the sun' and seek an instrument of revenge against the Cocoms.

Nachi Cocom's attempt to repeat the Maya victory at Chichén Itzá with a new alliance was soon defeated. Hundreds of Maya were slaughtered in a battle around a temple pyramid which the Spanish fortified. With their position in the north-west consolidated, the invaders completed the conquest with campaigns remarkable only for their brutality. Disregarded was Montejo the Elder's pious injunction to El Mozo that in accordance with His Majesty's wishes they were to 'comport themselves like true Christians' and wage war 'with the least prejudice' to both races. 'Nero was not more cruel than this man,' wrote an outraged Franciscan in a letter to the Court dealing with an expedition to the south-east by El Mozo's lieutenant, Gaspar Pacheco. Women as well as men were pressed into service as he advanced through a landscape of burning settlements and abandoned milpas. Guerrilla methods were met with reprisals. Prisoners were garrotted or torn to pieces by dogs, women thrown into the lagoons with weights on their feet; arms, legs and breasts were cut off in punishment. Small children were stabbed when they failed to keep up with their mothers. On the march, in which the porters were chained together by their necks, those who fell ill were removed by the simple method of cutting off their heads and pushing the bodies to one side. What had been one of the most populous areas of the Yucatán became the most desolate as famine followed Pacheco's ravages. No priests were with the expedition, as the Franciscans were to note pointedly in their later reports to the Crown of these and other atrocities. By 1544 resistance around Chetumal had collapsed and Pacheco was able to report that his new provincial capital on the shores of Lake Bacalar was secure.

Elsewhere, the conquerors took advantage of the ambiguities in the Crown's views on slavery and branded as slaves those who had opposed them. In the still-resisting province of Chel, in north-eastern Yucatán, Pedro Alvarez burned alive or hanged the caciques. In one town the leading inhabitants were chained up inside a hut which was then burnt. Women were hanged from trees with their children suspended from their feet, and, in an incident which became legendary among the Spaniards as well as the Indians, a young virgin and a newly married woman, both unusually beautiful, were hanged because the commander wished to remove a temptation to his troops and to impress on the Maya that his men were not interested in their women. The last spasm came in 1546 when the semi-slavery inherent in the encomienda system provoked the Maya to a final rebellion in which they proved they could be as cruel as their masters. The uprising started in the north-east, around the newly established town of Valladolid. El Mozo had gone to Campeche to welcome his father to the pacified province and many settlers were on their encomiendas (and therefore not grouped together in the Valladolid garrison) collecting tribute so that the revenues would not appear too discouraging when the Adelantado took a look at the books. The Maya nobles and priests selected the date for the uprising after consultation with the oracles: November 8th, 1546, which in the Maya calendar is 5 Cimi 19 Xul, signifying Death and the End.

A score or so of encomenderos were tortured and sacrificed. Two children were roasted alive over a fire of copal incense. The new alcalde, or mayor, of Valladolid was among those who perished. He was tied up and dragged through the villages for display. For a time his reputation for courage awed his captors and no one would kill him, but eventually his head was cut off. With an almost manic determination to erase every sign of Spanish rule, the rebels massacred between 500 and 600 Indians who had sided with the Spaniards and slew cattle, horses, dogs and cats and every alien creature, including hens, the Spaniards had introduced to the country. Even their new trees and plants were torn out of the ground and their farm buildings burnt down. The limbs and heads of the human victims were given to couriers for distribution throughout the land as evidence that the uprising had succeeded. But at Valladolid a garrison of only twenty men held off a horde of Maya until relief arrived from Mérida. Elsewhere, the local caciques decided to wait for more solid evidence of success than severed limbs before they joined the uprising. Before long the fighting subsided and the guilty were punished. Five or six rebellious priests were burned, among them one Chilam Anbal who, blending the old religion with the new, had proclaimed himself the Son of God.

Perhaps if the conquest of the Yucatán had proved a profitable venture the reaction against the Adelantado would not have been so severe, but as it was he was caught between the Court, the Church and the settlers. He was accused of cruelty and corruption. He had burned Maya priests and intimidated the *cabildo*, or town council, of Mérida by appearing fully armed in their midst (having seen to it that he was the only man permitted to enter the chamber in arms), the system of taxation was inadequate and he had failed to administer justice. A Judge of Commission instituted an inquiry and found him guilty of numerous offences. No less than three Montejos (the Elder, El Mozo and Francisco, the Elder's nephew) were suspended from office. Heavy fines were imposed and Montejo the Elder lost his lands at Champoton, because he had used forced labour and in any case had taken them illegally. The Montejos had become anachronisms and the Court turned a deaf ear when, not long before his death, Montejo the Elder journeyed to Spain to appeal for the return of his hereditary and other titles.

The fine palace he built in Mérida in the main plaza, close to the cathedral, is still there, with its club-wielding wild men standing guard on the stone façade over the door. Like their friends, the Xiu, the family fell on hard times, and the house was sold in the 1840s. The interior, refurbished during the sisal boom of the 1870s, has a faded, neglected look nowadays. The male line vanished some time ago but continuity has been maintained through the female side. According to the elderly guide who escorts one through the palace, three generations of those who claim an increasingly tenuous relationship with the Adelantado live in a wing of the house, beyond a large refrigerator and a crate of empty Coca-Cola bottles.

5
'Are They Not Men?'

With the Maya, who hardly had time to have a history in our sense of the word, the record is all seams, darns and embroidery. There is a sequence in which myth or semi-myth merges into history, then becomes micro-history as the power to make events is vested in the Spaniards, and finally even that gives way to archaeology and anthropology, sociology's terminal ward where before the undertakers move in there is a chance to examine the institutions and inter-relationships that, magnified and shifted into new patterns, form our own societies. In the collapsing, inarticulate world of the Maya, the scholars became the spokesmen for the past and in a sense its major figures. That is an ethnocentric view, of course, and a modern Maya might quarrel with it, arguing in much the same way as Africans who complain that Dr Livingstone was not the discoverer of Lake Nyasa, merely its first tourist. However, the 'meek panthers', as a modern Mexican writer called the Indians of Central America, interest us mainly because they once were people of genius and fierce passions who controlled a vastly more impressive realm than their present one; and the revelation of the extent of that realm came from outside the enclosed Maya world.

To pursue the past of a subjected people requires compassion, an inwardness that recognizes in broken cultures and broken buildings the unity of civilization, however cruel and unsympathetic the early structures. It is not a particularly modern development; in Central America, where conquerors were for the first time tormented by the dilemmas of colonialism, it emerged in the first half of the sixteenth century through a fierce debate over the responsibilities of Church and Crown to the Indians. 'Are these Indians not men?' a Dominican friar asked rhetorically in a sermon in 1511. 'Do they not have rational souls? Are you not obliged to love them as you love yourselves?' Our own twentieth-century debate about the ethics of colonialism seems almost crude when compared with that carried on by the Spaniards. It was held within the framework of the prevailing Aristotelian philosophy and the main protagonists were a colonial bishop, Bartolomé de las Casas, of Chiapas, a Maya province, and Juan Ginés de Sepúlveda, one of the foremost theologians of his time. If there were such a thing as reincarnation, las Casas would undoubtedly emerge today as an Anglican bishop in South Africa, obstinate, bluntly outspoken, morally unchallengeable, basically sentimental in his view of the natives, and loathed by the majority of his fellow whites. 'The Apostle of the Indies' was a Dominican, the order that led the struggle for pacification through Christian love. At the same time, it was also a struggle for the conscience of a court trapped between its religious obligation to bring souls to God by morally acceptable means and an equal desire to produce wealth in the Americas. The unresolved question that prevented determination of the matter was: were the Indians men or 'beasts' in the philosophical sense of the word? On the one hand slavery was wrong and therefore forbidden; on the other, Aristotle had said that there were different orders of existence. Were the Indians 'Natural slaves?' The confusion was remarkable. Montejo the Elder, for example, was forbidden to make slaves of Indians who had been in bondage to other Indians, but was permitted to import Negro slaves, since Negroes were regarded as a lesser order than Indians. The issue was brought to a head by the settlers on the new encomiendas demanding that the system (which was at one time to have been abolished) should be made permanent. To accept that would have meant dooming the Indians to perpetual serfdom, a state not much different from slavery, whatever the laws said about the Indians being wards of the Crown and as such free vassals. It was las Casas' strength that he cut through the confusion and concentrated on the moral issues: he did not believe in 'just wars', or mass conversions (such as the Franciscans carried out) made more or less under compulsion without instruction in Christianity, and he refuted the idea that the Indians were inferior, with all that implied as an excuse for exploitation. The temples of the Yucatán were as worthy of admiration as the pyramids of Egypt or any other works of antiquity, he maintained. Las Casas' views so infuriated the Spaniards in the Yucatán, to which his ecclesiastical authority was extended for a time, that they refused to accept his jurisdiction or pay Church dues. The Bishop carried his campaign to Spain in 1547 when he was in his early seventies and two years later the Council of the Indies was swayed sufficiently by his argument that the Indians were being treated as of 'less worth than bedbugs' that it recommended the King to call a meeting of learned men to consider ways in which conquests could be made 'justly and with security of conscience'. The letter noted that: 'The greed of those who undertake conquests and the timidity and humility of the Indians is such that we are not certain whether any instruction will be obeyed.' In the spring of 1550 the King accepted this advice and halted all conquests until the special commission had met and reported its views. As Lewis Hanke, the historian, has remarked: 'Probably never before or since has a mighty emperor – and in 1550 Charles V, Holy Roman Emperor, was the strongest emperor in Europe with a great overseas empire besides – ordered his conquests to cease until it was decided if they were just.' The learned men met in Valladolid in 1550–1 and listened to a disputation in which Sepúlveda, speaking in defence of war against the Indians argued that it was lawful because of the gravity of their sins and the rudeness of their natures. The latter fault made it acceptable that they should serve those of a more refined nature. Las Casas' arguments we know. It need only be said that the debate expanded sensibilities and left the Crown better informed about conditions in its American empire, but was inconclusive, like so many Great Debates.

The moral crisis that hit the Spanish empire in the midsixteenth century is exemplified in the Yucatán by the career of

Yllmo. Sr. D. Fr. Diego de Landa, natural de Ci

Portrait of Bishop Landa

Bishop Diego de Landa, a Franciscan who came to the province in the year before the Valladolid debate. His portrait hangs in the sanctuary at the back of the huge monastery and church he built at Izamal, a Maya city some forty-five miles from Mérida. The face is ascetic, rather prim, with downcast eyes, and intellectual. It makes a disapproving contrast with the more robust expressions of other bishops and the conventional sweet-ness of the near-by copy of the Virgin of Izamal (the original one, which came from Guatemala in 1558, was burnt in a fire in 1829). Landa, as Prior of Izamal, built his monastery on the remains of a pyramid, flattening and covering it so completely that not a corner of paganism is visible. From the back of the church one can see across houses to another of the town's once numerous pyramids where a cross has been firmly planted. The paradoxical nature of his times was such that he was both a ruthless destroyer of Maya art and literature and the foundation rock of all scholarly investigation from the mid-nineteenth century onwards. His interest in the Maya was keen but there is something in the Bishop's face that tells one it was prompted more by a need to know the devil than love for his back-sliding flock. It is easy to imagine him writing (as he did in his apologia after he was recalled to Spain to account for his harshness at the Mani *auto-da-fé* in 1562) this brief, slightly puzzled account of the destruction of the Maya holy books, the painted codices: 'We found a large number of books in these characters and as we found nothing in which there were not to be seen super-stitions and lies of the devil, we burned them all, which they regretted to an amazing degree and which caused them much affliction.' The Maya codices – only four of which have sur-vived to this day – contained prophecies and astronomical information. They were the written 'language of Zuyua', the secret language by which the priesthood and the aristocracy kept their knowledge and the esoteric mysteries of the religion to themselves. So far as modern scholarship and our enjoyment of the past are concerned, the burning of the books was vandalism of the worst kind; but the friars had understandable reasons.

73

The Maya priests and their magic books represented a detestable and cruel religion. It was also uncomfortably similar to Christianity in some respects. Common to both were the central elements of blood and sacrifice, the importance of statuary and visual representation, ceremonies of baptism and confirmation, the use of incense; and above all, perhaps, the cross. Father Francisco Hernández wrote to las Casas in 1545 that

'. . . when our people discovered the Kingdom of Yucatán they found crosses there, and one cross in particular which was made of stone and mortar of a height of ten palms and was erected in a court . . . alongside of a sumptuous temple, and is very much frequented by a great number of people. This is on the island of Cozumel, which lies near the mainland of Yucatán. It is said that this cross was really adored as the God of Water or Rain . . . when asked whence or through whom they had first heard of that sign, they replied that a very handsome man had once passed through the country and that he had left it with them, that they might remember him by it. Others, it is said, answered that it was because a man more resplendent than the sun had died on that cross.'

The faiths were already tending to merge, the Spaniards mystified by the presence in pagan lands of what looked like the symbol of Christianity, the Maya clinging to the images of the old religion by offering spurious explanations which they knew would please the friars. Apart from their association with the rain god, the crosses may have represented the tree of life, the sacred ceiba tree; eventually they were incorporated in the Christian cross, changing the nature of the latter. For centuries the Maya worshipped the cross as a deity in its own right and apart from the crucified Christ. During the War of the Castes in the second half of the nineteenth century, the rebellious Maya of Quintana Roo prayed to the oracular 'Speaking Cross', while other lesser crosses were dressed in smocks and ribbons.

Landa became the Provincial of Yucatán in 1561, a position that fell short of giving him full episcopal powers. There was a good case, however, for claiming inquisitorial powers, and since he had for several years noticed signs of 'the very greatest knavery and idolatory' it was not long before his friars were out taking evidence in the towns and villages. In later years Landa was endowed with saintly attributes; an old woman was cured of tuberculosis when he baptized her; a star shone above his head as he preached. But at that time he must have been remembered largely as the man who collected maize for church dues at a time of famine and who had a rough way with heretics and idolators. There were ecclesiastical trials for blasphemy, bigamy and of a man who had expressed sympathy with 'some French Lutheran pirates', an event which may contain an echo of 'Antonio Martinez' in the books of Chilam Balam.

Among those who fell into the net were the Xius of Mani and their old rivals, the Cocoms of Sotuta. Both had advanced sufficiently in their Christian studies to understand the importance of crucifixion. Francisco Xiu, who a year before the *auto-da-fé* had been flogged and banned for six months from Mani for drunkenness, was charged with nothing worse than trying to burn down his home town (the charges were dismissed), but his relations were accused of crucifying a girl child. Juan Xiu, who died afterwards as the result of torture at the hands of the friars, claimed that the marks on the child's hands and feet were the stigmata. The mortally sick Juan Cocom, cacique of Sotuta, was the supposed beneficiary of the sacrifice of two boys whose hearts were torn out with these words, 'Lord powerful God, these hearts we offer you and we sacrifice to you these boys in order that you may give life to our governor.' Shortly afterwards two more boys were sacrificed in the church of Sotuta, where Cocom, a 'convert', was buried. Prophecies that there would be a repetition of the great storm that struck the country in the fifteenth century seem to have prompted crucifixions at the cenotes to appease the rain god. In some cases the victims were thrown in still nailed to the cross. Others were killed first and then thrown in and some had their hearts torn out before bodies and hearts were dropped in separately. Lorenzo, the brother of Juan, was one of the leaders of the return to the old gods. After he succeeded as cacique of Sotuta he sacrificed three boys who were thrown alive into the Well of Sacrifice at Chichén Itzá. During these and other sacrifices, there were frequent references to Jesus Christ; 'Let these girls die crucified as did Jesus Christ, he who they say was Our Lord, but we do not know if this is so.' And: 'You see the figure of Jesus Christ and we offer to our gods the hearts of these who are sacrificed.' In some cases the name 'Jesus Christ' was written above the victim and there seems to have been a preference for holding sacrifices in Holy Week. By far the most brutal crucifixion had no connection at all with Christianity. It took place in the Cocom town of Hoctun, where the cacique, Juan Iuit, used a wooden pole bound with thorns to beat to death, with blows on the breast, a girl who had been lashed to a pole.

With so many children the victims of sacrifices, it is not altogether surprising that it was the boys in a convent school who brought to the friars' notice the incident which touched off the Inquisition. It was not a case of human sacrifice, but a fairly innocuous one of idols and bowls of deer's blood found in a cave. To avoid the central part he would inevitably be cast for in the trials that would draw in most of the leading figures in Xiu and Cocom country, Lorenzo Cocom committed suicide.

Landa began the *auto-da-fé* in July or August, after obtaining the support of the civil administration through the governor of Yucatán, Diego Quijada. The accused were paraded in *sambenitos* of cotton dyed yellow with red crosses before being allotted the various tortures intended to produce confessions. Some were given as many as 200 lashes, others were hung up with stones attached to their feet (hanging up without stones was not regarded by the friars as a torture) while yet others suffered the prolonged pains of being tied to the burro, a wooden frame. To add to their misery, scalding hot wax sputtered on their naked backs as the friars stood over them with candles waiting for confessions or signs of penitence. For some tough cases there was the water torture: the mouth was held open with a stick while water was poured in. One of the torturers then stood on the victim's inflated belly until water 'mixed with blood' flowed out of mouth, ears and nose.

It is easy to imagine what Juan Cuoh, of Yaxcabá, must have suffered, probably quite deservedly, at the earlier inquisitorial trial at Sotuta. Cuoh had taken part in a sacrifice in a church where the victim, obviously a convinced Christian who may have been chosen because of that, replied to his killers' assurance that he was 'going to glory in the manner of our ancestors' that they should do what they wished 'for God is in heaven who watches me'. At his trial, Cuoh took the oath, crossed himself and promised to tell the truth. He then admitted to having three idols. Reminded that he had promised to tell the truth, he admitted to having twenty more. The trial took a nastier turn, with Cuoh questioned about the sacrifices he had participated in. As he still denied having any more idols he was put to the torture. He then confessed to three more. Still dissatisfied, the friars ordered more torture and Cuoh remembered another two, making twenty-nine in all.

With a remarkable desire to maintain precise records, the friars noted that 4,549 men and women were tortured and 6,330 fined. How many died as a result of burning and tortures is unclear, but one later estimate put the figure at 150, although this may have been an exaggeration. For later ages what mattered most was not the human suffering but the destruction of various artefacts. On the great plaza in front of the church at Mani, Landa supervised the destruction of 5,000 idols, 13 great stones which served as altars, 22 small stones, 27 rolls of hieroglyphs on deerskin and 197 vases. It seems appalling vandalism now, but in the light of the dreadful things done in the name of the religion represented by those stones and hieroglyphs, can one really blame him?

Bishop Toral, the first Bishop of the Yucatán, did. He arrived almost immediately after the end of the *auto-da-fé* and appears to have developed strong prejudices against the Provincial on his way to his see. The opponents of Landa and Quijada, a dapper ladies' man with a reputation for opportunism, were an unlikely combination of liberal friars and settlers. The latter regarded excessive Christianity as having an unsettling effect on the natives and there appear to have been at least two attempts by encomenderos to burn down the monasteries. Harsh treatment of the Indians was definitely out of favour in the Spanish empire when Toral arrived and he reacted strongly to the reports given him of the tortures used in the Inquisition. Prisoners were freed and an inquiry opened almost immediately. Leading citizens, many of them no doubt Landa's enemies, were persuaded to sit on the examining panel. Much of the evidence extorted from the Indians was repudiated and both Landa and Quijada were placed in humiliating positions. Quijada attempted to take his case to higher levels but was eventually charged with overstepping his authority and ordered to make restitution. Unable to do so, he went to prison for eleven months. Landa resigned and took his case to Mexico and then, on royal orders, to Spain, which he reached after a year and a half that included delays through shipwreck and illness. It was not only Toral who wrote complaints against him; so did the Maya, who by that time had discovered that central authority could be played off against local authority.

In Madrid Landa was censured severely by the Council of the Indies for having usurped the office of Bishop and Inquisitor. His legalistic defence, based on papal documents giving broad powers to monastic orders in remote places, irritated them still more and the matter was referred to the Provincial of Castile who established another panel, this time of seven Franciscans, who eventually exonerated Landa. During the eight years or so he was in eclipse in Spain, Landa spent his time in the monasteries to which he was assigned writing the document without which his name would account for very little indeed. He entitled it *Relación de las Cosas de Yucatán* (*An Account of Events in Yucatán*) and it reads like an apologia, an explanation of his own mixed feelings about the Maya whose souls had been entrusted to him. It gave a history of the Maya and an account of their customs but perhaps most important of all, for later generations at least, it described the Maya calendar, with drawings of the Maya day and month signs, and it contained a Maya 'alphabet' which even if it has proved of uncertain usefulness in deciphering the hieroglyphics, at least shows that the Maya knew about phonetics. It also includes a date from the Maya calendar which together with one from the books of Chilam Balam (of the founding of Mérida) formed the starting point for the successful attempt to correlate the Maya calendars with the Christian one. But as the incomplete manuscript was not discovered until 1813 in Madrid, an account of how nineteenth-century German, British and American scholarship tackled that problem will have to wait until later.

For the sources of his information, Landa relied impartially on a Cocom and a Xiu. One mentor was Juan Cocom 'a man of great reputation, learned in their affairs and of remarkable discernment'; presumably he was the one for whom the sacrifices were made while he was dying. His other informant was Gaspar Antonio Chi, a talented offspring of the Xiu aristocracy, who played the organ, spoke Spanish and Nahuatl as well as Maya, and was highly literate. His history of the Yucatán written in 1582 was a major source for the handful of Spanish historians of the Yucatán during the next hundred years.

Landa was restored to favour and in 1573, following Toral's death, he returned to the Yucatán as its Bishop and remained there until his own death in Mérida six years later. At Mani, so unfavourably associated with his name, one senses as nowhere else the harsh probity of that sixteenth-century argument between dogmatists and humanists, with the Indians, yearning for the realism of sacrifice and death rather than their symbols, as almost mute third parties. In Montejo Xiu's house the walls still bear the grey, cracking stumps of pegs from which long-gone sleepers hung their hammocks in the empty galleries and rooms through which one walks to reach the roof the house shares with the church. The house is half-ruined but it lives in a way. The priest has an office there and the sacristan and his mother occupy a sound part of the ground floor. The bright, hot light flows through the gaping windows. On the undulating concrete roof groups of girls sit close to the parapet chatting and giggling together, stopping every now and then, as if bored or exhausted, to stare blankly at the flat horizon. Beneath them there is a no-man's-land formed of the great plaza with a cobbled processional way and a dusty emptiness from which the low houses of the town seem to shrink. Somewhere down there the idols were smashed and the books burnt, the deerskin parchment damp enough from the humidity of the wet season to make a little smoke. Some of those who heard the hammers and felt the whips may have built the fragments into the huge walls of the church or turned them into limestone concrete for the roof. The church contains, like a thorn, an Indian processional cross, but despite that ambiguous symbol of death and survival one recalls that Mani meant 'the end' in Maya.

Ruined stairway, Copán

Maya house in the Petén

The arch at Labná

Tulum, the ruins on the cliff above the sea

6

Beneath the Vines, Beneath the Trees

For a century and a half after the collapse of the Maya in the
Yucatán, the Itzá, the despised 'tricksters and rascals' of the
ancient chronicles, survived unconquered and unchristianized
on the shores of Lake Petén-Itzá and in their island capital,
Tayasal, guarded by swamps, jungles and fevers. Beneath the
vines, beneath the trees, this last fragment of the great Indian
civilizations was created around the time of the fall of Mayapán
in the mid-fifteenth century, when the Itzá began to move
south with an instinctive nomadism as the new katun cycle
began, and gathered strength in the sixteenth and seventeenth
centuries as more Indians fled from the friars and the encomiendas. They increased greatly 'in numbers, pride, cruelty and
power', wrote the eighteenth-century historian, Juan de
Villagutierre. On their island fortress 'nothing molested them,
nor was it possible even to pass near their confines'. The
priests kept the rituals and practised heart sacrifices, and the
anahtes, or sacred books, were preserved and the knowledge of
how to read them passed on. Only the priests enjoyed the
prospect of old age, it was said, for all other men were killed at
the age of fifty for fear they became wizards. In the end the
Itzá did not so much submit as vanish: they leaped into the
water from their island city and swam for the shores and shelter
of their traditional friend, the forest.

By itself, nature might not have been enough to preserve the
Itzá. The new solicitude of the Crown towards the Indians
played a part. A seventeenth-century Spanish writer noted that

the word 'conquista' had been eliminated 'from these pacifications, for it is found hateful and they must not take place with the noise of arms but with charity and kindness'. The wooing of the Itzá was left to the Franciscans and for a century they pursued it sporadically with great courage and, in the last stage, subtlety, playing on prophecies and creating a wedge between the Canek, or secular ruler, and the priests who knew that Christianity meant an end to their power. It is one of the more remarkable episodes in the history of the Spanish empire and it is hard to think of any missionary exploits elsewhere which equal the drama of Andrés de Avendaño's visit to Tayasal when he sat drifting in a canoe on the lake, calmly eating the tamales offered to sacrificial victims, while the Canek and his escort reflected on whether to kill him.

The lake is the centre of the Petén, the focal point through which all journeys pass. It is shaped like a pothook, some twelve or thirteen miles long, with Tayasal's island (nowadays called Flores in honour of a nineteenth-century hero) in the short arm, just past the angle. Naturally, it is the provincial capital; the houses cluster around its slight, bowl-shaped hill on top of which is a large plaza with a modern church, a police station and a few administrative buildings. The same place was the centre of old Tayasal, where before its conquest there were nineteen or twenty-one (the counts vary) temples, the largest of which was the domain of the Quincanek, or high priest. It is described as having been square with a high parapet and an approach of nine steps of 'beautiful stone'. An idol guarded the doorway and inside was another of 'unwrought emerald' (possibly a large piece of jade). The Canek had his temple too, and inside were wooden and stone idols, stucco figures, a sacrificial altar and the sacred books. The Canek's palace was close to the lake, with a small square in front in which was a truncated stone column with a carving on top ('very ill formed', says Avendaño in his account). The column was called *Yax cheel cab*, the first tree in the world, whose fruit the Maya Adam, Ixanom, ate. The people wore cotton clothes which were regarded as more beautiful than those made in the Yucatán and plugged their ears and noses with small plates of inferior gold and silver or vanilla. Families, whatever their size, were restricted to one house each and conditions were filthy. The dead were taken to the mainland for burial in the milpas; those who were killed for sacrifice were eaten. Tayasal is circular and less than half a mile across; the four neighbouring islands, which were also heavily populated in the seventeenth century, look ridiculously small, like farthings. Contemporary estimates put the population at 25,000, with thousands more living on the lake shores. Teobert Maler, the German archaeologist, noted in 1904 that the lake had risen twenty-five centimetres in the past twenty-five years, so perhaps the islands are smaller now. Nevertheless, from a dugout canoe the waters look shallow, with the sandy bottom appearing as a weed-streaked beige through the slightly clouded water. A causeway joins the island to the northern shore these days but canoe-ferries, powered by outboards, stutter backwards and forwards to both shores and, farther afield, to the Indian villages of St Andrés and San José.

The lake is a gasp of relief, a psychological necessity, after the smothering gloom of the jungle. Le Douanier Rousseau drew inspiration from the Central American tropics but most of those who have had to cross them on foot have been glad to escape from their thorns, snakes, muddy pitfalls and continual damp. Maler, like Le Douanier, an ex-soldier with the Emperor Maximilian in Mexico, is sour and unable to say a good word about anyone until he reaches the lake, and then his German soul floods forth. The lake, he found, was 'especially romantic and beautiful by moonlight or by soft starlight in the stillness and coolness of the night. While the weather-hardened Indians of San José and San Andrés bend to their paddles and the cool water ripples and the stars in the dark firmament twinkle full of mystery, an indescribable feeling of melancholy involuntarily comes over one while pondering on the hard and thankless life of these representatives of a once great race. . . .' Désiré Charnay, a nineteenth-century French traveller, thought it was like an Alpine lake, but that is Charnay searching for easy, postcard descriptions. It is impressive but not grand. The surrounding hills are low and just steep enough for everyone to have a grandstand view of the lake; the water is a serious yet uncertain blue and the trees have that mat, generous green which, like everything else that grows between Capricorn and Cancer, comes from being blessed with a perfect compact of heat and fertility. At the southern end there are reeds and the slow merging of one vegetal texture with another over the shallows.

It must have been here that Cortés, the first European to see the lake, arrived with a weary army in 1525 on his way to quell a rebellion in Honduras. Although the march involved no fighting (the rebel leader Cristobal de Olid had been overthrown and executed by the time Cortés arrived) it was physically the most arduous journey he undertook. He envisaged it as an exploration and a princely progress, with a display of renaissance panoply and wealth. He took with him Guatemozin, the last king of the Aztecs and several other Indian leaders (so that he would have them under his eye while he was away), 250 Spanish veterans of the wars, of whom 130 were mounted, a number of recently arrived Spaniards, 3,000 Mexican warriors to escort their chiefs, a large train of domestics, four priests, including two Flemish theologians, and, in his own personal entourage, a chief steward and paymaster, a keeper of the plate, a major-domo, two household stewards, a butler, a confectioner, a chamberlain, a physician, a surgeon, several pages (including Montejo the Younger), two armour bearers, a master of the horse, eight grooms, two falconers, five musicians with sackbuts, dulcimers and flageolets, a dancer, a juggler and puppeteer and three Spanish muleteers. There was also a large service of gold and silver plate and, four days' journey behind the main body, a herd of pigs for consumption by Cortés and his household. Even while the army was starving these were kept out of sight and when Bernal Díaz, who described the journey in his *The True History of the Conquest of*

Mexico, asked the chief steward about them, he was told that they had all been eaten by alligators while crossing a river. In fact, some of them survived the journey and reached Honduras.

The journey from Espiritu Santo, near the southernmost curve of the Gulf of Mexico, to the trading post of Nito, on the Golfo Dolce, covered roughly 1,000 miles. Bridges had to be built across wide rivers, horses dragged through swamps and a road cut through the jungles. The Indian chiefs took to cannibalism; others starved. Most of the horses perished on the flinty mountains above the Sarstoon river. The dancer died from exhaustion, and so did many others. Only one musician

Probable route taken by Cortés in his march from Espiritu Santo to Nito in 1524–5

had the strength or will to play and he was greeted with shouts from the Spanish soldiery of 'Maize not music!' It was during this awful trek that Guatemozin was executed by Cortés shortly before Ash Wednesday, 1525, in an unjust spasm of suspicion and anxiety which he later regretted. Guatemozin was hanged side by side with one of his subjects, the Lord of Tacuba, from the branches of a ceiba, the Maya tree of life, after cursing Cortés with these words 'May God demand of you this innocent blood'. This famous, or infamous, event took place at the Acalan-Maya town of Itzamkanac, a once impressive but now lost trading centre on the upper reaches of the Candelaria river. Whatever the truth about Guatemozin's part in the alleged conspiracy against the Spaniards, Cortés suffered agonies of conscience and sleepless nights afterwards. Díaz reports that he was so distracted that he arose one night and walked to the gallery of a temple where idols were kept. There, he slipped in the dark and fell twelve feet, seriously cutting and bruising his head.

The approach to Tayasal was possibly the only time when the army marched on a reasonably full belly. There were deer to be speared or shot, iguanas and fish to be obtained from the Indians; so it was a reasonably contented force which halted on the shores of Lake Petén-Itzá and looked across at the glistening white temples and houses of Tayasal. Cortés thought they had reached an arm of the sea and Díaz believed they were on a wide river. The Canek agreed to ferry the army to the far side, and Cortés, by sending a Spaniard as a hostage, persuaded him to visit the army and listen to mass sung to the accompaniment of flageolets and sackbuts played by the now-recovered musicians. Díaz says that Cortés, escorted by thirty crossbow-men, paid a return visit to Tayasal where the Canek presented him with low-grade gold ornaments and some feathered mantles, but Cortés does not describe the Itzá capital in his fifth letter to Charles V in which he recounts the events of the march. But then, as W. H. Prescott noted in a letter to John Lloyd Stephens, Cortés never did have much to say about the cities he visited: '... one peso d'oro was worth all the antiquities of Anahuac to the old conquerors'.

If Tayasal made little impression on Cortés, Cortés left his mark on Tayasal. His horse, Morzillo, ran a splinter from a stake into its fetlock and the Canek undertook to take care of it, 'although I know not what he will make of it'. Cortés explained in his letter to King Charles. The unfortunate Morzillo was taken to Tayasal where he was accorded divine status and offered a diet of flowers and turkeys. According to one legend the Itzá assumed from the copper bit they had seen in his mouth that he also liked gold and this was offered to him too. Whether from his wound or from starvation, Morzillo died and at once took his place among the Itzá gods. He became Tzimin–Chac, god of thunder and lightning, possibly because the Itzá had been treated to an intimidating display of mounted Spanish fire-power. A large stone statue was made of him and he was worshipped in the Quincanek's temple.

Despite several attempts to penetrate the province of 'Tayca', no more Spaniards are known to have reached Tayasal for almost a hundred years after Cortés, although several expeditions travelled up the Rio San Pedro Mártir and one, in 1580, sighted the city from a distance. Tayasal was a stronghold of heathendom, a sanctuary behind the new frontier formed by the edge of the rain forests. The flight of Indian apostates was a constant worry to the friars and, for different reasons, to the encomienderos as well, but the situation presented no military threat. The Itzás, conscious of the diplomatic benefit to be gained by preventing the pressures from building up, sent an embassy to Mérida in 1614 and promised to accept Christianity, but that was merely an example of the famous Itzá trickery. The first serious attempt at their conversion came in 1618 when two Franciscan friars, Bartolomé de Fuensalida and Juan de Orbita, were dispatched from Mérida to the most advanced missionary outpost at Tipu, on the upper Rio Hondo, close to the present frontier with British Honduras. The journey from there to Tayasal was a difficult one. There were delays while a canoe was built to take them across Lake Yaxhá, which blocked their route, and their guides were fearful that they would all be killed by the Itzá, but at last they reached Lake Petén-Itzá, where the Fathers immediately put up a thatch and timber church and sent messengers to inform the Canek that they had arrived.

A delay of a week before the messengers returned caused anxiety, but the friars' reception as they neared Tayasal set their minds at rest. A fleet of canoes containing the Canek and the leading citizens came out to escort them to the landing place, where, under the light of candlewood torches, all drank the cup of peace, a frothy cocoa called *ʒaca*, and numerous presents, including a sabre for the Canek and a quantity of Tipu cacao (especially prized by the Itzá), were unloaded from the canoes. The friars were taken to the house which had been prepared for them close to the Canek's palace.

The next morning Father Fuensalida sang mass before a group of silent Itzá and appointed the Apostle Paul patron of the island. That done, the friars had a long conversation with the Canek in his palace, followed by an address by Fuensalida to the assembled zamaguales, or common people. At the end of a polite reception the friars were told by the zamaguales' spokesmen that unfortunately the time ordained in the prophecies for their conversion had not yet arrived and they would continue with their present religion. The Canek suggested to the friars that the best course would be for them to go home and return to Tayasal when the time was more opportune.

Fuensalida and Orbita were then taken on a tour of the city and its temples which eventually led them to the statue of Tzimin-Chac, now the principal god of the Itzá. No doubt Father Orbita was embittered by a feeling of having come on a fool's errand; he was obviously not the sort of person to appreciate the finer points of Itzá diplomacy, in which cautious 'maybes' at least left the way open for later negotiations. As he stood listening to the story of how Tzimin-Chac had come to the Itzá he felt not amazement but fury; 'It seemed as if the

spirit of Our Lord had descended on him,' wrote the seventeenth-century historian Cogolludo, 'for, carried away by a
fervid and courageous zeal for the glory of God, he took a
great stone in his hand, climbed to the top of the statue of the
horse and battered it to pieces, scattering the fragments on the
ground.' Chalky though limestone is, it is hard to believe that
the entire horse was destroyed, so perhaps there is some truth
in the legend that when Tzimin-Chac was being moved elsewhere by water his raft capsized and he was lost overboard
close to the end of the promontory of Nitun, less than a mile
from Tayasal, where on clear days he may occasionally be
glimpsed on the lake bed.

There was uproar from the zamaguales and demands for the
friars to be put to death as Orbita went about his destructive
work, but no one seems to have tried to stop him. He remained
calm when he had finished and Fuensalida delivered a sermon
in which he described the horse as being similar to the deer
which they killed with their arrows. Standing beneath his up-
held crucifix, he once again urged the Itzá to worship the true
God. Amazed, the people fell back to let the friars leave unmolested. The Canek, who was of course immediately told
about the incident, politely avoided all references to it when the
two priests went to see him after 'resting from the toil of the
spiritual battle' and he accepted the gift of a cross, but it was
quite clear that the incident had not changed his mind about the
potency of Christianity. The hostility of the zamaguales made
the missionaries realize that they would be foolish to stay any
longer, and although the Canek did not urge them to leave,
they asked for a canoe to be made ready. Some of the still
friendly Itzá gave them a parting present of clothes and small
idols, but on the way back across the lake they were chased and
pelted with stones. Only the intervention of a Tipu cacique
who happened to know the leader of the pursuers saved them
from being shot to death with arrows, like Tzimin-Chac's
brothers the deer. The cacique pointed out that the Fathers
were leaving and that should be the end of the matter. 'Then do

not bring those *xolopes* (pineapples) here again,' said the Itzá cacique.

Almost unbelievably, the *xolopes* were back again in the following year, 1619, this time with the backing of the Governor of the Yucatán (something they had not had the first time). It seems fairly evident that the friars had decided that the Canek could be worked on and divided from the Itzá priesthood by offering him continued temporal power provided he accepted Christianity and Spanish rule. The Canek received them with as much kindness as before and seemed more willing to listen to their arguments. Their meetings went so well that Fuensalida and Orbita were encouraged to begin talks on what hereditary powers he would retain under Spanish rule and the length of the tax holiday – ten years – before he was required to start paying a moderate amount of tribute. The Canek ordered the erection of a large cross near his palace, a move which caused no obvious resentment among the populace. But once again the appearance of things on Tayasal proved deceptive. The Canek's wife, who was under the influence of the Itzá priests, threatened to leave him for one of his caciques, Nacompol, unless the friars were expelled. The Canek, while reluctant to take this step, agreed to go with her to join in feasts and dances at nearby gardens on the mainland, probably on the Nitun promontory, where there are the remains of a temple pyramid. On the following day the friars saw that their second attempt at peaceful conversion had failed. An armed party tore down the religious ornaments in their chapel and bundled the friars towards the shore, refusing to allow them to talk to the Canek, who stood passively watching them from his palace. The fiery Orbita put up a resistance and was half strangled with the collar of his hood and flung unconscious to the ground. The friars were then thrown into a leaky canoe with three Indians from Tipu to paddle them, and it was only after a dangerous, hungry journey that they reached safety. They were so dejected that they decided to abandon their mission at Tipu and retreat to Mérida, a decision which was greeted with satisfaction by their backsliding congregation. A great tract of territory in the south-east of the Yucatán quickly reverted to paganism.

Before long yet another Franciscan, Father Diego Delgado, took the same route southwards, this time to martyrdom. His proposition that he should attempt the reconversion of the apostate Indians on the borders of Itzá territory was accepted and he founded a mission called San Felipe y Santiago de Zaclun. Unfortunately for Delgado, his new mission attracted an ambitious soldier, Captain Francisco Mirones, who for some time had turned over in his mind plans to subdue the Itzá by force. He put his ideas to a new Governor and, since the Franciscans had had no success, they were tentatively accepted, with the understanding that they must first be put to the Council of the Indies and the King. On the strength of this, Captain Mirones raised a force of fifty Spanish soldiers and marched to Zaclun. As he had nothing much else to do until final word was received on his plan of conquest, Mirones took to trade, and proved so unscrupulous that he drove the Indians to near revolt. In 1623 an order prohibiting the military expedition against the Itzá was received from Spain, and Delgado, who had been given permission to undertake a mission, decided to leave secretly on his own. Mirones, alarmed for his safety, sent twelve soldiers after him to persuade him to return or, if that failed, to go with him. Once again the Canek gave permission for a visit and Delgado, the soldiers and eighty Indian porters marched to Lake Petén-Itzá where they were picked up by canoes and carried with every sign of welcome to Tayasal. Once ashore, however, the two-facedness of the Itzá showed itself with a sudden, feral intensity. The Spanish soldiers were overwhelmed and disarmed and they, and the Indian porters, were bound and taken to the plaza for sacrifice. Delgado, who had been held apart from the others so that his attempts at preaching could not be heard, was confronted with the heads of his companions on stakes when he was led into the plaza. There were two reasons why he was about to be killed,

91

he was told: the destruction of Tzimin-Chac by Father Orbita and the fact that he had come accompanied by troops. Like his companions, Delgado had his heart torn out and his head placed on a stake. His body was cut to pieces. According to one story, the Spaniards' teeth were placed in the mouth of a stucco and mother-of-pearl mask of the sun in the Quincanek's temple.

In Zaclun, Mirones became more and more anxious as time passed and he received no word of what had happened. Finally, he dispatched two more Spaniards and an interpreter, Bernadino Ek, to Tayasal. When they lit a fire on the lake shore to signal there were strangers waiting for transport, canoes were sent and the new arrivals brought rapidly to Tayasal where they were tied up and placed in a palisaded enclosure for the night. Their guards celebrated so well that they became drunk and fell asleep, giving Ek a chance to slip his bonds and free the Spaniards. Unfortunately, the latter's wrists were so badly swollen and bruised from the ropes that they were unable to climb the palisade and fell back, awakening the guards with the noise. Ek, however, managed to escape and run down to the beach where he jumped into a canoe and paddled furiously for the far side. He was chased but managed to keep ahead and finally shook off his pursuers in the forest. Ek, but for whom nothing of what had happened might have been known for years, was tortured by Mirones, who disbelieved him, but his story was eventually accepted.

Mirones met his end in February the following year, 1624, when he, his soldiers and Delgado's replacement, Father Juan Enriquez, were celebrating the Feast of the Purification of the Blessed Virgin in the church at Zaclun. The soldiers' arms had been left in the armoury under the guard of only one man. The Indians, whose resentment of Mirones and his men had been at the boil for some time, took their chance, rushed the armoury and then made the Spaniards prisoners in the church. According to the historian Villagutierre, Father Enriquez had time to swallow the consecrated host without 'omitting any of the proper forms in doing so'. He then demanded in a loud voice that the Spaniards should be allowed to confess themselves like Christians. This the Indians permitted and the church was filled with the anguished hub-bub of the doomed men declaring their sins. Mirones, tied to a wooden roof prop on the epistle (the left-hand side of the church facing the altar), was the first to die, killed with his own knife snatched from his belt by Ahkimpphol, the leader of the Indians, who slashed open his breast and pulled out his heart. The other soldiers were similarly sacrificed. 'While these ministers of Satan thus glutted their infernal rage,' Father Enriquez was tied up to a prop on the gospel side, opposite the body of Captain Mirones. Some of the Indians wished to spare him, but Ahkimpphol dispatched him too with a rapid blow, silencing the voice that had continuously preached to the Indians on their impiety throughout this hideous slaughter. Ahkimpphol was captured later and taken to Mérida, where, perhaps remembering with contempt the Spaniards in the church calling on their God for forgiveness, he refused to confess himself before he was hanged.

7
The Fall of Tayasal

For almost three-quarters of a century following Delgado's martyrdom the Itzá were once again left to themselves. The population on the lake and in the forests continued to grow, and as it did so, the Church and the civil authorities became proportionately more anxious. An independent, pagan population defying Spanish control was an obvious threat to the settlements to north and south but perhaps it might have been ignored for a few decades more if it had not been for another factor: the presence of English loggers and buccaneers in Belize. There was a definite fear that they would play on Maya hostility to the Spaniards and extend their influence into the interior, perhaps forming an alliance with the Itzá as they had done with the Mosquito Indians on the Caribbean coast of Honduras and Nicaragua. Reports reached Mérida that a red-bearded man with a book, perhaps a Protestant with a Bible, was living in Tayasal (who he was and what happened to him, if he ever existed, remains a mystery). By 1689 the Council of the Indies was ready to sanction a conquest and three years later it was agreed that a road should be built between Campeche, in the Yucatán, and Guatemala, with armed expeditions pressing forward from the north and south and squeezing the Itzá into submission as bloodlessly as possible. In 1694 the expeditions were sent off; and before long they had all turned back. The Yucatán force skirmished with the Quehache Indians and the troops refused to go further without reinforcements. In the south, the Guatemalans lost a unit of forty-nine

Spanish soldiers and thirty-six Indian archers, slaughtered by the Itzá. The onset of the rains led to the decision of the remainder to retreat.

In the end, the conquest of the Itzá was accomplished from the Yucatán and without the assistance of Guatemala, although the Petén was to become a part of that country. As usual when under pressure, the Itzá sent an embassy to Mérida, where the ambassador, Can, a nephew of the Canek, announced to the Governor, Martin de Ursua, that his uncle wished 'to drink the same water and live under the same roof' as the Spaniards. The Canek's feather headdress was presented to Ursua as a sign of submission. Before sending Can, the Canek had consulted with four leading caciques and his senior subjects and councillors and they had all agreed that the time prophesied for conversion had come. The embassy of six Indians wished to be baptized at once, and Ursua arranged for this to be done with great pomp in the cathedral, to which they were taken by a large and magnificently dressed escort. Ursua was godfather to the ambassador, renamed Don Martin Francisco Can, and the Count de Miraflores performed the same function for his brother, Don Miguel Can. Loaded with presents, the embassy was sent home with an escort of thirty soldiers to protect them on the first leg of the journey.

In the meantime, the Franciscan friar Father Avendaño had heard that the Canek was prepared to accept a mission, and, despite a previous failure to reach Tayasal, he set out at the end of 1695 with two other friars and Indian guides and porters. There could hardly have been a better man for the task: he was brave, wise, humane, scholarly and devout. Like Bishop Landa he had mastered the complexities of the Maya calendar, about which he wrote a subsequently lost treatise, and he was familiar with the prophecies and the prophetic books, which he had seen in the Yucatán (evidence that a later generation of priests took a more tolerant interest in Maya art and religion).

The party which arrived to convey the friars to Tayasal included the Canek but was nevertheless alarming. The fleet of eighty canoes was manned by 500 armed men in warpaint and the friars were only slightly reassured by the fact that the warriors left their large quivers filled with arrows in their boats when they landed. Avendaño's attempts to welcome them with trumpets and a message of peace and goodwill on behalf of the King were disregarded and the missionaries and their followers were bundled aboard the canoes with 'very rude actions'. A nephew of the Canek demanded an image of Christ which hung from Avendaño's neck, and when it was refused, snatched a machete which had just been given to the Canek. With a quick pass in front of Avendaño's throat, he cut the string and took the image, replying to the friars' rebukes with a surly, 'Well, if you don't want to give it to me, what else am I to do?' The Canek, obviously a weak man, merely laughed.

What happened next is described in Avendaño's own words (the translation is Charles Bowditch's of the friar's 'Account of Two Trips to the Petén' as given in Philip Ainsworth Means' *History of the Spanish Conquest of the Yucatán and the Itzás*):

'In the long time that we were on the lake, a temptation was offered to the King, such as belonged to the devil who inspired it and natural to his inhuman and cruel heart, so as to inspire me with fear, so that my heart might suffer some sadness or disturbance; but his purpose found itself frustrated, first, because when I started from Mérida for this nation, I went prepared to die; and second, knowing that they were such savages in their ways, my courage stood prepared to suffer whatever insults they might say to me, as for instance to bear for God, who gives us courage, any unreasonable acts, whatsoever. Suddenly the said King placed his hand over my heart to see if it was at all agitated, and at the same time he asked me if I was so. I who was before very glad to see that my wishes and the work of my journey were being obtained, replied to him, "Why should my heart be disturbed? Rather it is very contented, seeing that I am the fortunate man, who is fulfilling your own prophecies, by which you are to become Christians; and this benefit will come to you by means of some bearded men from the East; who by signs of their prophets, were we ourselves, because we came many leagues from the direction of the east, ploughing the seas, with no other purpose than, borne by our love of their souls, to bring them, (at the cost of much work) to that favor which the true God shows them." I at this time, with some freedom on my part, also placed my hand on his breast and heart, and asking him also if his was disturbed, he said, "No". To which I replied, "If you are not disturbed, at seeing me, who am the minister of the true God, different in everything from you, in dress, customs and colour, so that I inspire fear in the devil, and if your heart is not troubled, why should you expect me to be afraid of you, mere men like myself, whom I come to seek purposely, with great pleasure, merely for the love which I have for their souls, and having found them, in order to announce to them the law of the true God, as you shall hear when we come to Petén." At this, changing the conversation, the devil tried to use him as his instrument for putting me in another greater temptation.

It is a custom among them, that, on the day before killing anyone or sacrificing him, especially if he is a stranger to their town, to give them something to eat, either the hot drink of barley and beans, which they use, or another of cacao, which is what they offer them. I was not ignorant of these rites, through what history relates that they had done on the two occasions on which priests of my holy religion had gone there; although in one case did they kill the Padre Fray Diego Delgado, through the fault of some Spaniards who followed him. When in the same way the said King asked me if I was hungry, I, though I had just eaten, realising the situation, said "yes", so that his wickedness should not see any cowardice in me; and I asked him if they had any-thing to eat, that they should give me some. At once he ordered that all the canoes should halt, and made them give red peppers and herbs, or tamales, which they brought on purpose to give us in the middle of that lake. I ate it eagerly and asked him very pleasantly if there was any more; to which he replied, "Then it has tasted good to you?" "Finely", I told him, "and I would eat more if there were any." I said this to him with some wit, at which they all laughed, but in a serious way, and they gave another which I ate with the same pleasure, at which they were all surprised – at the sight of my coolness. . . .'

The reprieved friar and his party landed at Tayasal and were taken on a tour of the island, including the Quincanek's temple where the friars thought they saw, rather indistinctly, the suspended leg or thigh bone of a horse. They were occupied with other things at the time and forgot then and later on during their stay to ask. The first day seems to have been spent in explaining a message from Governor Don Ursua and delivering a sermon. No mention was made at this time or later of Ambassador Can's journey to Mérida.

After this, the friars returned in the dusk to their lodging, accompanied by the Canek and a host of curious Itzás. At no time during their stay were they ever left alone 'since if any, satisfied with having seen us by day, went away to their houses at night, double the number came by night to see us and to sleep there, besides those who came first, and even those who had gone away satisfied with seeing us, did not fail to come back'. They were not, Avendaño complained, able to attend to their 'needs' without a crowd in attendance. Scolding by the friars and the Canek's order that they should be left alone produced nothing more than laughter. 'Their tediousness was such that if we sat down, they all sat down next to us, surrounding us; and then some on one side and others on the other would touch us from top to toe, not excepting (if we gave them the chance) the hidden parts of a man.' To obtain some respite, the friars arranged that the crowd would seat themselves on the stone benches of a temple while they conducted a service, a sight which the Itzás found very amusing. Just for the pleasure of being free from physical contact, the friars would continue with the movements of the service long after it was in fact over.

The Canek, the Quincanek and another senior priest still played for time, but finally it was agreed that they should all gather in the temple at dawn to discuss conversion. A feast had been prepared of tortillas, beans, squashes, wild pig, prawns and fish, which the Canek and his followers ate. All were extremely suspicious of baptism since they feared that it involved circumcision or some form of bloodletting. One of the Canek's numerous children had been held in readiness near the temple, and the Canek now brought him forward and demanded a demonstration. Avendaño asked whether, if baptism proved to be harmless, the Canek would assent to the rest of his children being baptized. The Canek agreed and as a result all the royal children were baptized. This example led to many other children being brought forward, so that in three and a half days, Avendaño baptized nearly 300.

More caciques from other Itzá settlements began to arrive on the island, their faces painted black and their bodies a fearsome red. They wore feather headdresses and carried long spears which were also decorated with feathers. Avendaño went down to the shore to greet them, displaying his usual calm by embracing them and offering food. As usual he made great play with the katun prophecies, prompting one cacique, Covoh, to ask testily, 'And what does it signify if the time *is* come? The sharp flint that points my spear is not yet worn away.' At that he raised the spear threateningly. Undisturbed, Avendaño replied that the time must have come because the cacique and the devil, Pacoc, with whom he was in league, had been unable to harm him. Covoh's previous misdeeds included stealing a suit of clothes brought by Avendaño for the Canek.

Avendaño and the Canek finally agreed that the older men would accept baptism in four months' time, but the arrangement was obviously very fragile. The friars prepared to leave and on the day before their departure were visited by Covoh, who asked for the loan of the two fattest of Avendaño's Indian servants so that when they broke their journey at his house 'they should have made me something good to eat'. Avendaño refused to let the men go but said he would stop at Covoh's house the next day. The cacique went off satisfied, to prepare, as Avendaño learned later, a cooking fire for the Indians and stakes for the friars.

As soon as Covoh had gone, the Canek warned the friars to leave at once by a different route than the one originally planned. The Canek's queen and her daughters backed up this advice and informed the friars that Covoh and his men intended to kill them by cutting them into small pieces, '. . . and they made gestures with one hand over the other, to show they were going to make mincemeat of us and eat us'.

Escorted by the Canek's son and son-in-law, Avendaño and his party made their escape by night. All went well until the escort left them, whereupon the friars became hopelessly lost and wandered exhausted and starving in the forest. Taking one of the two compasses with the party, the two younger friars decided to push on on their own, leaving Avendaño while they searched for a friendly village. Avendaño, who had been saved on two previous occasions by 'miraculous honey' and a 'miraculous' trail through a swamp, was now to benefit from yet another miracle. He was lying on the ground on his own, engaged in the prayers for the dying 'when suddenly, though there was no sapote (chicle or chewing gum) tree where I was, there came a squirrel down a low tree with sapote fruit in his little paws, and giving two jumps in my presence, it showed its little teeth and went away'. The fruit was 'ripe and sweet as honey' and Avendaño survived to make his way to Mérida, where he reported to Ursua.

A military attempt to take Tayasal appears to have been launched while the Franciscans were fleeing through the jungle. The force reached the shore close to Tayasal and apparently expected a friendly reception. However, the Itzás jumped out of their canoes, slashed the throat of a Spaniard, clubbed two Indians to death and carried off to the island a Father Buenaventura, a lay brother and another Spaniard, who were all sacrificed. Some forty of the Itzá were killed in a brisk battle but the Spanish force withdrew to await reinforcement.

In January 1697, Don Ursua set out from Campeche to join this force and supervise in person the surrender of Tayasal. He brought with him a force of cavalry, his staff, the vicar-general appointed by the Bishop of Yucatán and various priests. On his arrival at the lake, he was informed by his godson, Can, that the Itzá were set on war and were strengthening the island's defences. Marauding parties harassed Ursua's men as they cut the trees and built the boats (including a galliot, a small fast galley) that were to carry them to Tayasal. While this work was going on, a fleet of canoes with a white flag at its head was sighted. It brought the Quincanek. Ursua put on the best reception he could at such short notice, and the Quincanek was brought to the Governor's tent – the royal standard flying in front – between paraded ranks of Spanish troops, with a band playing. There he announced that the Itzás wanted only peace and that the Canek would shortly visit Ursua. But the Canek never appeared. Instead there arrived an entirely novel item from the Itzá armoury, a small regiment of women intent on romantic conquest. Their purpose was either to appease the Spaniards or weaken their resolve to such an extent that they would never want to set sail for Tayasal, but, under the stern eye of the vicar-general, they were politely received and sent home.

At last all was ready for the invasion. Ursua hoped to avoid force and his men were forbidden, on pain of death, to open fire without direct orders from him. The troops were confessed, mass was said and they then set sail in the galliot, encouraged by the finding of a small engraving of St Paul floating on the waters. As the sun rose over the lake, more prayers were said by the vicar-general and the troops raised a great cry of '*Viva La Ley de Dios!*' (Long live the Law of God). Following that, there was a mass repentance of sins by the men, with the words 'Lord, I have sinned, have mercy upon me,' and a general absolution by the vicar-general.

Half-way across the lake a reconnaissance canoe was sighted and shortly afterwards the Itzá battle fleet appeared from behind the Nitun promontory. A hideous noise of war cries rose from the canoes as the Itzá brandished their weapons and sped forward. Before long, the galliot was completely surrounded and the Indians fired volleys of arrows. Even so, Ursua refrained from returning fire and his vessel was driven close to the shore. Two of his men were injured by the arrows and one, Bartolomeo Duran, was so infuriated by the pain of his wound that he disobeyed orders and fired his musket. Discipline broke down and shooting became general, so that by the time the galliot reached Tayasal, the Spaniards' blood was up and they leaped into the water and fought their way ashore. Itzá resistance on land and water collapsed. Those on the island plunged into the lake, while the warriors in the canoes tumbled overboard in a panic to escape the galliot, from which twenty soldiers were firing with muskets. From Tayasal to the mainland, wrote Villagutierre, nothing was to be seen but the heads of Indians, men, women and children, all swimming as fast as they could.

Ursua's policy of clemency succeeded in persuading great numbers to return, including the Canek and Quincanek. The evil Covoh, who had caused Avendaño so much trouble, was caught and put in irons. So, after some initial festivities, were the Canek and Quincanek, who, Ursua discovered, were plotting to escape. Quincanek was put to the torture but refused to confess and awed his captors by summoning up a hurricane so tremendous and with such thunder and lightning and fearful howling of winds that, says Villagutierre, 'the island was like the centre of hell'. The curates were unable to exorcise the storm until three in the morning, by which time terrible destruction had been caused and 200 houses blown away.

The Canek and the Quincanek were baptized, becoming respectively Don José Pablo Canek and Don Francisco Nicolas Canek, but the Itzá were never completely subdued.

Ursua's godson, Don Martin Can, reverted to the old faith and took to the woods only a year after the fall of Tayasal; and in 1699 the problems of living in the rain forests surrounded by hostile Indians led to the withdrawal of the main Spanish force, taking with them the Canek and the Quincanek. Only a small garrison was left in Tayasal. Even in the mid-nineteenth century, the Itzá were 'still, in reality, an independent race', wrote Charles Fancourt, a former Superintendent of Belize. 'With respect to their actual condition, our information falls short of what was known to the Spaniards at the close of the seventeenth century.'

Following the fall of Tayasal, the conquerors spent nine hours smashing idols. They discovered in the Canek's palace copies of the sacred books of prophecies and histories, but what became of them is not known, although it has been suggested that the three codices now in Europe came from Tayasal (they could equally well have come from those seen by Avendaño in the Yucatán).

Another discovery showed that Avendaño and the friars had not been deceived when they thought they saw a horse's bones in the main temples. 'There was hanging from the top', wrote Villagutierre, 'by three strips of spun cotton of different colours, a leg-bone half decayed; and on the ground beneath were placed three braziers for burning perfumes or incense, with storax and other aromatic substances in them, which they used to burn in the sacrifices, and some dry maize leaves; on the top of this leg-bone was set a crown. It was explained that these bones were the fragments of what remained of a great horse which had been left in their care by a king who had passed that way a long time before.'

PART II

EXPLORATION

8

A Lost City Rediscovered

In Central America the Conquest was at last completed. In Western Europe a new era, both romantic and speculative, had begun. Lost cities enjoyed a vogue. Two years after the rediscovery of Pompeii in 1748 a party of Spaniards either stumbled upon or was led to the ruins of Palenque, in the Chiapas forests. They were known to the Indians as *'Casas de Piedra'* (houses of stone). There were no legends, except those that could be drawn from the splendid carvings, the princely courtyards and the tree- and vine-covered towers and temples. The literary imagination of the time was left free to do its best, or worst, with them; and therefore it was almost a century before they were prosaically connected with the people who had probably known about them all the time, the Indians. Discoveries are not, of course, discoveries unless the mind can make something of them. Fifty years earlier a party of Spaniards might well have walked through Palenque and nobody would have thought any more of the matter. After all, Avendaño probably saw Tikal, the grandest ruins in Central America, on his way to Tayasal, but he made only a passing mention of it or whatever it was he did see. Palenque's ruins are about eight miles from the administrative centre of the same name that was established in the mid-sixteenth century. Numerous forays against the Itzá and the Lacandónes were launched from there and it seems improbable that, in the 200 years before 1750, no one heard about the mysterious *'Casas de Piedra'* in the jungle. But in the eighteenth century even the intellectually isolated Spanish court and its empire were brushed by the romantic liberalism of Western Europe. Officials were instructed to report any interesting finds. A lost city in the jungles, the home of jaguars, apes and wild Indians, provoked enough curiosity for three official expeditions to be sent there between 1784 and 1807. Nevertheless, it was still quite a long time before news of Palenque reached receptive ears in Europe.

The first person to write about the ruins was Father Rámon de Ordóñez y Aguiar, the canon of the cathedral of Ciudad Real de Chiapas, who seems to have gone there on his own account in 1773. Palenque, he decided, had been built by Votan (another name for Quetzalcoatl), the legendary hero of the Maya-Quiché Indians, after he had received a divine command to leave Atlantis and lay the foundations of civilization in Central America. It was not until ten years later that a local official, José Calderón, wrote an official report that led to an Italian architect, Antonio Bernasconi, being sent from Guatemala City to carry out an official survey. He provided some remarkably misleading drawings that showed Maya nobles in Spanish kneebreeches with elaborate buckles on their shoes. The report reached the royal library in Madrid and disappeared into a large pile of unpublished documents. The next official visitor was an artillery captain, Antonio del Río, who brought with him an artist, Ricardo Almendariz, who was at least more painstaking. Del Río procured seventy-nine Indians with forty-nine axes and seven crowbars and began to clear the site with a devastating efficiency worthy of an artillery officer. 'A general conflagration soon enabled us to breathe a more wholesome atmosphere,' he reported. Following that his men set to work on the buildings, adding considerably to the effects of time and tree roots. 'Ultimately there remained neither a window nor a doorway blocked up, a partition that was not thrown down, nor a room, corridor, court, tower nor subterranean passage in which excavations were not effected from two to three yards in depth.' Roman influence, it was thought, had inspired the builders of Palenque, since the presence of an arched stone conduit suggested that members of that 'polished nation' had stayed there and passed on their arts as a return for hospitality. Finally there came in 1805–7, a retired captain of dragoons, Guillelmo Dupaix, who had been commissioned by Charles IV to make a survey of Mexican antiquities. He accomplished part of his journey trussed up and carried by Indians who mistook him for a bandit. They marched on stolidly as he shouted: 'Boys! Look, I am a captain and I am asking where the municipal centre is!' Alas, Dupaix seems to have had an unlucky face: he was later imprisoned on suspicion that his survey was merely a cover for fomenting revolution. His reports (accompanied by some imaginative but good architectural drawings by Luciano Castañeda) vanished into the Cabinet of Natural History in Mexico City where they remained until rescued nearly thirty years later by a French *abbé*.

In the end it was Del Río's report, which had lingered in Guatemala City, that touched off with, as usual, a very long fuse, the nineteenth-century explosion of interest in the Maya ruins. A Scottish geographer, Dr James McQueen, probably brought it to London where it was published in 1822 with a long preface about Votan written by Dr Felix Cabrera, an Italian antiquarian resident in Guatemala City. It was the first account of the ruins to be published anywhere. Involved in the venture was the German- or Austrian-born (but French by naturalization) 'Count' Jean Frédéric Maximilien de Waldeck, scion, supposedly, of the Dukes of Waldeck-Pyrmont, soldier of fortune, artist and possessor of what was once described as a 'Münchausen-like virtuosity' for telling tall stories about his adventures. He was living in London at the time and was responsible for touching up and generally improving Almendariz's drawings which were included in the book and signed by Waldeck as his own.

One imagines that Waldeck, who claimed to know the American continent from 'the Magellan Straits to Spitzbergen' – he was never very strong on geography – met either McQueen or Cabrera, or an Irish adventurer of Spanish extraction,

Colonel John Galindo, or perhaps all three of them, while he was in Central America shortly after being ejected from Lord Cochrane's Chilean navy in 1820 or thereabouts. He spent a great deal of his long life (if one can believe his very possibly bogus date of birth, he lived to the age of 109, an unequalled record for Mayanists) struggling with various rather unlucrative publishing ventures. Perhaps it was the Del Río book that lent a little authority to his claim that he was 'the first Americanist', or scholar of American antiquities. It was in this guise that he met the well-intentioned but dotty Viscount Kingsborough, an Irish peer, who died in a Dublin debtors' prison as a result of his expensive enthusiasm for Central American civilizations. In pursuit of material for his nine-volume opus *Antiquities of Mexico*, he was misguided enough to send Waldeck to Palenque.

In the early part of the year the jungle around Palenque is dark green and glossy, a sinuous exuberance of cascading creepers that pour from trees supported on equally twining, complex roots. A stream, the Otulum, runs down from the steep hills and passes through the middle of the ruins, adding its small noises to those of birds and dragonflies crackling their wings like innumerable short circuits. The jungle keeps its distance, thanks to the custodians; they have planted the main plaza with orange trees whose Mediterranean scent confuses the imagination just as much as does the name Otulum, which might easily have graced a sacred river in the Campagna or Sicily. One looks at the modest temples against their tropical backdrop and the word 'embowered' comes to mind. Palenque is charming, a little domestic, a feast of the picturesque. Almost any temple could have harboured an eighteenth-century picnic, with woodwinds breathing their musical enchantments in the background. What Rose Macaulay called 'ruin-sensibility' is heightened there as nowhere else on the American continent.

Thus one walks through the wild mint that cloaks the unreclaimed stones around the palace and temples of Palenque aware of one's own traditions as well as those of the Maya.

They are Waldeck's 'dear ruins' where he established himself at Lord Kingsborough's expense for a year or so in 1832–3, living in the building known as the Temple of the Count, entranced by the sculpture and an Indian girl whom John Lloyd Stephens later described as 'once the pride and beauty' of Palenque. Perhaps to flatter her, or maybe merely because he thought his patron would like to see a half-naked Indian maiden amid the sculpture, he incorporated her into his drawings of Maya nobles and priests. Waldeck's temple faces east and stands close to the edge of the shelf in the hills on which Palenque is lodged, overlooking the rich plain which once supplied its wealth, and in the mornings the elderly 'Count' was woken by the sun streaming across the plaza and through the open doorway.

Various vicissitudes, including seizure of written material by the Mexican government, saw to it that Waldeck's work at Palenque went unpublished until 1866, but nineteenth-century scholarship lost very little as a result of this delay. Waldeck's inventive approach to his work seems to have started the great

'Elephant's trunk', on right
near top of a stela at Copán

elephant controversy that has run through Maya scholarship for over a century: he drew elephants into the glyphs. Although he later decided they were tapirs, the damage had been done. Mayanists have been seeing elephants ever since. In some cases, such as the elongated macaw beaks on the stelae at Copán, their speculation was justified. They do look remarkably like elephant trunks, although a close study reveals the scale-like skin behind a parrot beak. Even as late as 1927, Eric Thompson

One of Waldeck's elephants from Palenque. A. P. Maudslay's accurate copy of the same hieroglyphs is on the left

was taking Waldeck's elephants quite seriously, although admitting the artist was not 'strongly blessed with the gift of accuracy'. Another English scholar, G. Elliott Smith, of London University, took the whole matter even further, spotting a mahout riding on an 'unmistakable Indian elephant' at Copán. Both Smith and Thompson were attacking what the latter called 'the Monroe doctrine of anthropology, or hands off America; home-grown American civilizations for the Americans'. Just as the early antiquarians were inclined to see Romans, Carthaginians *et al.* among the Maya ruins, so later ones found evidence of Asian origins. The elephants may be rather silly, but the argument itself is not foolish. Maya art does look 'oriental'. There are figures on the Copán stelae which are remarkably Chinese; one sees occasionally on pottery and jade ornaments a sensuous turn of a body which might have been executed by an Asian Indian carver. The Maya and other American Indians did come many thousands of years ago from Asia by way of the Behring Straits and perhaps the truth is that the 'oriental' elaborations and rhythms of Maya art were as innate within them as the nest-building instincts of chaffinches. If a face on a Copán stela looks Chinese, it may be because the Maya came from the same racial stock. However, that does not support the 'big bang' theory of cultural diffusion, which is what Thompson, Elliot Smith and others were championing. The diffusionists hold that civilizations are spread and do not evolve spontaneously. So far as America is concerned it is a romantic idea: Quetzalcoatl coming with the Norsemen or perhaps in the shape of an Irish monk to being enlightenment to the American savages; the inhabitants of Atlantis fleeing westwards from their foundering island; Indians or Indo chinese bringing with them nostalgic memories of elephants. Architectural and artistic styles did spread among the Indians, but all the evidence points to them having been their own styles indigenously evolved. The similarities within Indian art, from Alaskan house boards to Maya stelae, are much greater than those between, say, Maya pyramids and Egyptian pyramids. It is fairly widely accepted that if the Maya and the Egyptians (and many other peoples, including the prehistoric Britons, as at Silbury Hill) built pyramids it was because they felt a need to, not just because they had seen one somewhere else or had been told about them. Just as making a bowl reflects a need, so – on a higher and more abstract level – does making a pyramid. The same reasoning can be applied to calendars and the prediction of eclipses. Needs expand with intellectual capacity and, given the limitations imposed by circumstances, they are universal. Because several races dig their ground with mattocks, it does not mean that the idea of mattock was spread from some central source. As the structuralist Claude Lévi-Strauss has pointed out, it is the need or requirement, not the implement, which constitutes the species. In other words, the mattock is the symbol of a common requirement to dig and produce food, and pyramids are the symbol of a common requirement to get nearer to the sun and the stars which move on mysterious principles and may be divine.

It was the figures on the Palenque carvings that made the ruins so much more open to antiquarian speculation than those in the Yucatán. It is easy to see Phoenicians and moustached European faces, as well as elephants, on the carved slabs. Even though one can appreciate it nowadays within the context of the Classic Maya period, Palenque is still unusually strange. The art is not in itself uniformly good. The figures often seem weak and there is an overall feeling that the place was both

Heads of gods on hieroglyphics in the Palace, Palenque. Note the jaguar half-covering the first head

civilized and effete, its art lacking – with some notable exceptions – in vigour. However, decadence is often a great deal more enjoyable than solid virtue; and often, too, what we call decadence is really transition, the movement from one stage of civilization to another. Palenque was on the edge of the Mediterranean of the meso-American world, the Gulf of Mexico, where pre-Columbian art is often more humane, more inventive and freer than elsewhere, as in the remarkable clay figurines from Jaina, a Maya burial ground off the west coast of Yucatán.

There is a feeling of cultural surge there and in Palenque, possibly because an *élite* was becoming aware of individuality and personal beauty. Examining a Palanque carving, it is often the singular, arched noses that are immediately striking; they must have been a caste mark, a distinction that set them apart from the flat-nosed Olmecs (whose art, dating from before the Christian era, is among the most beautiful and vigorous in America) and other races who presumably had been subjected. The artificially compressed foreheads emphasised this feature even more, and in some figurines it is caricatured by carrying the ridge over the brow like a ramp. Perhaps the curious custom of pechni, flattening the nose before execution, had to do with the idea of removing the chief physical attribute of nobility, or superior race, of lowering the victim in his disgrace, to common levels before death. How odd it is that Europeans also admired the Roman nose, the Wellingtonian nose, as a sign of aristocracy and of a commanding personality.

To return to Waldeck: his elephants may reveal his personal inadequacies but they nevertheless stir the imagination; they are ludicrous but they create interest, which was Waldeck's contribution during his life to Maya studies. He was a crooked but important pollen-bearer in the cross-fertilization between eccentric or, more politely, unorthodox scholars and those following stricter disciplines, and if some day it is decided there should be a shrine, a Temple of the Mayanists, it would be hard to find a more appropriate and enjoyable place than his abode at Palenque. After all, he was a gold medallist of the French *Société de Geographie*, and the American Antiquarian Society in 1839 unanimously elected him a member together with John Quincy Adams, the sixth President of the United States. Prescott, the historian, who had been elected to the Antiquarian Society at its previous meeting, thought Waldeck talked 'so big' that he must be a bit of a charlatan, and quite a few others were not taken in, but it is surprising on the whole how many were. He was a mediocre but passable artist who claimed to have studied under David, Prud'hon and others and perhaps that gave him a certain basic standing; and, like any good international 'con-man', he was a skilled linguist, fluent in French, English and Spanish as well, presumably, as in his native German. There is a photograph of him in a book by Miss Mary Darby Smith of Philadelphia, an engagingly naïve

Waldeck

but really rather silly lady who is nevertheless a great source of information about Waldeck. It shows a man of about 70, with a well-brushed white beard, possibly rather burly, not at all bald and very alert; the eyes catch one's attention. They look a little sideways from behind gold-rimmed spectacles, as if asking 'What are you making of me?'

Waldeck claimed to have been born in 1766 but became a little confused between birth and baptism dates, so that sometimes he gave the year as 1768. His desire for a state pension may have had something to do with his assertions as to his age. Statements of where he was born also varied but it was probably within the boundaries of the Austrian Empire, although Paris seems to have been given as his birthplace on one occasion. However, he adopted, so he said, 'revolutionary principles', during his spell under David's real or invented tutelage and in time became a French citizen. His friendships ranged with remarkable flexibility for a revolutionary artist from Marie-Antoinette to Robespierre and Marat; later, in England, they covered the ground from George III ('a frequent guest') to Beau Brummell, Fox, Pitt and Lord Byron. The last encounter took place at the home of an unnamed Scottish laird where 'Lord Byron would swim and leave me to fish alone', Waldeck informed Miss Darby Smith, adding a few comments that the authoress noted primly she cared not to repeat. Lord Byron was probably thrown into Waldeck's list of notable acquaintances entirely for the benefit of Miss Darby Smith, whose book *Recollections of Two Distinguished Persons: La Marquise de Boissy and the Count de Waldeck*, featured in tandem with 'the first Americanist' the last mistress of Lord Byron. The Marquise was the former Contessa Guiccioli, who in later life in Paris kept in close touch with her dead lover by means of 'spiritism'. Miss Darby Smith first encountered Waldeck through the recommendation of an elderly 'savant' whom she met while visiting 'a celebrated Turkish bath establishment' near, suitably enough, Blarney, in County Cork. Waldeck was at that time (about the late 1860s or early 1870s) living in Bedford Square,

London, from where he had sent a letter to the 'savant' recommending his *The Ancient Monuments of Mexico*, published by subscription, 'The only means I have of undertaking the publication and combating the Jesuits who wish to prevent the execution of the plan . . .' He considered himself at war with the Jesuits because of their alleged distortions of history. Waldeck seems to have made frequent trips from Paris to England, at one stage, in the 1820s and 1830s, possibly to exploit Lord Kingsborough, and in later life for a mixture of business and family reasons. At the age of 84 – according to his estimation – he married his English housekeeper's 17-year-old niece, Ellen Henwood, by whom he fathered a son. Waldeck owed his obviously robust good health to horseradish, which he recommended warmly to Miss Darby Smith 'to be taken for six weeks every spring, grated horseradish mixed with crumbs of bread and flavoured with lemon-juice instead of vinegar; taken in large quantities by the tablespoon instead of the teaspoonful, three times a day at each meal'. His only problem was with his legs, which had been 'bitten by the rattlesnakes in the ruins of Palenque'.

Miss Darby Smith was clearly a wealthy woman and Waldeck no doubt traded his celebrity for her subscriptions to his work in progress. On one occasion he wrote asking for a loan of 10,000 francs so that he could take his unfinished diorama featuring the history of all countries 'from the heroic age to this date' to New York, where he hoped to establish a partnership with P. T. Barnum. The great showman ducked an invitation to discuss the matter with Miss Darby Smith and said that he felt too old 'and certainly your friend is, to engage in a new speculation'.

With his courtly manner and sonorous voice, Waldeck enchanted his biographer with the story of his life and adventures, the latter beginning at the age of 19 with a journey in the company of Le Vaillant, the noted French explorer, to southern Africa in 1784. There he engaged in a remarkable journey of his own, accompanied by Kaas, a Hottentot, and Kees, a trained ape. The Napoleonic wars saw him fighting side by side with the First Consul at Toulon, in the Italian campaign and in Egypt, where he frequently partook of Napoleon's 'humble fare' as they dined alone. Waldeck, an Austrian citizen at that time, had assumed a false name and, although he had been given the rank of captain, was in reality, so he said, a 'savant' charged with investigating some aspect or other of Egypt's past or its natural history. At this stage one begins to suspect that Waldeck's stories were designed to cover up a spell in prison, possibly for forgery or false pretences. He had, he told Miss Darby Smith, the ability to copy the handwriting of anyone perfectly, and on one occasion 'from mere caprice', he had imitated the signature of Napoleon Bonaparte. Hearing of this, Napoleon sent for Waldeck and, remarking on his success at forgery, handed him a piece of paper and invited him to sign it 'Napoleon'. The paper read 'Condemned to three months at Vincennes'. According to Waldeck, the Emperor released him after two weeks. It is not clear whether it was before or after this imprisonment (very probably before) that Waldeck was supposed to have made a famous journey from Egypt to Madagascar by way of the Desert of Dongola, losing his three companions *en route*. Anyway, his next remarkable journey came after he had joined Lord Cochrane in 1819 to lend his naval experience (allegedly gained on board the French privateer *Surcouf* in the Indian Ocean) to the Chileans in their war of independence from Spain. He parted from Lord Cochrane before long because of 'a difference of temperament and of money' and then made his way by river from Peru to Copán, Honduras, which as a glance at a map will assure the reader, is about as feasible as travelling by train from London to Reykjavik. But it was that trip to Copán, real or invented and however he got there, that entitled him to claim some initial expertise in the field of American antiquities; and that in turn brought him into contact with the unfortunate Edward King, Lord Kingsborough.

Kingsborough, an Irish peer from Cork, entered Exeter

College, Oxford, in 1814, at the age of 19, as a nobleman. He obtained a place in the second class of *Literae Humaniores* but never took a degree. However, his period at Oxford saw the germination of a scholarly obsession that was to ruin him. In the Bodleian Library one day he came across an Aztec hieroglyphic tribute chart in the collections of Archbishop Laud and 'the learned Mr Seldon' and he seems to have been completely carried away by its beauty and mystery. The founders of the Central American civilizations, he decided, were the ten Lost Tribes of Israel, and he set out to prove it, in the process spending £32,000, a 'larger sum of money on a literary work than ever were before expended by any nobleman', as one of his contemporaries noted. A spell as M.P. for Cork (he was the eldest son of a peer, the Earl of Kingston, and therefore his title did not exclude him from the Commons) from 1820–6 seems to have interfered not at all with his scheme for a nine-volume work that Prescott described as 'noble', 'magnificent' and 'colossal',while politely disagreeing with the theory about the Lost Tribes, to which Kingsborough devoted 307 pages of notes in Volume VI. An Italian artist, Augustine Aglio, spent five years researching and copying codices in Paris, Berlin, Dresden, Vienna, the Vatican, Rome, Bologna and Oxford. Seven volumes came out in 1831 (the two last ones were not published until 1848, more than a decade after Kingsborough's death), two sets of them printed on vellum at a price of £3,000 each. The price of those printed on paper, with coloured plates, was £210 and quite clearly there was not much demand for them then or later. By 1856 they were being offered at £63, a bargain, since they really are magnificent works, though so heavy and large that a trolley is needed to bring them from the library shelves to the reader's desk. Either out of kindness or with publicity in mind, Kingsborough gave away nine sets to learned institutions and various European crowned heads. Since the *Compendium of Irish Biography* laments that if he had only lived another year he would have inherited his father's title and £40,000 a year, it seems unlikely that he bankrupted the family. Possibly the family got tired of the expensive eccentricity displayed by the bachelor heir, for it seems no attempt was made to bail him out when, on the suit of an Irish paper manufacturer, he was arrested for debt and locked up in the Dublin Sheriff's prison. There he caught typhus and died in February 1837, at the age of 42.

Around the time of the publication of the first seven volumes he financed a trip to Palenque by Waldeck, who was to carry out further research there and make drawings. The noted Americanist was given a British passport in which he was described rather strangely as a British subject who had been engaged in London as an engineer in the English mining company of Tlalpuxahua, in Mexico. After his first visit to Palenque, Waldeck was not permitted by the Mexican government to return there. Civil war was imminent and as Waldeck (or his ghost writer) wrote in his account of his attempt to return to Palenque (*Le Voyage - Pittoresque et Archaeologique dans Yucatan*), 'These good people were unable to conceive that I received money from England to visit old monuments, and they imagined I was a spy in the pay of the British government.' The British were interested in the Yucatán and Mexico generally during the nineteenth century and were not above supporting the occasional gun-runner, so perhaps the Mexicans were not as unreasonable in their suspicions as Waldeck made out. In fact, it may be that the government had very good reasons for chasing him out of the Yucatán, where he spent more than two years. *Le Voyage Pittoresque* is an enjoyable book and perhaps the author deserved his gold medal from the *Société de Geographie*, but it leaves a feeling that not all is revealed. For example, in his account of the siege of Tabasco by rebellious forces, Waldeck mentions the return of his associate, a M. Pieper, from New York, bringing with him 100 English guns for resale. Why on earth, one wonders, would an archaeologist team up with a gun salesman at a time when civil war was erupting? However, Waldeck in his 'capacity of old soldier' put the guns to good use, loading them all so he and other defenders of his lodgings could keep up a running fire from behind bales of merchandise in front of which was a minefield of twelve demijohns filled with gunpowder and an obstacle

Waldeck's published version of a drawing by Almendariz of a stucco relief at Palenque (from Del Rio's report as published in London in 1822)

composed of 200 broken bottles strewn around to break the
charge of the barefooted rebels. In the end it was cholera and
not fire-power which lifted the siege.

Waldeck may not have reached Palenque again but he did
get to the ruins of Uxmal where he made some of his usual misleading drawings and named the Temple of the Wizard after
'*mon genereux protecteur*' Lord Kingsborough (he also dedicated
Le Voyage Pittoresque to him). He died in Paris in 1875, aged
109 by his own count, but quite possibly ten to twenty years
younger. A fall as he left a ministerial *soirée* brought about his
end, as the Countess Ellen explained to a saddened Miss Derby
Smith, who said goodbye to him on his deathbed and was
gratified by the way in which he looked at her for a few moments 'with the utmost clearness' before advising her to 'remember, my dear, there are few to be trusted, few who are sincere'.
The invitation to his funeral gave all his honours, including the
Venezuelan Order of Merit and honorary membership of the
Athenaeum, in London.

John Lloyd Stephens, who had a low opinion of Waldeck's
drawings, having been able to compare some of them with the
originals, happened to be in Palenque in 1840 when the Indian
beauty whom Waldeck had included in his sketches was buried,
Gravesides drew Stephens like magnets. Perhaps he foresaw
his own death in those fever-ridden regions, or perhaps it was
the lugubrious sentimentality of the age. The girl had had two
unhappy marriages since Waldeck's stay at Palenque. 'I could
not turn my eyes from her placid but grief-worn countenance,
and so touching was its expression that I could almost have
shed tears. Young, beautiful, simple and innocent, abandoned
and dead, with not a mourner at her grave.' He watched horrified but unable to tear himself away as the uncoffined and un-
shrouded body was covered. 'A small piece of muddy earth
fell upon one of the eyes, and another on her sweetly smiling
mouth, changing the whole expression in a moment; death was
now robed with terror. The women stopped to comment upon

the change; the dirt fell so as to cover the whole face except the nose, and for two or three moments this alone was visible.' Her 'sweet face speaking from the grave' remained in Stephens' memory for a long time afterwards.

9
The Race to Palenque

Twice a day the tides raise themselves just high enough to sluice the outer gutters of Belize, the capital of British Honduras. Occasionally, backed by the Caribbean hurricanes, they wash away the houses as well as the rubbish, but as such occurrences are comparatively rare, the little town at the mouth of the Belize river has an easy-going, confident air. It is an unpretentious place on an equally unpretentious river which arrives at the sea without the luxury of an estuary: one moment it is narrow enough to be crossed with a plunge and a few strokes – that is if anyone were foolish enough to dive into its suspect waters – the next, open sea. The Negro fishermen swoop round the point, lower their sails hastily and there they are, right in the heart of the capital, which is occupied by a fish and vegetable market. British Honduras was the creation of buccaneers who part-timed as loggers, thus earning sufficient respectability to entitle them to the protection of the Crown against the claims of the Spanish Empire. Despite Lord Palmerston's assertion that 'Honduras is ours by the best of titles, that of the sword,' its survival is really a modest triumph of diplomacy. It was always one of the less plausible parts of the British Empire, a muddy foothold in a region where British interests were never very much more than robustly ambiguous. Nowadays, of course, it is among those left-over bits of Empire which won't go away because of the inhabitants' fears that they will be swallowed up by someone else, in this case Guatemala, so colonial diplomacy exerts itself towards extrication rather than staying put.

A posting to Belize can never have been popular with British officials. The climate is wet and horrible for much of the year and in the past death from one of several varieties of fever was all too likely; and there was also the depressing feeling of being sent to serve in a *cul-de-sac* of Empire. For men of mettle, as nineteenth-century British officials often were, the best response was activity, which possibly explains the optimistic view they took of imperial prospects in Central America. The opportunities were fairly evident: the Spanish Empire had collapsed in the early 1820s and various forces struggled for supremacy in the chaos that persisted for many decades afterwards. The British consul to the Central American Republic in the 1830s and 1840s, Frederick Chatfield, a Palmerstonian Empire-builder, wanted to press ahead with the creation of a British protectorate embracing what are now the sovereign states of Guatemala, Honduras, El Salvador, Nicaragua and Costa Rica. From Belize, where the drunken Robert, King of the Mosquito Shore (which extends along the Caribbean coasts of Honduras and Nicaragua), had been crowned in the redbricked Anglican cathedral, officials had gone forth to place his subjects, the Mosquito–Sambo Indians, allies of two centuries' standing, under direct British guardianship.

It was in the same spirit that what has been called the 'Race to Palenque'* began. On 30 October 1839, John Lloyd Stephens and Frederick Catherwood (whom Chatfield was to refer to contemptuously as that 'Yankified English artist') sailed into Belize aboard the British brig *Mary Ann*. Stephens had been appointed by President Van Buren as his 'confidential agent', with the mission of discovering whether the Central American Republic really existed and, if it did, who was running it and where. He brought with him a diplomatic frock coat with braid and brass buttons, which he seems to have worn only once or twice, and a hat with an American eagle, which he put on more often because he found the eagle impressed local officials. His

* In David Prendergast's, *Palenque: The Walker–Caddy Expedition to the Ancient Maya City, 1839-40.*

diplomatic duties sat fairly lightly on him, and as he makes clear in his books (among the wittiest and most enjoyable ever written about Victorian travel) his main interest was archaeological exploration. However, his appearance *en route* to Guatemala City via the ruins of Copán evidently aroused the suspicions of the Superintendent of Belize, Col. Alexander Macdonald, a veteran of the Peninsular War and Waterloo and, according to Stephens, a person whose conversation was 'like reading a page of history'. The British had imperialistic competition in Central America: the French were interested, of course, particularly in Mexico, and the United States was on the verge of the expansionist phase which took it into Texas and California. Therefore, if an American special emissary arrived with talk of dangerous cross-country journeys to places such as Copán and Palenque (which Col. Macdonald knew so little about that he spelled it 'Polenki') there must be some ulterior motive. And, if in order to claim an interest in the region it was necessary to send expeditions to ruins, then Great Britain would be in the forefront. The Colonel entertained Stephens and Catherwood to dinner in Government House and after proposing the loyal toast to Queen Victoria, drank to the health of President Van Buren and expressed the hope that there would be strong and perpetual friendship between Britain and America. 'I felt at the moment, "Cursed by the hand that attempts to break it"', wrote Stephens. After another toast, this time to the successful voyage of the two travellers, Col. Macdonald put his arm through Stephens' and walked with him as he warned of the dangers of travelling in a 'distracted' country. If threatened, he must assemble the Europeans, hang out his flag and send word to Belize. As Stephens left Government House, the flags were run up, a salute of thirteen guns fired, the soldiers of Fort George presented arms and the government schooner lowered and raised her ensign. As if that were not enough, the captain of the steamboat which was to carry Stephens and Catherwood down the coast placed himself under the American envoy's orders. 'I have had my aspirations, but never expected to be able to dictate to the captain of a steamboat,' noted Stephens.

These civilities over, Col. Macdonald began to prepare the British expedition which was to travel cross-country through the hardly known Petén to reach 'Polenki' first. A colonial outpost like Belize boasted no archaeologists or scientists, but the Superintendent chose the best of what was to hand and selected Patrick Walker, the Keeper of the Public Records, and Captain John Caddy, Royal Artillery, the Belize Harbour Master. Walker was a remarkably sober and reliable person, a model of propriety and industrious application; not the sort of person one would automatically choose as a companion on a journey through rain forests, but nevertheless better than most when it came to keeping discipline and not getting lost. Caddy was a more genial soul, a good draftsman and painter (which was why he was chosen for the trip) whose main interests were hunting and fishing. Neither knew anything about ruins and, in fact, seem to have passed through one group of Maya pyramids in the Petén without realizing what they were. The expedition had a surprisingly military character and Walker and Caddy were accompanied by a non-commissioned officer and fourteen men of the 2nd West India Regiment (a Negro unit), Caddy's servant Private Carnick, of the Royal Artillery (he died of fever on the border of British Honduras and Guatemala), Mr Nod, the interpreter, and nine pitpan men. Travellers on the rivers of Central America frequently voyaged aboard such exotic craft as pitpans and bongos. The former were large dugouts with a canopy in the mid-section for protection against the sun and rain. A team of six or more men with six-foot paddles propelled them from the bows, while another man steered with a paddle in the stern. Bongos were keel-less sailing craft, broad-beamed with two masts.

No time was lost. Stephens and Catherwood were hardly aboard their steamship when, on 13 November, the Walker–Caddy expedition was off in its pitpan, with the rains making life a misery as they moved slowly up the steamy Belize river towards the interior. On his own initiative, Col. Macdonald had drawn £200 from the colony's military chest to finance the expedition. The Colonial Office would, he hoped, give its approval and he wrote to Lord Russell, the Colonial Secretary, to assure him that the pencil of Lieutenant Caddy would 'convey to your Lordship's mind a perfect idea of the appearance of Polenki'. He carefully avoided mentioning that Stephens had just passed through Belize, observing only that in 'recent American papers' he had read that 'Mr Stephens', a well-known traveller, had been appointed by the Government of the United States to proceed to 'Polenki'. The *Belize Advertiser* was more blunt. The American expedition had 'roused the jealousy of our Settlement', it noted. Apart from visiting Palenque and charting the exact position of Lake Petén-Itzá, Walker and Caddy, it appeared, were to inquire into whether the 'province of Palenque' had been destroyed in recent warfare and acquaint themselves with the commercial aspects of the Central American Republic.

It is surprising how smoothly the journey across the Petén to Palenque went. Caddy kept a diary and blazed away at the animal life, and Walker made notes on the political and scientific aspects of the journey. Neither was much of a writer, but Caddy's diary has a Victorian prolixity with a charm of sorts: '. . . we were soon delighted by preparation for a meal, whose savourship we augured well of from the odour which ever and anon was wafted by the gentle breeze from the *cocinera* to our olfactory nerves'. Similar journeys by Stephens and Catherwood were full of drama, with descriptions of adventures, encounters with all sorts of people, pleasant and unpleasant, disabling fevers and all the hazards of a country in the middle of a civil war. Stephens, the writer, needed adventures for his books and he often went out of his way to find them. Perhaps Walker and Caddy were both more stoical and more efficient at the business of getting from A to B. Nevertheless, dull people make dull journeys, and neither official was exactly brilliant. They reached Palenque, made their observations and drawings and departed after adding their signatures on the stuccoed arches of the palace to those of Noah O. Platt, of New York, and William Beanham, a young Irishman who made a remarkable journey into the interior on his own, at times living on wild roots. Having survived many hazards, he was found dead one day in his hammock, his arm hanging over the side, his head split open with an axe and the book he had been reading lying on the ground beneath him.

Contrary to Col. Macdonald's hopes, the Colonial Office took a poor view of the whole episode. The expedition's report gave no real scientific description of Palenque and Walker's theory that the ruins were of 'Egypto-Indian origin' was very sketchy. His political speculations were taken amiss and excised from the report, even though it was never published. The British Government was not at all interested in adding to Her Majesty's territories in Central America, although Walker had written encouragingly that 'these abject wretches' might well be grateful if they were brought within the imperial fold: 'Throughout the spacious savannahs of the commandant and priest-ridden Petén, as well as at every place on the banks of the magnificent Usumacinta, the inhabitants expressed an ardent anxiety to be under such a government as the English . . .'. Two years later, while Macdonald was still fighting with the Colonial Office for approval of the expedition's expenses, an official in London was noting that the expedition had been a waste of time and money. 'An American named Stephens made the same journey and has published a full account of Palenque with drawings, etc. far more complete than any which were made by Captain Caddy and with a far more extensive range of general observation.' Shortly afterwards another official wrote: 'The motive was merely that we might not be outstripped in this case in scientific zeal by the Americans. This was not very wise, and the result is that we have been beaten by these new rivals in scientific research, who will now boast over our inferiority instead of having to boast only over our comparative inactivity. After all, the drawings and travels have not been

published, and now it is hardly to be supposed that any book-
seller would hazard the publication. In short, the whole affair
has been a blunder, though a very well-meant one.' Caddy did
read a paper on 'The City of Palenque' to the Society of
Antiquarians in London in January 1842, but that, alas, was not
published either.

Stephens, who had heard in Guatemala that Walker and
Caddy had been speared to death by Indians, was glad to learn
of their safe arrival when he got to Palenque well after them.
The thought that he had been beaten in a race never occurred
to him.

Not long before the Walker–Caddy expedition, another
British subject (although he had no wish to be one), Col. John
Galindo, had made some worthwhile drawings and observations of the Maya ruins. He has been called by Ian Graham, a
present-day British Mayanist, the 'first archaeologist in the
Maya field', and his reports on Copán, in Honduras, were
partly responsible for drawing Stephens and Catherwood there
while on their way from Belize to Guatemala City, where
Stephens was to present his credentials, presuming he could
find a government.

Galindo was born in Dublin in 1802 of an Anglo-Irish
mother and a father whose Spanish ancestors had settled in
England a hundred years earlier. Both parents were unsuccessful actors who no doubt filled the more hopeless corners of
their lives with compensatory fictions; at any rate, there is in
the life of John (later Juan) a feeling of a background of
generous but unfounded expectations and small achievements.
Philemon Galindo, the father, was also a fencing master, and in
that role he was employed by Sarah Siddons, the actress, with
side-duties as a lover. It was a well-known relationship in
Dublin where a bawdy contemporary cartoon showed Mrs
Siddons' foil lightly touching Philemon on the heart while his
prodded her in a less refined portion of the anatomy. At the
time of John's birth, Mrs Siddons was in her mid-forties and
fourteen years older than Philemon, whom she had set up in

Portrait of Juan Galindo

one or two unremunerative theatrical ventures. Perhaps he was
flattered as well as rewarded by the relationship, and no doubt
she enjoyed his romantic genealogy as well as his youth. It was

presumably Philemon who instilled in John the notion that he was a descendant of Clovis the First, the fifth-century king of France, and the kings of Aquitaine, a lineage which Galindo honoured by naming parts of the Petén 'Aquitaine' when he was the province's governor. John's character was compounded of the traditional stuff of which Irish heroes are made: he was hot-blooded, headstrong, liberal, fanciful (to put it mildly) and, despite a desire for English esteem, almost instinctively anti-English. The Spanish world attracted him just as it had a great many full-blooded Irishmen anxious to find temperamentally congenial surroundings well away from the English, and at the age of sixteen he set out to help Lord Cochrane (a Scot, not an Irishman) free South America from tyranny. I am not clear whether he ever actually served in Cochrane's fleet or was way-laid by the charms of Jamaica, where a relation had a sugar estate. But if he did reach his destination it is possible that there was a meeting between the bogus cadet member of the family of the Dukes of Waldeck-Pyrmont and the descendant of King Clovis. One could speculate that Waldeck's Irish connection grew out of such a meeting, but on the whole it seems unlikely, Galindo would have been quite young at the time and although self-assured and a good French-speaker (his mother Kitty applied herself to his education) it is doubtful whether he would have had anything to say about Lord Kingsborough.

In his early twenties Galindo joined the staff of another Irishman, John O'Reilly, the British consul in Guatemala City, where he worked as a secretary and Spanish translator. For one of his temperament it must have been a rather boring job, and he soon left to join the army of the liberal General Francisco Morazan, who invaded Guatemala from El Salvador. As an Irish liberal, Galindo had no difficulty in winning the confidence of Morazan's federal government. It granted him naturalization papers, and under its leader's patronage he was rapidly promoted from major to colonel to commander of the army to military governor of the Petén – all before he was thirty. From having been more Irish than the Irish, Galindo changed to being more Central American than the Central Americans. Between him and Chatfield, the British Consul, there started a remarkably bitter feud caused, in the first place, by an argument over the Belize boundary. It was Galindo, said Chatfield, who first installed in Central American minds the idea that the British had no firm legal rights to the territory. No man had done more, he wrote, than Galindo to cause 'the unpopularity with which the English are viewed in Central America'. He had proposed Dutch and American settlers for Belize and the Petén, American capital to replace British capital and sanctions against Belize. Finally, he was appointed by the Central American Republic as a special emissary to inform liberal opinion in Britain, France and the United States on the Belize question and to negotiate with Lord Palmerston on the boundary. Chatfield, who by this time regarded him as a scoundrel, wrote to the Foreign Office to warn it of the imminent arrival of a 'common adventurer'. Galindo stopped in Washington for interviews with President Andrew Jackson and his Secretary of State but aroused no enthusiasm, thanks to successful British attempts to discredit him. In London he was resolutely cold-shouldered by Palmerston on the grounds that whatever he might think to the contrary, he was still a British subject and therefore could not represent a foreign country. Moreover, he held land in the area under dispute and so was an interested party. After writing some entirely fictitious reports on the success of his mission, Galindo returned to Central America, having achieved nothing useful except the establishment of good relations with several learned organizations interested in the archaeology and natural history of the region. He was clearly humiliated and infuriated by his failure, which he blamed on Chatfield who – he was to write to Palmerston – had driven him into chauvinism by attacking his credibility as an emissary. The depth of his bitterness became evident when the British seizure of the Caribbean island of Ruatan prompted him to call on every true Central American to revenge himself on the British.

Frustrated in Belize, Galindo went ahead with his own plan for the colonization of a place called Boca del Toro, the bull's mouth, which is on the Caribbean coast of Panama near where it joins Costa Rica. There, on the disputed coast and among the islands of the Chiriqui archipelago (one of which was promptly rechristened Isla Galindo) the equivalent of a sultanate was to be established, confounding the designs of English traders, King Robert of Mosquitia and various other contenders. Father Philemon was to be commandant and governor, younger brother Felipe Augustin was appointed secretary, with the promise of a 'brilliant destiny' as a landed proprietor, while brother Philemon, an undergraduate studying for the Anglican ministry, was offered the bishopric of a new see. The colony's subjects were to be 700 emigrants from Jamaica, where Galindo's uncle James was also enlisted to help with plans for exploiting coal mines and the non-existent gold mine of Tisingal and the building of a trans-isthmian railway. Father Philemon and Felipe arrived in the new colony without any money in 1836 and were fortunately befriended by a British trader. Costa Rica, which was not in possession of the area concerned but had aspirations, sent Philemon a copy of its constitution and appointed him *Jefe Politico*, but New Granada (now Columbia; at that time Panama was part of New Granada's territory) dispatched a military expedition. Father Philemon was allowed to escape to Jamaica, from where he returned home to England.

The feud with Chatfield was brought to a head in 1838 when a 14-year-old English boy, James Dearing, fled to the sanctuary of the British consulate claiming that Galindo had enslaved and cruelly beaten him. Demands by Chatfield for the boy's clothes and wages were answered by an angry Galindo storming into the consulate and insisting on the boy's return on the ground he had been entrusted to him by his mother. Chatfield refused to hand over James and Galindo retreated into the street where he bellowed that he had been insulted and would take the law into his own hands. Careful to avoid making a gaffe, Galindo turned to the acknowledged experts on diplomatic etiquette, the French. A helpful secretary at the French legation drafted a note challenging Chatfield to a duel and undertook to deliver it on Galindo's behalf. Naturally, the challenge was rejected and Galindo relieved his fury to some extent by dashing off a note to Lord Palmerston, complaining that he had been grossly insulted and only consideration for an agent of Her Britannic Majesty's Government had prevented him from adopting 'the common resource of posting', i.e. putting up notices advertising the consul's failure to act like a gentleman and give satisfaction. After some strenuous diplomatic activity, young James passed to Galindo, to the Central American government and finally back to Chatfield, who presumably sent him home to his mother, having preserved what he called 'the inviolability of the British flag'.

The British, particularly Chatfield, have often been blamed for the break-up of the Federation. There is some argument about the degree of their responsibility, but it is certainly true that as the Liberals' – and Galindo's – fortunes declined, so those of the British improved. Outmanoeuvred by his rival, his hopes of riches continually dashed, Galindo left Guatemala City to join the army with which the Liberals were trying to restore the authority of General Morazan. His end was more tragic than he deserved. In 1840 while retreating from the Liberal defeat at the battle of El Potrero, in Honduras, he was trapped and slaughtered with machete blows in a village. In a casual p.s. which began 'I forgot to mention . . .' Chatfield noted his death in a letter to Col. Macdonald, the Belize Superintendent. And in an official report he recorded with savage finality: 'Thus ended the career of this ill-judging and mischievously intentioned person.'

Recklessness and great curiosity often go together, with unguided energies leading to dead-ends and marvels, the mind adventuring with hardly a glance at the map or the signposts. Galindo was like that. It must have been a lonely life, but one full of exotic impressions, that he lived in whatever passed for a governor's palace in Flores, formerly Tayasal, the city of the Itzás. There he dreamed up disastrous schemes for colonizing jungles and exploiting tropical coalmines and at the same time threw himself into a dimension of intellectually profitable activity, travelling to Palenque, exploring the ruins of Topoxte Island in Lake Yaxhá, not far from Flores, describing the geology of the Usumacinta and Pasion rivers, and making, from Guatemala City, the journey to Copán which, through the ensuing report and drawings, was to titillate the anticipations of Stephens and Catherwood. His account of Palenque in the *London Literary Gazette* in 1831 may have helped persuade Lord Kingsborough to send Waldeck there. Both Galindo and Waldeck were competitors for the *Société de Geographie*'s gold medal in 1838 for the best work on Palenque, a prize which went to Waldeck for *Le Voyage Pittoresque*. Galindo had to be content with the Society's silver medal presented to him several years earlier when he visited Paris at the time of his abortive mission to London. He was an eager correspondent ('Our zealous corresponding member', he was described as by the editor of a paper sent to the London Royal Geographical Society) writing in his excellent copperplate to learned institutions and journals in France, Britain and America, enjoying the recognition implied by the thanks he received for the stucco glyphs from Palenque he sent to the Society of Antiquaries of London and the *Société de Geographie*. Some of his gifts can still be seen in the *Musée de l'Homme*. Perhaps it was all part of a promotional effort, but the idealistic element in his character and the attempt to give a broader picture than would be required to draw in trading companies and foolhardy independent settlers makes me rather doubt it. Once, camping in the Petén jungle, I was woken by an animal scuffling among the pots and pans. I caught him in the beam of a torch: a small foxy animal. A few months afterwards I came across what must have been a description of his species in a paper by Galindo entitled 'On Central America', read to the Royal Geographical Society in 1836: 'The zorillo is a small fox, whose wind is extremely offensive; it stupefies and has been known to cause the death of a dog that killed it; the same wind leaves a blue dye on every beast and on everything it comes in contact with.' This description, with its slightly comic sensationalism, captures something of the essence of Galindo, expressing his desire to describe as much as he could, however insignificant the item.

10

Incidents of Travel

When John Stephens and Frederick Catherwood said goodbye to Col. Macdonald, they were on their way to Guatemala City, with an important side trip *en route* to Copán, in Honduras. Once they had ascended the Rio Dolce in their steamboat and landed at Isabal they were in what the colonel had quite rightly called a 'distracted' country. It was engaged in civil war and all the dangers to be expected in that situation attended the pair as they set out on muleback over apallingly muddy mountain trails on which the mules fell down, broke down, collapsed on the travellers and stood unmoving under the lash and the rain. Stephens' diplomatic credentials made no impression when one night, as they prepared for bed, or rather their hammocks, a band of ragged mestizos and Indians, led by a drunken mayor and a captain with a sword and a 'wicked expression' burst into their hut and, by the light of blazing pine torches, arrested them. Their captors, wrote Stephens, were men 'who would have been turned out of any decent state prison lest they should contaminate the boarders'. Muskets were pointed at their breasts, hands placed in readiness on the handles of machetes. Stephens' servant Augustin, always bellicose himself as a result of a machete blow on the head in a previous engagement, urged his master in French to give his party the order to fire. They had eleven charges, all sure, in their weapons and one round would have scattered the ruffians. But fortunately it never came to that. A man of a better class entered and was more impressed than the others by the passport and the endorsements from

Commandant Penol and General Cascara of the Federal government. Permission was given to the travellers for a courier to be sent, at Stephens' expense, to General Cascara informing him of the arrest. That presented another problem. Stephens was unable to write Spanish; in fact, to judge by the mis-spellings in his books, he knew very little of the language. However, Catherwood was fluent in Italian, and as General Cascara was Italian the letter was written in that language and signed by the artist in the role of secretary. Stephens had not come equipped with an official seal, but the tails side of a half-dollar piece was employed without anyone observing them, and the letter was handed to the mayor for dispatch. 'The eagle spread his wings and the stars glittered in the torchlight,' Stephens remembered of his make-shift seal. They were locked up for the night in the mayor's council chamber, with twelve men guarding them, but the travellers drank a bottle of wine given them by Col. Macdonald, felt better and went to sleep. When their door burst open again, it was only the mayor come to inform them that on second thoughts they were free to continue to Copán where yet another obstacle awaited them in the form of Don Gregorio, the black-whiskered richest man and petty tyrant of the place – but more of him later.

It is almost a banality to say it, or more accurately repeat it, but in the first half of the nineteenth century a man of talent could still be almost anything he chose provided he had the means. He rarely needed qualifications and he was not confined to one speciality. The boundaries of the sciences and the near-sciences had not been defined and enthusiasm and intelligent curiosity added rapidly to a small stock of knowledge. In that respect at least it was a more human and more enjoyable world than ours. It is always better to be a free-lance explorer than a settler with a patent on your land. Stephens was a diplomat, an archaeologist, a writer, later on a railway builder and at all times just a bit of a showman. His diplomatic career was not very important; it lasted a year or so and served largely to provide him with some measure of protection as he travelled

John Lloyd Stephens

through the Central American Federation collecting material for the books with which he was to build on the success of previous books on the Middle East and eastern Europe. At the same time he hoped to collect material for a Museum of American Antiquities. In pursuing this last ambition, he became disastrously involved in a 10,000 square-foot panorama of Middle Eastern antiquity designed by Catherwood and displayed first in Leicester Square, London, and later – at the time of their departure for Central America in 1839 – New York.

What Stephens called 'our great inducement' to visit Copán was not the scanty report of Galindo, although that was important because it proved that there was an extensive ruin, but a more ancient account of a swinging stone hammock forming the portal through which the visitor entered. No such Maya engineering miracle was mentioned by the first man to describe Copán, Diego Garcia de Palacio, in the sixteenth century, but at the end of the eighteenth century, Don Francisco Fuentes y Guzman (another charlatan, I regret to say) not only described the hammock but added for good measure a Circus Maximus and statues of men and women in Castillian costume, the men with hose, frilled collars, swords, caps and short coats. As an historian, Don Francisco was naturally entitled to respect, and his description was incorporated in the work of another historian, Juarros, who wrote:

> 'Entering by this gateway one admires two fine stone pyramids, broad and high, with a hammock slung between them, and in the hammock two human figures, one of each sex, dressed like Indians. But the most surprising thing is that, although it is of such great size, there is no joint or rivetting to be seen, and, notwithstanding its being all of stone and of such enormous weight, it swings with a slight touch of the hand.'

If such a creation had existed it is very likely that Stephens would have wanted to dismantle it and float it down the Copán river on the first leg of its journey to New York. He made inquiries about the feasibility of doing this with some of the magnificently carved stelae to be found in Copán, but was informed that the river was not navigable. It is a shallow, fast stream which, in the dry season, is comparable with the middle reaches of a Scottish salmon river. As well as being '*El Padre de Mayismo*', the man who put future studies on a sober basis, Stephens was also the father of the site-looters who are plaguing the region more than a century later. Carved wooden lintels, vases, figures and various relics were taken by him from Uxmal, in the Yucatán, and other sites and shipped to New York where they perished in what he called 'the general conflagration of Jerusalem and Thebes', meaning poor Catherwood's panorama, lit by 200 gas lamps. Catherwood lost $2,000 in that particular pyre of his never-too-secure fortunes. Stephens had the sad experience of seeing his lintels, incinerated but still in shape, amid the ashes next day. Some large limestone panels from Kabáh, which is near Uxmal, fortunately arrived in New York too late for exhibition and were given to a friend who built them into the wall of a folly. They were discovered in 1918 by Sylvanus Morley and removed to the American Museum of Natural History.

It was their common enthusiasm for instructional showmanship that drew Catherwood and Stephens together in London after the writer's return from the Middle East. Stephens had been aided in his travels by a map of the Nile drawn by the artist and knew and admired his work and perhaps enjoyed his lectures on Jerusalem which accompanied the panorama. He gave Catherwood's show a considerable puff in the introduction to one of his earlier works, presumably as part of a build-up for his illustrations to the Central American volumes and the New York exhibition of the panorama. Stephens, although independently wealthy, was a financial success by his own efforts, which Catherwood most certainly was not. His first books had been bestsellers and those on Central America were to do even better, in Britain as well as in America. Combined with his literary abilities was a sharp eye for the spectacular, that touch of showmanship I mentioned. There is a warmth which reflects a sense of affinity, when he mentions a Mr Handy and his elephant and two dromedaries who were passing through Guatemala on foot (and in the middle of a civil war!) and a Mr Clayton who had come to Mérida after reading Stephens' first volumes on Central America, bringing with him from the United States 'an entire circus company with spotted horses, a portable theatre, containing seats for a thousand persons, riders, clowns and monkeys, all complete'. Years later, his account (in Vol. II of *Incidents of Travel in Central America, Chiapas and Yucatán*) of a padre's story of climbing a mountain on the edge of the Petén and seeing 'at a great distance a large city spread over a great space, and with turrets white and glittering in the sun' stirred the imagination of a less scholarly showman. Maximo, a boy, and Bartola, a girl – two 'living Aztec children' – were put on display by Barnum's American Museum as the human booty from an expedition to the '4,000 year-old city of Iximaya'. An American and a

Canadian perished at the hands of the Indians but one man survived to bring back with him to civilization the royal children. They visited England and were inspected by the Prince Consort, and it was some time before they were recognized as a hoax. The padre's tale of Indians living in the city 'in the same state as before the discovery of America' was fantasy. Perhaps it was based on legends of the still-undiscovered ruins of Tikal or Yaxchilán, deep in the Petén jungles.

Despite his homely affection for such things as circuses, Stephens clearly had little desire for the everyday comforts of life in New York or New Jersey. He never married, and even if he had lived to a ripe old age, it must be rated doubtful whether he would have settled into the pleasurable tranquillity of a Victorian bachelorhood. He had a flippant susceptibility to girls (and a morbid interest in their burials) but it is hard to say how much these inclinations were genuine or how much they merely reflected the tastes of a readership which could be equally stimulated by death and the passing fancies of a handsome adventurer. Graham Greene has said there is a splinter of ice in the writer's heart and that is certainly true of Stephens. There is often a tombstone carver's relish for the funerals of the young, the apparently sensitive and the beautiful. He is constantly flirtatious, but there is a distance, an ultimately genteel conventionality about his descriptions of pretty women and transitory love. Female feet are admired, an unveiled harem ogled in Turkey, the hand of an ailing maiden 'born but to bloom for a season' is held on a 'physician's pretext', a beautiful unknown nun visited at her Guatemalan convent for the sake of an embrace before she says farewell to the world (which is uncomfortably like another funeral); and he is rendered sleepless by the offer of a carteret (a folding cot) whose usual occupant is a high-minded girl with a fancy for strangers. Once, in his earlier travels in Egypt, he bought the loin-cloth of a Nubian girl, leaving her entirely naked. 'She was not more than sixteen, with a sweet mild face, and a figure that the finest lady might be proud to exhibit in its native beauty.'

Times certainly change. These days one might get away with a description of ravishing her in the sands, but buying her loin-cloth would be regarded as the grossest exploitation.

Everything except inner feelings is finely observed, but, of course, to have leaned too much towards personal expression in a Victorian travel book might have been regarded as ill-mannered. It was not the fashion of the times. Stephens' faults, however, are more than compensated for by his urbanity, fluency, and marvellously sharp intelligence. He was a quick observer of people, a meticulous and vivid describer of land-scapes, towns and ruins, and he had, rather unexpectedly, a well-tuned political instinct that enabled him to perceive that the 23-year-old half-breed, Carrera, would dominate Guatemala after the break-up of the Federation. Several years afterwards, Catherwood, who was planning to settle in California, suggested his friend should also emigrate there and stand for the U.S. Senate. If he had, he would have done very well.

In addition to these considerable talents Stephens had another, one of particular importance to nineteenth-century travel-writers: he could write fast and at length without the usual signs of exhaustion, such as patchiness and fluctuations in style. His four books on Central America (*Incidents of Travel in Central America, Chiapas and Yucatán*, Vols. I and II, and *Incidents of Travel in the Yucatán*, Vols. I and II) all came out in a four-year period which included two journeys of ten and seven months respectively.

Unlike Stephens, a rich man's son who set out on his jour-neys to the Middle East to clear up a streptococchic throat, Catherwood was a struggling professional who went to the Middle East for the sole purpose of painting and sketching. Nothing else mattered very much in his life, although later he must have felt disillusioned, for, like Stephens, he became a railway engineer: an unsuccessful one, for he was sacked from his job of supervising South America's first railway in British Guiana. He married late, when he was in his forties, but one imagines that at heart he was always a bachelor, although of a very different type from the vivacious, outgoing Stephens. Catherwood's character has been rather a mystery to those who have read *Incidents of Travel*. Stephens never refers to him by his first name or the abbreviation 'Cath' used by earlier acquaintances and friends; in Stephens' pages he is always 'Mr Catherwood' or 'Mr C.' Perhaps he was never quite elevated to the position of friendship on an equal footing. He was employed by Stephens for the South American journey for a fee of $1,500, with deductions of $25 a week for Mrs Catherwood and their son who were living in New York. None of his fellow artists, so far as I know, ever painted or drew Catherwood and he appears only once in one of his own drawings, a tall, burly man in a long jacket helping Stephens measure the front of Structure 25 at Tulum. Catherwood was of Scottish origins, the descendant of forebears who had come south to make their fortunes in London, and perhaps he revealed his ancestry in his reserve and an intense application to his task. He was a practical rather than an imaginative artist, one who, to bring out his best, needed as a model the results of other men's imaginings. He conveyed the masterly fantasies and elaborate delineations of the Maya to audiences in Europe and America with dedication, accuracy and sensitivity. That he was very much more than a draftsman can be seen from his drawings of the Copán stelae, where he captures better than any photograph the strange yearning, beseeching quality of the sculpture (one can see, too, the harm exposure to the heavy seasonal rains has caused since he was there: much fine work has deteriorated).

Like so many English writers and artists of his time, Catherwood's first journey abroad was to the Mediterranean. He arrived in Rome in the early autumn of 1821 at the invitation of his friend, Joseph Severn, a painter who had gone there with Keats. 'We have this morning (Severn wrote in a letter) seen St Peter's – and the Vatican – with which he is quite delighted or I should say astonished.'* Astonished but not delighted: there was too much of the meticulous Scot in him

* Quoted from Victor von Hagen's, *F. Catherwood, Architect-Explorer of Two Worlds.*

for delight, but it is a sound reaction, one that lasts, to be astonished. It is the expression of curiosity and humility, and those basic characteristics were always with him whether he was travelling up the Nile with Robert Hay's (later the Earl of Tweedale) task force of artists, architects and antiquarians, or dressed as an Arab and armed with his seven-barrelled gun, journeying through the Levant as architectural adviser to Mehmet Ali (and nearly getting torn to pieces by a furious Muslim mob while drawing inside the Dome of the Rock in Jerusalem).

Anyone who has travelled in remote places in troubled times will know how subject one is to suspicion and how dependent on the will of one man, whether he be the local sheikh or district commissioner or, as in Stephens and Catherwood's case at Copán, a landowner, Don Gregorio. The Don, a fierce-look-ing, unshaven man of about fifty, found the travellers waiting for him at his hacienda as he rode up. He cast a cold eye on them, dismounted without a word and strode inside for his dinner. Sons, servants and labourers equally ignored them; even the women turned away their heads. Stephens wanted to tumble his and Catherwood's luggage into the road and curse Don Gregorio for an inhospitable churl, but the sensible Mr C cautioned against this, warning that an open quarrel might lead to them being prevented from seeing the ruins. The Don also had a few second thoughts about the embarrassments that might come from an outright row and he finally pointed to a chair and asked Stephens to take a seat. That was as far as his hospitality went and the travellers were largely ignored for the rest of the evening while the men shelled corn, throwing the grain on to an ox-skin. Don Gregorio's wife, however, did offer to bake them bread, provided they were prepared to pay for it.

Their evening tasks finished, the Don's family prepared for sleep. Stephens wrote, 'The Don's house had two sides, an inside and an out. The Don and his family occupied the former and we the latter.' Even outside there was so little room that

Stephens hung in his hammock like a new moon, his heels as high as his head.

In the morning the two sides ignored one another as best they could. Fortunately, one of the Don's sons, a young man more civil than the rest, brought over a guide for the travellers. Then as now one approached Copán through cornfields and bright-green acres of tobacco. The site lies in a valley where the Honduras mountains have subdued themselves to the status of steep hills. They are not now as thickly covered with jungle as they were in Stephens' day but they are still tropical and lush, unless one is there in the dry season when the leaves have fallen and the trees are wispy. At such times, the light is a dusky gold on the grand plaza and there is an orderly stillness of a just-opened tomb, the sense of an unknown moment revealed.

Stephens and Catherwood entered the woods around Copán and before long came to the bank of the river which in those days swirled beneath the eighty-feet high wall at the back of the acropolis.

'With an interest perhaps stronger than we had ever felt while wandering among the ruins of Egypt (wrote Stephens of Copán), we followed our guide, who, sometimes missing his way, with a constant and vigorous use of his machete, conducted us through the thick forest, among half-buried fragments, to fourteen monuments of the same character and appearance, some with more elegant designs, and some in workmanship equal to the finest monuments of the Egyptians: one displaced from its pedestal by enormous roots; another locked in close embrace of branches of trees, and almost lifted out of the earth; another hurled to the ground and bound down by huge vines and creepers; and one standing, with its altar before it, in a grove of trees which grow around it; seemingly to shade and shroud it as a sacred thing; in the solemn stillness of the woods, it seemed a divinity mourning over a fallen people.'

The only sounds came from troupes of monkeys, forty or

Altar G, perhaps the most magnificent at Copán. It is carved in the form of a double-headed serpent. The date is the latest so far deciphered at Copán: 800 A.D.

Hieroglyphics and ornamentation on Stela C, Ceremonial Plaza, Copán

Head of the rain god, Ik, from Temple 11, Copán

fifty strong, who moved through the trees in long processions. It was the first time Stephens and Catherwood had seen these 'mockeries of humanity', and they looked to the travellers like the departed spirits of those who had once lived in the ruined city around them.

The carvings on the Copán stelae are the most elaborate, the most deeply undercut, complex and fluent in the Maya world. They are the nearest thing to statuary in the round that the Maya ever produced. No space is wasted and glyphs cover the sides and backs of the stones. The difficulties for Catherwood were enormous. He found the complicated designs 'perfectly unintelligible'. Added to the problem of unfamiliarity was that posed by the poor light. It was the rainy season and the foliage was thick, casting a deep shade. Burning away the trees would have been hard in the perpetual wetness and in any case, an attempt might have brought down the wrath of Don Gregorio. Finally, they decided to clear a few trees around one idol with the machetes of the Indians they had hired. It was slow work and Stephens found himself thinking nostalgically of the ring of the woodman's axe at home and wishing for 'a few long-sided Green Mountain boys' from New England. As was to become his customary task, he cleaned and scrubbed away the dirt and moss on the sculpture. Then, while Catherwood prepared for his first drawings, he explored the site with two mestizos, Bruno and Francisco, who although living near by had never seen the sculpture before. Their enthusiasm grew with his and before long they were raking the ground with machetes, stopping when metal rang on stone so that Stephens could scrape away the soil with his hands and uncover the carvings beneath the humus. Stephens was overwhelmed by the beauty, the stillness and the sense of desolation.

He returned to Catherwood to find him consideraby less enchanted. His feet were in mud and he was drawing with his gloves on to protect his hands from the mosquitoes. Even with the *camera lucida* he found it impossible to master the intricate designs; what he had done satisfied neither himself nor

Stela B, Copán, as drawn by Catherwood (from Volume I of *Incidents of Travel in Central America, Chiapas and Yucatan*).

Stephens, a less exacting critic. The *camera lucida* was a device in principle rather like a periscope which by means of prisms projected an image on to paper (Catherwood used squared paper) where it could be traced. They moved into a hut on the edge of the forest, where they were to spend the night in a depressed frame of mind. However, the recovery of a pair of waterproof boots in a bag which had fallen into the river cheered Catherwood up somewhat, and both men had their spirits revived even more by watching the sun set over the jungle with a gorgeousness Stephens had never seen surpassed. The following morning Catherwood returned to his stelae wearing his waterproofs and with a piece of oilskin normally used for covering luggage on which to stand. The light fell exactly as he wished and he was much more successful.

Aldous Huxley has called Catherwood a 'martyr to archaeology'. In a most appallingly hot, sticky climate he stood patiently for hour after hour putting down what he saw on damp paper, bitten by all sorts of insects against which he had no protection except his clothes and a free hand. No one at that time connected mosquitoes with the *calentura*, as malaria was called, so he was not fully aware of the risks he ran. He stayed on at Copán after Stephens had left to carry out his diplomatic mission and became seriously ill. Fever was to strike him again later and in the end made him so ill that Stephens felt obliged to call an abrupt end to their first trip.

Don Gregorio continued to make trouble for Stephens and Catherwood at Copán, even though the ruins were not on his land. He convinced the mayor that such a suspicious pair would undoubtedly bring about a visitation from troops; moreover, they were forcing up the price of labour. The mayor paid a visit to the travellers who as usual were each carrying a brace of pistols and a gun. Their appearance was so formidable that the mayor bowed himself out of their presence at top speed and nothing was said of the need for them to leave at once. It was clear, though, to Stephens that if Catherwood was to continue working at the ruins, or he was to visit them again without disturbance, it was necessary to have some established right to the place. If the British are a nation of shopkeepers, the Americans are a race of real estate agents. Stephens entered into negotiations for the site with one Don José Maria who was as much surprised as if the writer had proposed buying his poor old wife (whose rheumatism had been treated by the travellers) to practise medicine upon. On examining the title, Stephens, who had attended law school, discovered that Don José only leased it. That obstacle was evidently not over-emphasized and Don José, although hesitant, was obviously anxious to garner the windfall promised by Stephens. After a day or two his indecision was ended by the diplomat-archaeologist producing his letters of recommendation and finally opening his trunk and dressing up in his diplomatic coat, a panama hat and white pantaloons yellow to the knees with mud. 'Don José Maria could not withstand the buttons on my coat; the cloth was the finest he had ever seen,' wrote Stephens. All present realized that an illustrious *incognito* was in their midst. The 'sale' was agreed and paper prepared for the execution of the deed.

In a well-known passage Stephens describes the transaction:

'The reader is perhaps curious to know how old cities sell in Central America. Like other articles of trade, they are regulated by the quantity in the market, and the demand; but, not being staple articles, like cotton and indigo, they were held at fancy prices, and at that time were full of sale. I paid fifty dollars for Copán. There was never any difficulty about price. I offered that sum, for which Don José Maria thought me a fool; if I had offered more, he would probably have considered me something worse.'

Stephens entered into negotiations for two more ruins: Quiriguá, in Guatemala, and Palenque. The former was visited by Catherwood alone, but on receiving his report Stephens approached the owner, a Señor Payes who was then in Guatemala City. The site is close to the Motagua river and Stephens and Catherwood had ideas of transporting the great sandstone stelae (they are rather eroded but very high – one is thirty-five feet, probably the tallest pre-Columbian carving there is) and everything else movable down the river and then by ship to New York, where the site would be reconstructed, in the way that later Americans moved churches and small castles from Europe. Señor Payes said he would be happy to contribute to science in the United States, particularly as such things were not appreciated in his own country, but unfortunately – or perhaps fortunately – he consulted with the French Consul-General (the same helpful one, presumably, whose aid Galindo sought in his quarrel with Chatfield) who no doubt saw another opportunity to embarrass his national rivals in Central America. He pointed out to Señor Payes that it had cost the French government hundreds of thousands of dollars to transport the obelisks of Luxor to Paris, and therefore the price of obelisks at Quiriguá should in some way reflect the cost of getting them to New York. Stephens, who had hoped to buy them for a few thousand dollars, thought Payes' asking price 'exaggerated'. It rose even higher later when Payes read a 'eulogistic' version of part of Catherwood's comments on the site which had been published in a New York paper and sent back to Guatemala. The proprietor demanded $20,000 and then sat back and waited for better offers from Britain and France, which never came.

Negotiations for the purchase of Palenque proved equally difficult and unsuccessful. There was, according to the Prefect, no obstacle to a sale provided Stephens married a daughter of the country, as required by the Mexican law governing the sale of land to foreigners. For two years the Prefect had had on his hands an order from the provincial government of Chiapas for the sale of the land concerned, with no exception for the ruins, but there had been no offers. There were moments, Stephens admitted, when alone and friendless, buffeted and battered, a stranger might be rooted to any spot on earth by a lovely woman. He looked over the ladies of Palenque and found that the oldest young one was only fourteen and the prettiest (who contributed most to his happiness by rolling his cigars) was already married. A widow and her sister, both about 40 and good-looking and amiable, had their attractions, particularly as with either of them would have come a pleasant house containing two tablets taken from the ruins. Stephens decided diplomatically that it was impossible to choose between them and instead agreed with the Prefect that he should seek to make the purchase through Mr Russell, the American consul at Laguna, who was married to a Mexican. Despite a passing reference to a plan to 'fit up the palace and repeople the old city' it is likely that Stephens hoped to shift the ruins, or part of them, and the stone tablets to New York. Mr Russell, in fact, offered $2,000 towards the cost of that project. A latecomer to the expedition, Henry Pawling, a young American who had formerly distributed handbills for Mr Handy's circus, was left behind in Palenque to make plaster casts and to complete the purchase. But before that could be done the Prefect received a letter from the Governor of Chiapas noting that Walker and Caddy had visited the ruins with fourteen armed men and that the Prefect had failed to stop them and had not provided the Governor with any information on the matter.

. . . 'Now he is again informed that some citizens of the United States of the North are doing the same; in virtue of which, His Excellency orders me to tell you to inform him immediately upon the truth of these facts, that he may take the necessary measures.

God and Liberty.

Enrique Ruiz'

In addition to the Governor's quite justifiable alarm, there was a new proprietorial interest in the ruins by the leading citizens of Palenque. Three of them petitioned the Governor over Pawling's plaster casts which he was shipping to the north where they might be used to 'supply the world with these precious things without a six cents piece expense'. Mr William

Brown, an American married to a Mexican and resident in Palenque, had offered from $8,000 to $10,000 just for leave to extract four or six principal stones. Either Mr Pawling should be refused permission to take away his casts or he should be made to pay $4,000 or $5,000. In the end Pawling was ordered to leave the ruins and the casts were seized by the Prefect. The Governor sent him orders to keep a 'watchful eye' in future on strangers who visited the ruins; they were not to be allowed to excavate or remove anything, however insignificant it might appear. Stephens never managed to buy his ruin.

The rains made life in the ruins of Palenque a misery for the travellers. Fierce winds blew out their candles at night as they camped in a gallery of the palace but luminous beetles 'of extraordinary size and brilliance' provided them with alternative lighting. These, Stephens noted, were the *locuyos* described in ancient Spanish chronicles. Men tied them to their big toes and thumbs when they went hunting and fishing. Among their supposed peculiarities was that of answering to their name; thus they were caught easily. Stephens and Catherwood caught their beetles with a hat and found that four together lit up an area of several yards' radius. By the light of just one, Stephens was able to read the debates in Congress contained in a newspaper. Catherwood, digging through the pockets of his shooting jacket, found a Broadway omnibus ticket on which could be discerned *"Good to the bearer for a ride, A Brower,'* which served to make Stephens nostalgic for home and the good beds into which his friends were turning at about the same time.

The assaults of mosquitoes, ticks and *niguas*, which had laid their eggs under his toenails and inflamed one of his feet, forced Stephens to retreat from the ruins to the village of Palenque. On his return he found conditions were even worse than when he had left: the rain poured into the gallery and saddlery, boots and clothes were green with mildew and the guns and pistols covered with rust. Catherwood's appearance was startling as a result of a recurrence of fever. 'He was wan and gaunt; lame, like me, from the bites of insects; his face was swollen, and his left arm hung with rheumatism as if paralysed.' When they left Palenque it was with joy. They even began a poem which started '*Adios, Las Casas de Piedra*', but got no further for lack of inspiration.

From then on *coches*, or litters, and even a *silla*, a chair carried on the back of a sturdy Indian, were used as means of transport, all modern prejudices about employing their fellow men in the same way as mules having been overcome. They continued the journey to Uxmal, in the Yucatán, where Stephens decided that for the sake of his companion's shattered constitution they must return to New York at once. Catherwood was carried in a *coche* to Sisal, where there was a brig bound for Havana, a first stage on the way home.

The first two volumes of *Incidents of Travel* end with Uxmal and an appeal to Britain and France to leave American antiquities to the Americans. The United States was a 'destitute country' so far as museum collections were concerned, whereas London and Paris had already been enriched by collection in the Old World. The plea was not heeded, of course. The pre-Columbian remains could hardly be considered a regional resource, although there is an argument of sorts, based on possession being nine-tenths of the law, for considering them national property, in which case they belonged to Mexico, Guatemala *et al*. In any case, it was another fifty years before American archaeologists took to the field in the Maya area.

It says a lot for the fortitude of Stephens and Catherwood that once the first two volumes of *Incidents of Travel* had been published they went straight back to the Yucatán to finish their journey. They arrived eighteen months after they had left, towards the end of 1841. This time they brought with them a useful addition, Samuel Cabot, a member of a famous Boston family. Besides being a doctor of medicine, and an ornithologist, Cabot, who was 26, had another attainment: he had held the bare-knuckle boxing championship at Harvard for two years. The doctor brought his surgical instruments and

Stephens and Catherwood a daguerreotype machine, with which they were to achieve very limited results. It was not the first time photography had been introduced in Maya exploration. In the previous year Baron von Friederichstal, a student of Lord Kingsborough's volumes, had taken a daguerreotype to the Yucatán after first seeking Stephens' advice on where he should go and the dangers of the journey. He was the first European to visit Chichén Itzá out of purely archaeological interest.

Stephens' and Catherwood's second journey began with a stay in Mérida, where they inquired about ruins. The Yucatán has always been a rather isolated and distinctively different part of Mexico and it is evident that the travellers were aided in their search by the separatist mood of that time. Nationalism needs roots in history and the Yucatán Creoles were evidently eager to help their visitors trace them. Mérida was feeling the strains of civil war, but it was still relaxed enough to appreciate a diversion, particularly one so novel as a daguerreotype machine with which the owners were anxious to take portraits for the sake of practice. On foot and by *calesas*, the two-seater carriages with blinds which were the principal means of transport (they still ply the streets, often with red Coca-Cola advertisements on the back), mothers arrived with daughters dressed in their best, with flowers in their hair. The prettiest of all was so grateful that on the day of their departure she sent the travellers a three-foot-wide cake which had to be stuffed into a pair of saddle-bags. The prevalence of *strabismus*, or cross-eyes, once a mark of beauty among the Maya, has often been noted in the Yucatán, and Dr Cabot had come prepared to carry out the new operation pioneered in France by M. Guerin. A brave small boy was offered as a guinea-pig and after he had been dealt with successfully, word spread rapidly. Dr Cabot was required to demonstrate the technique to the town's surgeons and physicians.

Stephens and Catherwood returned to Uxmal to pick up where they had left off, which from Catherwood's point of view was courageous considering how ill he had been there. The architecture there and in its vicinity is the most magnificently embellished in the Maya world, but it is nevertheless a depressing place, or at least I find it so; and that may have been because for most of the time I was there, *el norte*, the evil north wind which brings illness, was blowing. The landscape and vegetation is no more boring than it is elsewhere in the Yucatán but, trying to set aside subjective feelings, there is a lack of architectural organization or central dynamism about the place. Something is missing, anyway, that one finds at the other great sites. Yet Catherwood did some of his best work there, including a masterpiece, his panoramic drawing of the Governor's house, 320 feet long, superbly ornamented in the Puuc style and one of the greatest of Maya works. Uxmal is one of a few sites where there is evidence of phallic worship: a stone phallus which was once ten feet high can be seen in broken condition in front of the main steps of the Governor's house.

Stephens, Catherwood and Cabot were so worn out by fevers at the end of their stay at Uxmal that all three were carried out in *coches*. Catherwood was more seriously ill than the others during their travels yet he seems to have emerged with a hardened constitution. At least, he survived to meet a different fate: drowning with 300 passengers of the S.S. *Arctic* in the Atlantic after a collision with the S.S. *Vesta* in 1854, the first important steamboat collision in history. A tropical disease, probably yellow fever, was to kill Stephens ten years after his second Yucatán trip. He was stricken while working in Panama on the trans-isthmian railway and returned to New York to die.

It was Uxmal that completely convinced Stephens that the buildings they were examining were built by the descendants of the Indians still living nearby. During his stay at Mérida he had seen documents from the second half of the seventeenth century which noted that the Indians were still worshipping there 'notoriously and publicly'. At an earlier date the historian Cogolludo, who for some reason, perhaps nerves and vertigo, had been temporarily struck blind on the steps of the Temple of the Dwarf (so called because of a legend of an old woman who hatched an egg which produced a dwarf who, despite his singularly small size, won a trial of strength with the occupant of the Governor's house, breaking his skull into pieces with the blow of a stick), mentioned finding signs of recently burnt copal in one of the chambers. The linking of the ruins with the Indians and not with some fanciful Phoenician or Hebrew ancestry was Stephens' great contribution to Maya archaeology.

By the time Stephens and Catherwood had completed their journeys they had visited the sites of forty-four 'ancient cities'. It was a very remarkable journey and the last two volumes of *Incidents of Travel*, in which are described a voyage down the east coast to Tulum and visits to hacienda after hacienda seeking information on new sites, are still the most detailed guides there are on Maya remains in the Yucatán. One is continually impressed by Stephens' clarity, the lawyer's skill with which he dismisses the arguments for exotic origins: perhaps he had produced no historical evidence linking the present Maya with the ruins, but then where were the traditions of Paestum or the round towers of Ireland? It was argued that the present-day Maya were too degraded to have ever produced a magnificent culture. Maybe, but who would connect the Creoles of the nineteenth century with the Spanish conquistadors of the sixteenth? Which had become more degenerate?

As they left, Stephens noted that the blast of civil war was sounding through the Yucatán's borders. No one could see then how it would pitch the country into a racial conflict that would last for the rest of the century. The Maya, no longer protected from the Creoles by the Crown, were ready for revolt. Stephens describes meeting a party of them in the forests. 'Naked, armed with long guns, and with deer and wild boars slung on their backs, their aspect was the most truculent of any people we had seen.'

11

The Cruzob, People of the Cross

The wars of independence which overthrew the Spanish Empire in America grew out of Napoleon's occupation of Madrid and the collapse of Spanish power. Self-government was thrust on the Creoles, or white middle classes in the towns, and in Central America the taste for it spread from liberals to conservatives who together achieved independence in 1821. The governments which followed were beset by civil wars and strife and were only intermittently enlightened, but a stock of new ideas from Europe on capitalism and individual rights (not that these were to be over-applied to the Indians) managed to take root, even if they never flourished. Europeans and Americans find it hard to believe how truly disturbing and alien those ideas can be to non-Western cultures; in fact, communism can be interpreted as profoundly unrevolutionary, a move back towards a simpler, more ancient and therefore more understandable world of communal life where the individual has no latitude outside whatever is ordained for his station or his office. Taxation to the Ladinos (a term which embraces all the white and near-white population, in short, anyone who is not an Indian) meant a step towards a modern society, with the Maya being drawn into the economy. The opening of the common lands on which the Indians grew their maize meant more efficient farming to feed a rapidly growing population. Of course, white avarice was a factor in these changes, but then avarice was in a sense essential to economic dynamism.

To the Maya the new regimes that succeeded one another at a fairly fast pace were tyrants. It is doubtful whether the Ladinos in the towns and the settled areas were aware of the ferment among the Indians, for those on the haciendas and in menial jobs in the cities were as tractable and seemingly stupid as ever. The urban life that centred on the gracious plazas, each dominated by a cathedral and frilled with the low arches and columns of arcaded public buildings, flourished in a modest way, with culture and education enjoying a boom under the new freedom. Mérida was beginning to prosper; Campeche remained the most beautiful of the cities but was not doing well economically since more and more trade was moving through Mérida's new port of Sisal; and in Valladolid, ruled by the most exclusive white aristocracy in the peninsula, the *élite* in their large airy houses were, if anything, more unbending than before the revolution.

According to the Ladinos, the Indians were people who learnt through the lash on their backs. Santiago Mendez, Governor of Yucatán in 1841–2, wrote:

'The character of the Indians of Yucatán is such that, were they to be judged only by their customs and habits, we would have to qualify them as stupid and devoid of reason. It would seem indifferent to them to be in the shade or exposed to rain or the scorching rays of the sun, even if they could avoid it. It does not matter to them whether they go dressed or naked. They never try to obtain commodities they see other races enjoy, even though the trouble or sacrifice it would cost to get them might be small. ... Reward does not encourage them, nor does punishment admonish them; in the first place, they think they deserve more – perhaps because they were always accustomed to be made use of – and in the second place they consider punishment as a kind of fatality from which it is quite useless to try to deliver themselves: hence they do not reform. So long as their hunger is stilled, it is quite indifferent to them whether their meal is exquisite and varied, or whether it consists only of tortillas and chile, devouring their food in either case with astounding voracity.'

The overthrow of the Spanish Empire was for the Maya almost an un-conquest. Over the centuries they had survived the spiritual and political crisis caused by the loss of their native priesthood and rulers and learned to accept a new priesthood, new rulers, in the shape of the Catholic church and the officers of the Empire. The church and Spanish systems of government began to fit the Maya. They adapted them so that old traditions and new impositions intertwined to make a different society that nevertheless still had its most important roots in the original culture. That is not to say the Maya were entirely subdued. There was a revolt in 1761 in which a chieftain had himself crowned as Canek, after the Itzá king (the Spaniards, with an equal reverence for tradition, had him drawn and quartered on Mérida's plaza). But generally there was an uneasy settling into a pattern of life that accommodated Christianity without disturbing the rituals and modes of the fundamental economic activity, the annual growing of maize. With the ending of the Spanish imperial domination, the church lost its authority, and for the Maya that meant almost that they had to start all over again. Mannoni, the author of *Prospero and Caliban, the Psychology of Colonialism*, has written of the crisis of abandonment which follows the ending of colonial authority. The shock caused the Yucatán Maya by the collapse of the Spanish Empire led to the chaotic barbarism of the cult of the Speaking Cross, with its arbitrary 'patrons' and other dignitaries; they even reached out to Queen Victoria in their desperation.

The wild party of Maya that Stephens and Catherwood encountered in the forest were on their way to join General Iman, a Yucatán federalist who had rebelled against the central government of Mexico. Nursing two successive defeats, he had conceived a new alliance that in time would have the most awful consequences for the territory: he enlisted the aid of the Indians. Under the governments that succeeded the Spanish Empire, Indians were conscripted for military service like everyone else. Although that aspect of their new citizenship was to prove useful to them, they detested it. There were few greater disasters than to be sent away from home for service. Among General Iman's inducements to join his side was a promise that military service outside the Yucatán would be ended.

It was on Valladolid, the most isolated and vulnerable of the Yucatán cities, that General Iman descended with his ragged army of Maya. Its first occupation was not a slaughter but those that followed were to be notable for their savagery. No other body of rich citizens suffered quite so much. Families were hacked to pieces in their homes, their daughters raped and then murdered spreadeagled on the window grills. Even today there is a harsh atmosphere about the town, as ineradicable as the legendary bloodstains on the floors of old houses.

It may simplify things to divide up the wars and unrest that covered more than six decades in the Yucatán. The first phase was a civil war that began in 1838 with General Iman's revolt. It was between liberal federalists who wanted more autonomy for the provinces and conservatives who wanted a strong government in Mexico City. The civil war culminated in the disaster of the Mexican–American war of 1846 and was succeeded in the Yucatán by phase two, the Caste War, a racial struggle between the Ladinos and the Maya that lasted until 1855 when it was officially but inconclusively ended. During that phase, Valladolid was occupied for a short period by the Maya and Mérida and Campeche were threatened. Only the onset of the rains and the need to plant corn saved the last two. Approximately 250,000 people, half the population of the Yucatán, may have died. Phase three saw the establishment, among the Maya, of the Cult of the Speaking Cross and more or less continual expeditions and forays by and against the Cruzob, the People of the Cross, in circumstances similar in many ways to those which plagued the British Empire on the North-West frontier of India. During this time the Maya achieved *de facto* independence and were accorded a limited degree of recognition by the British. The Cult of the Speaking Cross was finally ended and the Maya conquered once again in 1901 with the occupation of the 'capital' Chan Santa Cruz by General Bravo.

There were Indian wars throughout the American continents in the nineteenth century, but the Maya were the only native people who managed to maintain themselves in a state of independence, however precarious. It is puzzling, in a way, that the American Indians have never achieved the political success of other races who have experienced colonialism. The Arabs, the Asiatic Indians, the Africans and the peoples of south-east Asia have all achieved nationhood, but the American Indians never did. It is not entirely, I think, that they were partly integrated with the Spanish conquerors, or that the Spanish, like the British in North America, were colonists in bulk and therefore permitted no rival nationalisms. The answer seems to lie in the great lack of ambition of which Governor Mendez spoke, and it may be that there is another important reason: a chronic instability in individual characters which communicates itself to any body politic under pressure. Indians often react like depressives, moving from one extreme to the other. The drunken Indians of Gallup, New Mexico, represent one symptom of their failure when the modern world is too insistent; the nationalists who took over Alcatraz (where a visitor could move straight from the company of drugged psychopaths to that of enlightened souls who wanted to talk about Summerhill and progressive education) and then fell to feuding and fighting until they were removed, are another example of their malaise. What I am saying is based on relatively casual observations, but the beauty of the art produced by the Indian civilizations and the appalling bloodiness of their religion may have been a pact, an accommodation of beauty and the beast, that alone permitted their societies to survive and grow.

In nineteenth-century Yucatán there was, just as there was in the United States, a frontier. It occurred some eighty to a hundred miles from Mérida, much closer to Valladolid. The new taxes and the attempts to draw the Maya into a more unified society had led to a flight into the forests where government could not reach them. The history of the years after the conquest was repeating itself. In the wars to restore Ladino authority the Maya showed that they were adept at learning the art of war. As in the past, they would usually avoid head-on assaults, relying instead on ambushes, flanking marches to cut off supplies and the slow attrition of the enemy. Walls were built across lines of march to provide cover for the defenders, and where there was no cover and the enemy was encircled they would build walls by lying on their backs and pushing boulders forward with their feet, protected from the defenders' fire by the size of the stones. But the reason why the Maya were so uniquely successful among the Indian races in fighting their rulers was rather more than their skill or their valour or the terrain in which they lived. They had an ally in the British at Belize. The muddy River Hondo, where the Maya believe a golden crocodile lives in a cave, is the border between Mexico and British Honduras; across it came a steady supply of gunpowder and weapons without which the fight could not have been carried on. It was not until 1893, when the Mexicans recognized the British Honduras frontier, that the supply dried up and Mexican bolt-action rifles were able to win the day against Maya muzzle-loaders. The British, pursuing their diplomatic tightrope walk in Belize, were anxious not only for Mexican recognition but for a guarantee against Maya raids and rebellion by the Indians within their own territory. A people who had defeated the armies of Mexico, the Yucatán and the Emperor Maximilian (as well as having given a contingent of American volunteers a drubbing) could clearly have taken over the colony at any time they wished. So there was a considerable element of *Danegeld* in the British gunpowder.

Although clearly well aware of their power, the Cruzob were also great admirers and respecters of Queen Victoria. Their leaders, recognizing that they could not continue on their own for ever, wished to place themselves under her protection, and one of them even suggested journeying to England for talks with the monarch. The idea of finding a larger protector was not entirely Maya. The Yucatán separatists on one occasion offered their territory to the United States, France or Britain, whichever first took up the offer, and President Polk of the United States eventually felt impelled to declare to Congress that the peninsula was as much subject to the Monroe Doctrine as anywhere else. But in any case, whatever local officials may have felt on occasion, the British Government never showed any real interest in extending its authority into the Yucatán. Nevertheless, the idea that a promise had been given and that one day the Queen would take up her responsibilities, persisted long into this century. In 1922 Sylvanus Morley and a party of Americans who had landed at the ruins of Tulum (where a Maya witch took up residence during Speaking Cross days) were mistaken for Englishmen by local Indians who inquired when they could expect the Queen's rule to be extended to them. In 1959, Nelson Reed, the author of *The Caste War of the Yucatán*, found himself listening at Felipe Carillo Puerto, formerly Chan Santa Cruz, to a prophecy that 'one day the English will give us arms and the people will go to war to throw out the Yucatecans. The sign will be when money disappears from the hands, Mexican money; that will be the balance of the year, the end of the world.'

The cross, as has been said earlier, was a Maya symbol as well as a Christian one. Families had their own crosses, worshipped apart from the saints or the Christ they were supposed to bear. In the old Maya religion the cross was associated with the rain or water god, and when the Cult of the Speaking

167

Cross was first observed, it was discovered close to a small *cenote*, a grotto where the water level never varied. The cross, cut on a mahogany tree, had the power of speech and served as an oracle. Ventriloquial acts of this sort had been a feature of Maya shrines before the conquest, the most famous being on Cozumel, where a voice spoke from within the clay figure of the moon goddess. The Speaking Cross was the instrument of the rulers of the Cruzob, who knew about the ventriloquism but nevertheless believed they were listening to divine messages transmitted through a medium. That the messages came direct from secular authority and no trance was involved was fairly conclusively proved by the story of a captured dragoon who was unlucky enough to win twenty-eight pesos from the Patron of the Cross, the religious and secular leader, in a card game. The next day the Cross condemned him for sacrilege for playing cards in the vicinity of the church and sentenced him to twenty-five lashes and a fine of twenty-eight pesos to be spent on candles.

In the early days of the cult, there was not just one cross but several, the junior ones smaller, but all dressed in *huipils*, the smocks worn by the women, and decorated with ribbons. The smaller ones were not used for prophecy, although they had a family relationship with the main cross and were known as its daughters. Perhaps there was an element in the new religion of the stela cult of a thousand years earlier, where carved and painted images of ancestors were worshipped with offerings on round stone altars set before them. In Palenque the crosses and the ancestors come together on the tablets in the temples. So the Cult of the Speaking Cross may have gone back further than it knew, although the Cruzob were aware of their more recent history. Long before the cult began, Indians in Mérida had taunted Ladino patrols with the names of past Maya kings; and in a message delivered to the people after a successful Ladino raid had destroyed the shrine of the Cross, the Cruzob Patron, José Maria Barrera, had spoken of calling on the 'governor who lives in Chichén Itzá' (probably a king of the Itzá whose spirit was supposed to still dwell there) for assistance.

As the cult survived its early vicissitudes, it grew in power and wealth. The sacking of the small town of Tekax and the taking of the garrison town of Bacalar (accomplished in twenty minutes) in 1857 with over a thousand Ladinos slaughtered and hundreds taken prisoner brought in a great deal of loot, which was traded across the Hondo. The British magistrate at Corozal, the northernmost town of British Honduras, found that success had forced up prices when he tried to ransom the survivors of Bacalar. The Cross, speaking in squeaky Maya, wanted 4,000 pesos. Before he had time to recross the border and find the ransom, all except a few women and children had been slaughtered on fresh orders from the Cross. (Indian prisoners who fell into Ladino hands were dealt with as ruthlessly, but without the divine guidance.) Those Ladinos who were not slaughtered were enslaved; a few years later there were several hundred white and mestizo slaves in Maya hands.

By 1857 the cult was sufficiently established to build the new church of Balam Na, House of God, a massively constructed barrel-roofed building of austere design which can still be seen. Just as the Spaniards had built their cathedrals facing a town plaza, so did the Cruzob at their new town of Chan Santa Cruz. The official residence on the eastern side faced the church to remind the Patron, also known as West Wind, of the source of his power. Specifically Maya touches were four small chapels, one for each cardinal point, and in the centre of the plaza a sapote tree reserved for executions. The town surrounding the plaza was laid out on the usual grid-iron pattern familiar to the Maya from the towns of the north.

Some of the best accounts of the rulers of the Cruzob and the Cross' method of conducting business have come from British officers who were sent across the border to negotiate or communicate complaints. Their reports, bound together in rather haphazard order, can be found in the British Honduras

Archives in Belize, where the librarian, newly out from England, hands the reader a small brush to remove the dust and the tiny mites which scurry across the pages of clear, Victorian handwriting.

The Belize Superintendent, who in 1861 sent two Royal Engineers officers, Lieutenants Plumridge and Twigge, to Chan Santa Cruz to deliver a stiff note of protest against border incidents, clearly had little idea of the type of person they would have to deal with. Plumridge was firmly instructed 'not to listen to the superstitious oracle of the cross or take part in any such mummeries unless under compulsion'. Their first encounter with Cruzob realities occurred at Bacalar where they were not allowed to land as the local commander was asleep. That proved to be a slight euphemism, as when the commander was fetched on the insistence of the two officers he proved to be drunk and capable of standing only with the aid of his men. In the evening when he had sobered up he proved to be civil enough and agreed to provide the envoys with mules and an escort. Whatever qualifications Plumridge and Twigge may have had for their mission, they did not include a knowledge of Spanish or Maya. Fortunately, they found at Bacalar a trader from British Honduras, José Maria Trejo, who was very likely engaged in selling arms. He agreed to accompany them as an interpreter, but almost turned back in alarm when *en route* to Chan Santa Cruz he was shown the peremptory letter to be delivered to the Patron, Venancio Puc, a brutal drunk inclined to take arbitrary measures with those who offended or bothered him.

Just how right Trejo was to be alarmed was demonstrated as soon as the party arrived at Chan Santa Cruz. A body of soldiery took them, with cocked muskets pointed at their breasts, to Puc, who read the letter and said rather ominously that there could be no reply until 'god came'. While awaiting the event, the party was locked in a small shed and the officers' arms, including their swords, were removed. Accompanied by their guards they spent from eight in the morning until midnight in the shed. At that hour they were taken to the church where god was speaking. The plaza was crowded and the officers noted the excitement their arrival caused. Inside the church they were made to kneel before the Cross which asked in a shrill voice, which seemed sometimes near and sometimes far away, what they wanted. When Trejo replied in god's language, Maya, the envoys were informed that the raiders were entitled to the cattle and other things they had taken, but as they had removed them without permission, they had been flogged. Plumridge's account mentioned that Trejo 'appeared very much frightened' by the way in which the Cross spoke. The interpreter's more graphic description of events says that god described the letter as 'very insulting'. The British could come in thousands if they liked; in fact, it might be better if they did, for that would make it easier for god to dispose of them all at once. 'I was very frightened,' wrote Trejo. 'I knew that they had chosen the hour for bringing us before the Cross when they usually execute their prisoners. Our lives were in great danger.' The place of execution was the previously mentioned sapote tree in the plaza, where prisoners were dispatched with machetes.

Trejo was so terrified that he ignored the officers' instructions to demand a reply to the letter and when asked specifically by god whether they had come about 'that letter' said their mission was to seek trade and peace, not to complain. In that case, said god, 1,000 kegs of gunpowder would be acceptable. There was no need for the Belize government to get involved in the transaction, which would be paid for in gold and mules; the traders could handle it. God's message delivered, the officers were returned to their hut where they were left until a drunken Puc sent for them next day. Twigge had a spoonful of pepper poured into his mouth and was made to drink aniseed, while Plumridge escaped with merely having to drink aniseed until he vomited. 'They objected very much to their treatment,' said Trejo. Noticing this, Puc asked the interpreter: 'Are they angry? Tell me? For if they are, I will have them chopped to pieces at once.' After that Plumridge and Twigge offered no more objections to the Patron's orders. They kissed and hugged him, danced and sang for his amusement, swallowed their aniseed without complaint and allowed him to slap their heads and pull them about as he felt inclined. The Patron and his men were so pleased by his guests and the amusement they afforded in a normally rather dull town that they were forced to endure three days of his hospitality before Puc sent them home with a reminder not to forget about god's gunpowder.

Another cause of trouble for the British on the northern frontier was General Marcus Canul, chief of the Icaiche Pacificos, a group pacific only in regard to the Mexican government, with whom they were in alliance. They were sporadically engaged in fighting with the Cruzob and at the instigation of the Mexicans, raided into British territory. One raid in 1866 left two dead, including a mestizo storekeeper known as 'Black Devil'. Canul, mounted on a stolen horse, retreated back to his stronghold in southern Yucatán with 200 cattle and a captured log-cutting gang consisting of thirty-seven men, fourteen women and eight children whom he proposed to ransom for 12,000 pesos. The Commissioner in the north, Gustav von Ohlafen, a Prussian, counselled against retrieving them by force, and in the end an inter-mediary, Franco Salazar, beat the price down to 3,000 pesos after having been subjected to 'a number of outrages, indig-nities and menaces which I cannot here explain'. The ransom was supposed to be back payments for thirty years of log-cutting on Canul's territory. Other attempts to buy him off with goods delivered 'on credit' failed. The general was given to cryptic warnings that he might go personally to Belize for gunpowder and statements such as 'When you have to cry, don't say I didn't warn you.' The British were particularly concerned that he or one of his allies would descend on Orange Walk, the main settlement in the north, and at the end of the same year, 1866, sent a platoon of the 4th West

Indian Regiment to stop him near the settlement of San Pedro. The men lost their shoes in the mud and by the time they neared their destination they were in no mood to fight off an ambush. The commander Captain McKay estimated that he was under fire from between 400 and 500 men. With five dead and fourteen wounded, the platoon fled after half an hour, passing through Orange Walk and barely stopping until it reached the sanctuary of Belize, which was soon in a high state of alarm, with the Governor ready to sail and refugees streaming in from the north. Even poisoned rum left behind for the raiders proved ineffective, since years of experience had taught them that it was always best to make a prisoner drink the first toast. In the confusion of the retreat from San Pedro it was not at first noticed that the Orange Walk commissioner, Mr Rhys, had been left behind. Captain McKay reported that he had been told by his men that efforts to induce him to leave had failed since 'he could not be prevailed upon to move from the spot where he had stationed himself'. Mr Rhys was never seen or heard of again. A court of inquiry eventually exonerated McKay of responsibility for the débâcle, although it found he had shown a lack of judgement. In the following year a stronger British force accompanied by a rocket detachment of the Royal Artillery proved more effective and the Maya retreated before a display of unmatchable firepower.

With the border still vulnerable to forays by Canul, the Belize administration sent Captain John Carmichael, a member of the recently formed colonial militia, to Chan Santa Cruz for talks with the new Patron, Bonifacio Novelo. The Cruzob, who had just suffered a rather nasty setback at the hands of the Ladinos, were anxious to impress their cautious allies from south of the Hondo and Carmichael was met at the wharf when he landed at Bacalar by a guard of honour and a band playing bugles and beating drums. He was then accompanied to Chan Santa Cruz where after a short wait outside the walls he entered through the ranks of a 200-strong guard of honour

173

backed by a thirty-man band. Passing under triumphal arches, with soldiers presenting arms at each intersection of the streets, he arrived in the plaza. There, 1,000 soldiers had been drawn up to greet him before he proceeded to the house of West Wind, the Patron. After a few minutes Novelo appeared from behind a curtain which divided the room and without looking at Carmichael prayed before an altar dominated by a cross profusely ornamented with gold and jewels. After such a splendid reception the envoy was susceptible to being impressed by Novelo whose countenance he found 'decidedly pleasing'. He was a man of about sixty, very fat, with a complexion lighter than the average Indian. 'He was dressed in a many coloured blouse made of cloth of Indian manufacture, white loose cotton drawers trimmed from the knee downward with rich lace, sandals of embroidered leather and scarf also of Indian manufacture round his waist, while round his neck was hung a massive gold chain with a cross attached.'

Novelo claimed to be purely a religious leader and not concerned with warfare. Foreign affairs was in his province, however, and before long Carmichael was engaged in discussions with the governing council of three, including Novelo, on whether the British would take over the territory. The Council had just turned down an offer of autonomy from the Mexicans because they doubted their sincerity. The Cruzob army, he learnt, was 11,000 strong and the men were obliged to serve in it for fifteen days of every month, receiving their weapons from the Chan Santa Cruz government but providing their own staple diet of corncake and red peppers. Obvious concern for his regime's image abroad prompted Novelo to deny that ventriloquy was employed under his control; children were taught to say their prayers to god through the Cross, which Carmichael noted dominated an otherwise bare church.

The effect of this diplomatic encounter on General Canul's activities seems to have been small. He captured Corozal in 1870 and launched his last raid in September, 1872, when he crossed the Hondo at Panting's landing with 150 men and moved on Orange Walk. There he besieged a platoon of the 1st West Indian Regiment with their surgeon in a single-roomed barrack building. The raiders set the kitchen ablaze and badly wounded the platoon commander, but they failed to overwhelm the defenders who, under the command of a sergeant, drove them off, giving Canul his death wound in the process. His successor, Rafael Chan, wrote the Lieut. Governor of Belize a letter of apology for the raid, asking pardon of 'Our Queen who has much reason to be annoyed'.

While the modern Maya endured a long agony, there took place two important discoveries concerning the ancient Maya. One was far away in Madrid, and was to have a purely scholarly impact; the other occurred in the heart of the Petén and demonstrated that, as Stephens had suggested, there were great cities still to be discovered. The last was a prelude that had to wait almost sixty years for the full symphony. War, the sheer inaccessibility of the Petén and a lack of organized effort were to have inhibiting effects on archaeological exploration.

12

The Greatest Discovery

The nineteenth century was the heroic age of archaeology, a time of great discoveries. It opened in the jungles of the Petén in 1848 when Governor Ambrosio Tut, a Maya to judge by his name, and Colonel Modesto Mendez, corregidor or chief magistrate of Flores (once Tayasal), wandered together among the jungled ruins of Tikal, in size and grandeur the Rome of the Classic Maya world. It was the greatest discovery in the archaeology of the Maya and remains so today. If there was, regrettably, no symbolism in the joint expedition of an Indian and a Creole, there is at least poetry in the thought of Ambrosio and Modesto among the temples, speculating on whether the city's unknown inhabitants had possessed cattle since Tut's grandfather had once seen a 'beautifully carved bull' not far away. Tikal means in Maya 'The place where spirit voices are heard' and Tut's ancestors must have always known about it and held it in some awe. Teobert Maler, the Austrian archaeologist who was the first to explore it thoroughly (but not until 1904) wrote: 'The Mayas believe that at midnight (especially during the great festivals) their ancestors return to earth and adorned as in the days of their glory, wander about in the forsaken temples and palaces, where their spirit voices are heard in the air. Therefore all important ruins in this land are regarded as enchanted, *encantadas*, and timid people do not like to sleep alone in their chambers.'

Tut was really the first to reach Tikal; he was on his way home along the trail he had blazed when he met Mendez and

Temple of the Dwarf, Uxmal

Caracol, Chichén Itzá

Castillo, Chichén Itzá

returned to the ruins with him. But Tut, despite his title of Governor of the Petén, was almost certainly illiterate and therefore unable to communicate his discovery to the civilized world. That honour fell to Mendez. Like so many Maya events, the discovery and its announcement took a long time to mature. The difficulties of travel in the almost trackless Petén and the rebellion farther north were between them sufficient to deter a thorough exploration of the heartland of the Classic Maya (Copán and Palenque are only its fringes) until towards the end of the century.

Tut lived in San José, a large Maya village a few miles across Lake Petén-Itzá from Flores, the provincial capital. It is doubtful whether he was much more than cacique or that his sway extended very far. The real ruler was Colonel Mendez, who performed a function similar to that of a colonial district commissioner. Mendez seems to have heard about the ruins some time before the expedition but to have been refused permission by the Guatemalan government to undertake a journey there because of the troubled conditions in the area. However, Stephens' books had come out in the first half of the decade and had stirred considerable speculation on lost cities existing in the hinterland, and finally Colonel Mendez had his way. He gathered together a party of five from Flores, including Eusebio Lara, a local 'artist' drummed up for the occasion, and travelled up the lake in two canoes. At its eastern extremity weeping women at a base camp informed Mendez that Governor Tut had set out for Tikal eight days earlier and had not been heard from since. Savages, wild beasts or the evil spirits lurking in the forests and ruins had no doubt done for them. But one day's journey along the trail brought the colonel to a spot where he encountered Tut returning from the ruins quite unharmed by spirits but complaining about marauding wild beasts and a lack of surface water. The trail to Tikal had been blazed and his men were able to return to San José while he accompanied Mendez. Two casks of water were sent ahead to await the party at the ruins and *en route* they refreshed themselves with the liquid which, with a slash of a machete, can be obtained from the water vine. At last they arrived among the great temples (Mendez thought they were palaces) of Tikal; the colonel made a mark signifying the ruins were the property of the Guatemalan government, which no doubt had become more aware since Stephens' and Catherwood's journey of the political value of ruins, and experienced a 'noble pride' in the accomplishment of his mission. He and his party clambered over the temples and palaces, then as now a difficult task, marvelled at their size and the carved sapote wood lintels and beams which were once a feature of the site, and speculated on the ambition that had prompted Tikal's creators to commemorate themselves in such a way. Lara sketched a few drawings which bear some resemblance to what he saw but not very much.

Mendez's report was duly written and sent back with Lara's drawings to Guatemala City where, following precedent, they were not published. The colonel's local fame was to rest more in the next few years on a peace mission he carried out on behalf of the Mérida government to the rebellious Indians at Chichénha, across the border in the Yucatán. To the amazement of the Indians, he arrived without a military escort and accompanied only by a priest. Perhaps he knew from the history of relations with the Itzá of Tayasal that when dealing with the Maya it was best to take either a lot of troops or none at all. His protection, he told the rebels, was granted him by the Virgin Dolorosa. After two days, a peace treaty was signed with the chief, Angelino Itzá, and sealed with a fiesta. The peace lasted one month.

Again following precedent, it was the foreigners in Guatemala City who paid most attention to Mendez's report. The Prussian envoy, Hesse, sent a copy to Germany where it was published by the Berlin Academy of Science in 1853. The stir was sufficient to prompt the British Government, still showing a flickering interest in Maya archaeology, to ask its by then retired consul Frederick Chatfield to find out more about

Tikal, which he did through his son in Guatemala City who sent him copies of Lara's drawings.

Tikal is one of those rare places which overwhelm the expectations, that give the viewer more than he or she could ever have anticipated from photographs, paintings or written accounts, and thus it belongs to a very special category of magnificence. Its peers are Chartres, Delphi and perhaps the great Bronze Age fortress of Dun Aengus in the Arran

Temple 1, Tikal (note stelae at foot of temple)

Islands. That is a personal list, of course. Anyone can make their own. But let me say that the pyramids of Tikal were for me more marvellous than those of Giza, and I could understand why Stephens and Catherwood on their first encounter with the works of the Classic Maya at Copán had viewed them with an 'interest perhaps stronger' than they had ever felt while wandering among the ruins of Egyptian antiquity.

Tikal was not the capital of a civilization; it was a civilization's greatest creation. Perhaps it is best visualized as a city state, although that is possibly a bit misleading since there was no city wall, none of the great purely civic buildings and fixed agriculture that one would expect with a city. Only one defensive work, a fosse on the northern side which appears to have been a protection against an attack from its considerably smaller neighbour, Uaxactún, has been found. Tikal was primarily a religious centre with a suburban sprawl the full extent of which is still not known. All that has been charted is six square miles with more than 3,000 buildings including

Courtyard of Maler's palace, looking across to temple on right

temples, palaces or monasteries, the shrines of the various clans who used Tikal rather as the British establishment uses Westminster Abbey, ball courts, great terraces and innumerable huts built on the small burial mounds which are a feature of the landscape around any site (they existed into modern times in the form of *ermitas*, open-sided sheds used as communal meeting places where the dead were buried close to the altars and crosses of Maya Catholicism). Nowhere else in the Maya world is there such evidence of an *élite*'s pride in the continuity of its achievements. The site represents some 1,100 years of effort which ceased around 900 A.D., although the site was probably still occupied for a few centuries after that. The earliest stela at Tikal is dated 292 A.D. and the latest 879 A.D., and those dates encompass its florescence.

When one considers the size and splendour of Tikal the wonder is that it left no historical legend. The only Classic site which has a tradition that can be regarded as even faintly historical is Copán, where in the sixteenth century the local Maya told Palacio that in ancient times a great king from the Yucatán had built its edifices and at the end of some years had returned to his native land, leaving them entirely empty. But at Tikal all we have are dates: the dedication dates of stelae commemorating the accession of unknown kings and priests (the Venancio Pucs and Bonifacio Novelos of more than a thousand years ago). It is a grave of the anonymous, a place free of personality, so that one is made more acutely aware through contrast of the obsessional concern of the priesthood with the abstractions of time. Mere bakhtuns (144,000 days) and katuns (7,200 days), the largest units required for the computation of dates from a base equivalent of 3,113 B.C., were not enough to appease the thirst of some high minds for penetration into even remoter regions of time. They dealt in calabtuns of 57,600,000 days and kinchiltuns of 1,152,000,000 days. Unless it has been misinterpreted, Stela 10 records a passage of time of more than 5,045,000 years.

Why they were so concerned with time no one knows.

Perhaps it was an outlet for otherwise constrained intellects; just to demonstrate that such a vast and, to mortals, meaningless stretch of time could be conceptualized in stone was a major achievement, an offering of the greatest worth to the gods. Whatever the reason, one is aware of the curious energy of those minds as one explores Tikal. It is like going over an abandoned millworks, a complex prayer wheel that once worked not by the race of water or wind but by the flow of time, the movement of the stars, moon and sun. Not very much would be needed to set it in order again, to bring back for longer than midnight the owners of the spirit voices.

The other great mystery of the Classic Maya is why their civilization collapsed more or less simultaneously at all the rain forest sites without a successor. There are various theories: a conquest by barbarians; the ruling *élite* grew over-demanding of the peasantry which supported them and their great projects and was destroyed by an uprising; a population explosion that led to exhaustion of the land and migration; recurrent plagues; a climatic change. The last seems to me the most plausible as the main reason, since it is hard to believe that a civilization of the sort that built Tikal could have flourished in circumstances where up to 200 inches of rain fall every year. Perhaps it was considerably drier in the Classic Period, and a slow increase in the annual rains made milpa agriculture, the mainstay of the society, increasingly difficult. The mahoganies and other forest trees would grow increasingly large and hard to cut with stone axes for new slash-and-burn fields, the nutrients would be more rapidly leached from the soil and the weeds would take over in two years or so, as they do today. For centuries the Petén has remained largely uninhabited as a result of its climate, and even now, when an effort is being made to develop it, the population is scanty. Only one Indian culture, the Itzá, has survived there in the thousand years following the collapse of the Classic Period, and they were a refugee society whose culture was not remarkable by earlier standards.

The Tikal that Tut and Mendez discovered was covered by trees with only the conical shape of the pyramids and the occasional gleam of limestone to indicate what they were. The tops of Tikal's pyramids do rise well above the forest (Temple 4, 212 feet high to the top of its roof comb, is the tallest pre-Columbian building in the Americas) like the heads of swimmers on a green sea, but seeing ruins from a distance in the jungle is extremely hard. I recall once travelling with Ian Graham on a compass bearing to find the ruins of Ucanal in the eastern Petén and being surprised to find that one could pass within twenty or thirty yards of a large mound or a temple pyramid without seeing it. It was like searching the seabed for a wrecked fleet. I experienced then at about third or fourth strength some of the satisfaction Tut and Mendez, Maler and other explorers in the Petén must have felt on discovering a site. For the sheer exhilarating joy of it, I clambered up the eroded cone of a pyramid, clutching vines and tree roots, gingerly feeling for footholds on tumbled stones, until I emerged into the open air and could see the Mopan river in its valley.

The forest retained its hold on Tikal until the second half of this century. Earlier visitors cleared away some of the trees for photography and exploration but as soon as they had gone the forest returned with all the surprising speed of tropical vegetation. It was not until 1956 that the University of Pennsylvania under contract with the Guatemalan government, began Project Tikal, the extensive clearing, exploration and restoration of the site, the results of which the visitor enjoys today.

The great plaza has been cleared, so that one can appreciate its immensity, the marvellous poise of its two temples and the retreating terraces of the North Acropolis and Maler's palace. The best time to see Tikal is just after dawn when the light is oblique and gentle and the wildlife in the surrounding jungle strolls or forages through the grounds – a few peccaries rooting around in the Plaza of the Seven Temples, a coati mundi in the Great Plaza, its tail waving above the grass like a snake-charmer's cobra, and once as I stood in the courtyard of Maler's palace, an oscellated turkey, a green-bronze bird, wild and limber, which when it saw me raced away across the walls, its head held low. Maler mentions in his report on Tikal that they roost in the trees where, the Indians informed him, a small owl sometimes pecked out their eyes, leaving them to wander blind and starving through the forests like cast-out kings.

Palenque, Copán and the Yucatán sites were all receiving a thin stream of visitors throughout the nineteenth century but Tikal was largely left to its isolation. There were no roads into the Petén, only mule tracks, and the best way of reaching the site was a matter for argument until as late as 1910. The foreigner had a choice of three routes, all of them difficult. He could travel up the Usumacinta and de la Pasion rivers and then strike across country via Flores; he could come from Guatemala City and the mountains and take to the jungle tracks near Cobán; or he could take a steamer to Belize, travel by canoe to Cayo, close to the frontier, and hire mules there for the rest of his journey. The last was probably the simplest. Mendez, who lived more or less on Tikal's doorstep, went there again in 1853 but left no account of his journey. The next visitor was a Swiss, Dr Gustave Bernouilli, who arrived by the Usumacinta route with a young German companion, Herr Cario. They were collecting specimens for a herbarium but at Tikal they turned to other things. They commissioned Indians from the lake to remove some of the carved lintels of sapote wood and today they can be seen in the Völkerkunde Museum, in Basle. Bernouilli, who suffered from a lung disease and was ailing during his journey across the Petén, never returned to Europe; he died in San Francisco. Next came Maudslay in 1881–2, followed by a few looters, and then Maler in 1895 and 1904. Maudslay was the greatest of the nineteenth-century Mayanists, but somehow it is Maler who sticks in one's mind at Tikal: moody, solitary, complaining, soulful, suspicious and incomparably energetic. A German who became an Austrian by adoption in his early twenties, Maler was born in Rome (where his father was the Duchy of Baden's envoy to the Vatican) in 1842. A rootless and restless person, he threw up the prospects of a career in architecture and enlisted as a cadet in the corps of Austrian volunteers raised by Count Thun-Hohenstein for the Emperor Maximilian's adventure in Mexico. Hard times of which he seldom spoke followed Maximilian's downfall, but Maler earned enough – by photography – or had saved enough money to survive and undertake several expeditions to ruins. His photographs and personal accounts persuaded the Geographic Society of Paris in 1878 that there was more to be explored in Central America than they had hitherto believed and may have been a decisive factor in the Ministry of Public Instruction's decision to send Désiré Charnay, a French traveller and writer who had visited Mexico in the 1850s, on a second expedition in the 1880s. Purely as an explorer, Maler reigns supreme among the Mayanists. He surveyed the Usumacinta thoroughly for the first time, discovering or revealing, among other sites, the Altar de Sacrificios; on the other side of the Petén his most important find was Naranjo, with its rich trove of 32 stelae. Maler's success was due not so much to the toughness necessary in a captain of Maximilian's army as to his Teutonic thoroughness. He explored systematically, helped by the reports of chicleros and natives as well as by a good eye for country when it came to spotting a likely place for a Maya site. The Peabody Museum, whose entry into the field at the end of the century had been beset with difficulties, including the death of the expedition leader from fever, employed him in 1897 as an archaeological leg-man, and it was for the Peabody that he did his greatest work.

One of Maler's Peabody colleagues was to complain later about the 'all too much unimportant babbling' in his reports, by which he meant that Maler was given to describing the context of the ruins in all its wretchedness and splendour. A misanthropic loathing of those he had to rely on in the jungle runs through his works. The only people he had a good word for were Negroes, and then only, one suspects, because there were not too many of them in the Petén. All that he wanted from human kind was praise and recognition; there is no indication by him or from those who knew him that he ever loved anyone or needed love. The jungle provided the solitude which was his chief requirement and his work was spurred on by an intense jealousy of all rivals; no one could claim a discovery without a sarcastically phrased rejoinder from Maler that he had heard of it first.

A lack of charity is not necessarily a defect in a writer and Maler's 'babblings' have a quality that places them above the average for the output of archaeologists. His labours for the Peabody spanned his sixtieth birthday and age joined with eccentricity in those years to harden an unexpected and possibly unconscious literary theme: man is the only degraded creature in the tropical Eden which sustains Maler's crippled soul. This extract from his report (translated from the German by the Peabody) on the exploration of the upper Usumacinta catches the flavour, I think:

'On the 10th of July we continued our journey without stopping until we reached the cabins of Plancha de Piedra on the left bank of the river, where lived two men, Navarro and Gama, for whom things had grown too hot in Mexico and who had met on Guatemalan soil. Although I was instantly aware that I was dealing with individuals of extremely doubtful character I was nevertheless obliged to engage their services for large pay, since the lazy fellows I had brought from Sacluk refused to accompany me further. These two men were also well acquainted with the ruins of Altar de Sacrificios, which were in the immediate vicinity, and I therefore felt it expedient to appear unconscious of any irregularities in their lives.

'The filth and degradation of the lonely hut, in which I

was to spend the night, beggars description. I cleaned out one corner in which I was to sleep but I could not avoid hearing and seeing many disagreeable things.

'In all my journeyings on the treacherous waters of the Usumatsintla (Maler used the old spelling of the name), between El Cayo and Saiyaxche, I have been forcibly struck by the extraordinary contrast between the lavish beauty of nature and the extreme degradation of the remnants of humanity existing there. Luxuriant vegetation of emerald hue bends in flower-laden branches to the water's edge, overarched by a sky of purest azure; brilliant-hued butterflies and humming birds with metallic sheen fly from flower to flower; gorgeous birds build their nests in every tree; even the snakes and iguanodons are graceful and beautiful; but humankind produces no such splendid forms as are to be seen in the Caucasus or in Asiatic Turkey. It is long since a respectable, stationary population inhabited these fruitful shores, and the dubious elements sunk in sloth, filth, and every possible vice, whose miserable habitations are met with here and there, are constantly shifting since they acquire no fixed property rights.'

At Tikal in 1895 Maler had, as usual, a row with his guides and labourers, Indians from San José, who doubtless resented his obvious contempt for them. So he moved away from their encampment to sleep on his own in one of the long chambers of the palace or monastery (now named after him), on the white-plastered inner walls of which he wrote his name. From the same walls he copied down meticulously the graffiti left by its occupants a thousand years before.

'Sometimes in my lonely chamber during the night I found myself so surrounded by roaring panthers with whom other creatures, perhaps more harmless, mingled their cries that I was forced to maintain a great fire at the entrance of my chamber, even occasionally to barricade it with timber. Of course, I always kept a carefully loaded rifle by my side,

Graffiti copied from plaster walls of the palace at Tikal by Maler

but otherwise in perfect tranquillity of mind. When I am sleeping in a ruin or under a tree in the primeval forest or in a little cave, I am not at all disturbed by the serenades tendered me at the midnight hour by the felis onca, the felis pardalis, the felis concola, or any of their kin. It always seems to me to be part of the situation, so I listen with careful attention. The darkness of the night makes no difference to my feelings because I am convinced that the same of good and evil always exists whether our planet bears us in sunlight or shadow.'

Maler would pause during a temple excavation to note the reptiles brought to light from their sanctuaries beneath the stones: a rose-coloured tiger lizard, a small coral snake and a toad 'which the Spaniards call *maʒamorra*, probably because it lives in its dark, subterraneous prison'. Sometimes he is constrained in his reports by a curious decorum. A 'dreadful error' committed by one of his men turns out in a letter preserved in the Peabody archives to have been wife-murder. Also reserved for the privacy of a letter was a note on the alleged anatomical peculiarities of Lacandón women. He had treated as 'somewhat incredible and ridiculous' reports by Ladinos that the women had four breasts, but he had now heard the same thing from a Mr Lederer who had informed him that a woman he had seen living with a Ladino had 'distinctly formed four breasts $\begin{smallmatrix} (.) & (.) \\ (.) & (.) \end{smallmatrix}$ (*vier Brüste*)!' Mr Lederer was of German origin and an intelligent man and Maler had no reason to doubt his assertion.

When he returned to Tikal again in 1904 he lived more amicably with his crew in one of the palace quadrangles. This time he lamented the damage caused to the Great Plaza and Temple 3 by the milpas fires lit by refugees from the war in the Yucatán. They had been chased away eventually by swarms of vampire bats, he noted gleefully. His men showed great reluctance to scale the temple tops to clear away vegetation so he could photograph them. The ladders of light guaramo wood he had built failed to persuade them it could be done safely until he offered extra pay as an inducement. Even Maler had to admit it was dangerous work as the crumbling stonework and the removal of trees that both destroyed and held the roofs together threatened the alternatives of being pitched to death or crushed to death.

Maler was the first archaeologist to castigate those who removed carvings from the temples. They were 'vile people' who carried out 'infamous destruction'. In one of the first cases of speculative looting for profit, an unnamed Spanish business-man 'heavily in debt', a drunken chiclero and a master shoe-maker from Flores had hacked out two beams from a Tikal temple and shipped them out through Belize, then as now a convenient outlet for looted art. Maler was never able to discover their eventual purchasers. He particularly criticized those – such as Bernouilli – who hired Indians to do the work of removal. Since they did not possess saws, they freed the timbers by burning the ends with slow fires, often leaving them unattended while they consumed their posole. They were quite undisturbed if a pair of sacerdotal feet, the plume of a helmet or some interesting hieroglyphics were consumed in their absence. He found a half-charred beam in a heap of rubbish in Temple 11, and suspected that others had been thrown away by the Indians on the road out of Tikal because they were heavy. More damage was caused by Indians smashing the faces on the stelae out of fear their spirits would harm the milpas. Even the esteemed Maudslay, who had preceded him at Yaxchilán, on the Usumacinta, as well as at Tikal, was not immune from criticism. To his 'great disappointment' he found that Maudslay had removed some of the carved lintels at Yaxchilán, taking them with him to England.

Maler was hired by Charles Bowditch, the director of the Peabody and driving force behind its first ventures into Maya regions, for $100 a month to include all his personal expenses. In return, the contract stipulated that, in addition to his labour, the Museum would have the rights to his photographs, although Maler was free to have prints made at his own expense. It was a pretty hard bargain even when one takes into account the greater value of the dollar then (Catherwood had earned considerably more almost sixty years earlier under his contract with Stephens) and Maler undoubtedly resented it. Add to that resentment his suspicious crankiness and there is the making of the row that blew up over his work at Tikal. The Peabody, Maler decided, wanted to make money out of his map of Tikal – the only one in existence – and he evaded all their efforts to obtain it, stepping up his demands for money as he did so. The Peabody was obliged to send out an expedition in 1910 to explore and chart the ruins once again. Bowditch wrote to its leader, Alfred Tozzer, that he hoped Maler would not hear of some productive work they had carried out at a site Maler knew of but had not visited, otherwise 'he would think we owed him a hundred thousand dollars more'. Maler, who finally broke off all communications with the Museum, retired to his house in Calle 59, Mérida, and spent his days tending the coconut palms in his garden and drinking in the town's bars. He made a sparse living from photography and occasional sales of pottery he had collected during his journeys. He died in 1917. The map was never found.

Little of Maler's work would have been possible without the booming sales of chewing gum in the United States. The Ladinos of the Petén he so despised, abandoned the arduous and unprofitable work of cultivating milpas and took to the forest in search of sapote trees (the same as those from which the temple lintels were made) to tap chicle for gum. Praçtically every discovery after Tikal seems to have been made in the first place by a chiclero during his wanderings in the wet season when the sap is rising. In fact, I have come across only one case in which the finder was an archaeologist. It was Maler, of course. He spotted the extensive ruins of Yaxhá as he was being paddled across the lake of the same name, and he describes the event with a brusque economy that conveys the tension, the unique egotistical pleasure of discovery: '... I carefully examined the green outlines of the forest on the rising north shore, clearly outlined against the cloudless blue sky. In so doing I became aware of an extended chain of elevations appearing here and there. I felt convinced that they indicated an extensive ancient city, the exploration of which I determined to put into execution at once.'

13

La Cité Lorillard

Archaeologists and scholars generally never like to admit that they are prone to the narrow emotions caused by nationalism, for knowledge is after all international and to be shared. Nevertheless, there was a whiff of national rivalries among the Maya ruins on various occasions during the nineteenth century and even into the first decade of this. It emanated mainly from the French who alone of all the nations represented by individuals in the Maya area spent government money on expeditions. They had, of course, political aspirations in the area; and they had too a competitive eagerness to be first with something, as they had been in Egyptology with Champollion and the Rosetta Stone. But despite the key discovery of a document by the Abbé Brasseur de Bourbourg and a great deal of impressive work by the philologist Count Hyacinthe de Charencey, they produced no Mayanists to compare with Ernst Förstemann, of Germany, or Maudslay, or the American scholars who have dominated the field since the end of the nineteenth century. The expeditions which the Ministry of Public Instruction helped finance were under Désiré Charnay, a travel writer of some renown, and Count Maurice de Périgny, another aristocratic scholar. Bowditch sniffed at their efforts. He wrote to Tozzer in 1910, 'the Comte de Périgny is not going to be a very formidable competitor if he intends to spend no more than two weeks in his work [in the eastern Petén]. I am afraid that is the way that most of the Latin races prefer to work. They pick up

Toltec figure above serpent head, Temple of the Warriors, Chichén Itzá

Temple 2, Tikal

The Great Eastern Court, Tikal

what they can and then make up the rest out of their imagination.'

In a letter to Bowditch, Maler gave a typical jeer in his odd English at the French efforts: 'It seems now the French are mixing then in the exploration of the Maya ruins to make up for the great failure of Désiré Charnay, which with great resources and noice [*sic*] has done nothing! They are very jealous now at Paris, and laughing at Mr. Charnay . . . ! When knowing that I did go to Tikal they did send the Comte Périgny to Yucatán and El Petén, to enquire if there are any cities remaining not yet explored by T.M.'

Charnay was the nineteenth century's equivalent of those intrepid impresarios of the remote or primitive who lead television teams into the jungles or mountains. When he arrived in Central America in 1880 he had already taken one expedition there, in the late 1850s, on behalf of the Ministry of Public Instruction. It had not produced anything very remarkable, but Charnay had a considerable reputation as a travel writer with notable qualities of intelligence, resourcefulness and leadership. A wealthy New Yorker of French origin, Pierre Lorillard, was also anxious that Charnay should lead an expedition in search of Maya ruins, and he added his backing to that of the Ministry.

Weighed down with seventy pieces of baggage, including photographic equipment and materials for making papier-mâché mouldings, Charnay, at that time in his early fifties, set off into the jungles. He had heard stories of a ruined city in a great omega-shaped bend of the Usumacinta, on the Mexican bank, and while he was in Tenosique, a small town on the lower reaches of the river, he questioned the mayor, Suarez, who claimed to have visited them in 1869, or thereabouts.

The picture drawn for him was an exciting one. The city was large and completely hidden by the jungle which clothed its terraces. In the river at its foot was a pile of stone which was believed to be the buttress of a great bridge that once

'*A travers la forêt*'. Désiré Charnay on the march (from Charnay's *Les Anciennes Villes du Nouveau Monde*)

194

spanned the Usumacinta. The river was over two hundred yards wide at that point and beginning to run fast as it headed for a turbulent drop through a grey-green throat of rocks and huge trees: ceibas, mahoganies, cedars, sapotes and palms. The falls were so rocky and dangerous that to attempt to take heavily laden canoes through them would have been very risky indeed; so Charnay decided on an overland journey to the ruins.

A great city and a great bridge which, according to Charnay's report, had never been visited by a European scholar or explorer were, as an archaeological lure, equal to Copán and its legendary swinging hammock of stone. Charnay decided to visit the site and name it in honour of his patron Lorillard, who clearly deserved some reward since all archaeological trophies recovered by the expedition were to go to the Ministry in Paris.

It seems evident that Charnay believed that the ruins might be those reported by Stephens' padre, who saw 'turrets white and glittering in the sun' from a mountain ridge overlooking the jungles. He set out in March 1882 for the Paso de Yalchilán, the crossing near the ruins, with a sizeable party. Ahead of him had gone a small group entrusted with the task of cutting and hollowing out tree trunks for the crossing. Charnay described the journey and its denouement in the book that came out of the expedition, *Les Anciennes Villes du Nouveau Monde*. British and American readers who feel they would like to know more about Charnay and his travels should be warned that the 1888 English translation is a much shortened and at times considerably changed version of the over-long original. Still, Charnay, who had visited England and had taught in the United States, must have spoken good English and no doubt he approved the translation. Like Stephens, Charnay gave his readers a good measure of dark-eyed beauties. Their sweet faces and the ample figures he observed under their transparent *huipils* (before Charnay's gaze only; no one else seems to have noticed see-through dresses in the Yucatán at that time) were several times on the point of making him give up 'ancient monuments, the world, my possible career', but, of course, like Stephens he had to produce a book for a publisher and therefore next day rode on. The Commandante of Piste, near Chichén Itzá, appears to have decided that Charnay's mind was not entirely focused on ruins. Late at night, when everyone else had gone to bed, Charnay looked up from the paper on which he was writing his impressions and saw before him 'a ravishing maiden more like an apparition than a mortal being. Was this the shade of a Maya princess conjured up by my imagination?' The 'beauteous figure' smiled at Charnay who sat dumb-struck. The spell was broken by the Commandante, who emerged from the shadows to inquire, 'You are surprised at our visit?' Charnay admitted that he was, especially at such a late hour, and the Commandante replied smoothly, 'Time is of no account when you wish to serve a friend. I heard that you required a cook. I brought you mine, that's all.' Charnay wondered at the Commandante's 'self-sacrifice' and regretfully declined the services of the fifteen-year-old cook, Josepha, to whom he slipped a coin. She in return gave him a drink from a bottle of *staventum* she was happily carrying and went her way back to Piste with the Commandante.

Drenched with quinine and fortified with an abundance of good food, Charnay strode through the jungle to the Paso de Yalchilán. In legend, at any rate, nineteenth-century English travellers sought to make the best of adverse surroundings at the main meal of the day by putting on their dinner jackets. If Charnay is typical, the more down-to-earth French merely rolled up their sleeves and ate almost as if they had never left home. Charnay has left us a luncheon menu:

Soupe: Purée de haricots noirs au bouillon d'escargots. Olives de Valence, saucisson d'Arles. Poulet de grain, sauté à l'ail et au piment rouge. Morue frite. Chives, pointes de petits palmiers en branches d'asperge. Fritures: haricots noirs rissoles. Crêpes. Fromage americain. Vins: Bordeaux et Aragon. Café, habanero et cigares de Tabasco.

Years later Ian Graham was to find an empty Bordeaux bottle at an old camp site near Yaxchilán. It's name, he learned, was Campo de los Gringos.

Hardly had Charnay arrived at the Paso de Yalchilán than his men, who had been sent to find a mule which had given up under its enormous load, produced a young boar which was received with 'joyful shouts', roasted and devoured down to the last morsel at a luncheon sitting. Recovering from this, Charnay fired shots to summon the men he had sent on ahead to build canoes for the crossing to the ruins. His inquiries, when they appeared, uncovered that they had done nothing. Taking their lead from their master, they had lived, as Charnay put it, 'like lords' on the supplies they had been given, supplementing them with better fish taken from the river than Charnay's dried cod.

The exploration and naming of the Cité Lorillard should have been the greatest accomplishment of Charnay's career, one that would have won him renown. But as he stood on the banks of the Usumacinta, he sighted a large canoe manned by three Ladinos. A 'horrible suspicion' flashed through his mind: he had been beaten to it. Another expedition had reached Cité Lorillard first. The men, he learnt, had been on a foraging expedition among the Lacandones and were returning to their master, Don Alvaredo, with nothing more than a few miserable tomatoes.

'Who is this Don Alvaredo?' he demanded.

'He is . . . well, Don Alvaredo.'

'Very well, but what is he doing there in the ruins?'

'He walks around.'

Charnay had more in his remarkable larder than tomatoes.

'Look here, my good fellows, take my card to your master with my compliments, together with half a wild pig, salt meat,

Travel by *silla* – a chair hoisted on an Indian's back (from *Les Anciennes Villes du Nouveau Monde*)

rice, biscuits, and in return ask him to lend me his large canoe, which these men I send with you will bring.'

A severe attack of malaria delayed Charnay the next day and when he was well enough to embark for the ruins he was still so weak that he could hardly sit up in the canoe. After three hours on the river he saw rising from the brown waters, like a ruined pharos, the pile of stones he had heard about in Tenosique. Charnay stumbled up the steep river-bank towards the ruins hidden by the jungle. He had gone only a short way among the ruins when he was met by Don Alvaredo, whose fair appearance (and 'elastic step', adds the English edition) revealed him at once to Charnay as an Englishman and a gentleman. The English edition continues:

'We shook hands; he knew my name, he told me his: Alfred Maudslay, Esq., from London; and my looks betrayed the inward annoyance I felt. "It's all right", he said, "there is no reason why you should look so distressed. My having had the start of you was a mere chance, as it would have been mere chance had it been the other way. You need have no fear on my account, for I am only an amateur, travelling for pleasure. With you the case of course is different. But I do not intend to publish anything. Come, I have had a place got ready; and as for the ruins, I make them over to you. You can name the town, claim to have discovered it, in fact do what you please. I shall not interfere with you in any way, and you may even dispense with mentioning my name if you wish".'

This noble indifference was clearly not meant to be condescending. It was kindly, and Charnay was touched and charmed, as everyone was by Maudslay. His nature seems to have had the sort of natural generosity and ease which instantly communicates itself and comforts. The men he employed obviously felt it, for he rarely had trouble with them. Like all good men he shaped the reactions of those he dealt with. In contrast to the ill-tempered Maler, he found his Ladinos 'truthful, good-tempered and remarkably honest'. So, wrote Charnay, 'We lived and worked together like two brothers, and we parted the best friends in the world.' Charnay named the ruins Cité Lorillard and the name had some currency for almost fifty years; the last date on which I have come across its use is 1928. Mr Lorillard had satisfaction for his money and presumably died believing that the immortal past had immortalized him. Nowadays the ruins are known as Yaxchilán, after the Paso de Yalchilán with the 'l' transformed into an 'x'.

Charnay decided that it was not after all Stephens' 'phantom city'; nor was the pile of stone part of a bridge, since there were no signs of abutments on the banks. What the stones were for is still a matter of speculation. Perhaps they supported an altar for the river god. Maudslay noted gratefully that Charnay 'kindly added his ample supply of provisions to my somewhat meagre stock'. He read Charnay's book later and thought it was 'interesting'. Maudslay was not inclined to elaborate on encounters but he found Charnay's companionship at Yaxchilán 'pleasant', which is often the reaction of shy and polite people when they are forced into acquaintanceship with strangers. They explored the ruins together and Charnay made his moulds for the Trocadero Museum in Paris, while Maudslay worked on slimming a lintel so that it could be carried up river and some 200 miles through the jungle to Belize, from where it could be shipped to the British Museum in Bloomsbury. It weighed half a ton but after a week's work with chisels and a broken pickaxe it had been reduced to a quarter of a ton. He reduced it still further later with a saw after it had been towed and paddled up stream in a canoe. It completed its journey to Belize via solid-wheeled ox-cart and a pole carried by sixteen Indians.

Maudslay named the ruins Menche-Tinamit, from other local names, and despite his remarks to Charnay, never called them Cité Lorillard. He had heard of them in Guatemala City through a Professor Rockstruh of the *Instituto Nacional*, who had visited them in the previous year and seems to have been the first person to write a description of Yaxchilán. Maudslay journeyed to the site from Cobán and then down the de la Pasión and Usumacinta rivers. It is a tranquillizing journey: the rivers carry one along effortlessly and on the whole evenly between a limited but softly beautiful landscape that repeats without a visual stammer the same trees, the same herons and macaws and little parrots, the same green turtles motionless and wary on fallen trunks and the same slow curves that prevent repetition becoming boring. On a good day the boat-men made thirty miles. In Maudslay's time, the traveller could lie in his hammock during the long tropical night and listen to one of the less soothing sounds of the river: the alligators snapping their jaws. Maudslay notes in his 'personal narrative' (unlike Maler, he was very careful to detach his own impressions from strictly factual details about ruins) on 'Menche' in the *Biologia Centrali-Americana*, a privately financed scholarly work on the region, that they noticed several signs of Lacandón Indians. Even then they were rarities, little seen by travellers, but once while they were examining a canoe a man came forward, followed by a woman and a child who kept their distance. Maudslay described him as 'an uncouth-looking fellow', with sturdy limbs, long black hair, very strongly marked features, prominent nose and thick lips. He was dressed in a long brown garment of rough material like sacking which had been marked with blots of red dye. Later in the same day they visited a *caribal*, or Indian village, which they approached along a path marked by two jaguar skulls stuck on poles. The men were away searching for wild cacao but the women received them courteously and invited them to rest. One assumes they had the normal number of breasts, for Maudslay makes no mention of the duplication which Maler's friend Herr Lederer claimed to have observed.

The Lacandóns, of whom there are now only about 150 left, are the last unbaptized Maya. In Maudslay's day and until well into this century they burnt copal and held rituals in the Yaxchilán temples. Until a decade or so before his arrival,

Yaxchilán seems to have been their main religious centre, but the collapse of an idol (probably one of the stuccoed figures the remains of which can be seen on the temple façades) led to a rapid decline in its use. On his way back from Yaxchilán, Maudslay visited the village again and this time met the men. 'I was much impressed by the striking likeness which the features of the elder man, who appeared to be the leader of the village, bore to those carved on stone at Palenque and Menche. The extremely sloping forehead was not quite so noticeable in the younger men, and it may be that the custom of binding back the forehead in infancy, which undoubtedly obtained among the ancients, is being now abandoned.' He noticed that they still used stone-tipped arrows with their bows.

Maudslay possessed a fortunate combination of wealth and scholarly tastes. He took his degree in the natural sciences at Cambridge (where he became a convinced Darwinist) and distinguished himself enough to be elected a fellow commoner of his college, Trinity, which in his old age recognized his work with an honorary fellowship. The family fortune was founded on steam engineering and Maudslay was the first Mayanist to recognize the difference the advent of the steamship and the railway had made to the exploration of the Petén and other Maya areas. The points of departure in the United States were in the last two decades of the nineteenth century only two weeks away from the jumping-off points for expeditions into the interior and it had become possible for American foundations, such as the Carnegie Institution, and universities, to undertake archaeological exploration of the area. There was still time, he urged in the *Biologia Centrali-Americana*, to record the remains and make exact copies of the hieroglyphics before climate and the mutilations of man disintegrated them. Maudslay was never principally concerned with trying to decipher the inscriptions but he was deeply aware of the need to provide materials for scholars to work on. He was only twenty-two when he first journeyed to Central America, in 1872, and satisfied an ambition to see a tropical forest, but it

A. P. Maudslay, 'My room – Chichén Itzá, 1889' (from *A Glimpse at Guatemala*)

was to be another ten years before Maya archaeology became his central interest. In the interim he served as a colonial official in the south Pacific, where he was Acting Deputy Commissioner for Tonga and Samoa. His interest in the Maya started as a result of what he called a 'journey of curiosity' to

Copán; between 1881 and 1894 he undertook seven archaeo-logical expeditions. One to Quiriguá in early 1884 taught him how detailed and exacting a thorough archaeological survey has to be, and in the following year he arrived in Copán with the best-organized and equipped expedition – not excluding Charnay's – that the Maya area had seen to that date. Mr Giuntini, a skilled plaster-moulder who was to make casts of the carvings and hieroglyphics, was brought out from England, and he was transported across the mountains together with machetes, axes, pickaxes, spades, crow-bars, wheelbarrows, surveying and photographic apparatus, dry plates and chem-icals, a barrel of lime, four tons of plaster of Paris and between four and five hundredweight of moulding paper as well as food, personal baggage and camp kit. The plaster of Paris had to be repacked at Isabal, the port, into waterproof sacks before being carried to Copán on mules. Maudslay calculated that the plaster for which he had paid fifty shillings a ton in Carlisle had cost him £50 a ton by the time it reached Copán.

Thanks to the British Foreign Office, General Bogran, the President of Honduras, was aware of Maudslay's expedition and had arranged for a commission to wait on him at Copán. He entered the village beneath triumphal arches and was surprised to find that the commissioners (an ex-minister of state and a professor) had been there for a week, much to the distress of the villagers who felt no good could come of having such people around. With great tact Maudslay managed to get rid of them after a week and then set about putting his relations with the locals on a sound footing. His gentle and sympathetic manner soon won the confidence of Copán's inhabitants. They worked hard for him and even the wheelbarrows were used successfully; in Chichén Itzá later he had great difficulty in persuading the Indians, almost proverbially ignorant of the uses of the wheel, to push them along the ground and not carry them on their heads fully loaded.

Occasional visitors turned up, including a general who followed him around the ruins, notebook in hand, as Maudslay did his best in Spanish to explain them. Before Stela A, on which a previous visitor had carved his name 'J. Higgins' in deep letters, Maudslay discoursed on the probability that one day the hieroglyphs would be interpreted. The general began to draw and after a while Maudslay glanced at the sheet of paper. He had carefully printed 'J. Hig' and was starting on the second G. 'These hieroglyphics are very much like the characters we use now,' explained the general.

Maudslay was such a diffident man that it is doubtful whether he would ever have written very much at all about his work, other than factual details of ruins, if it had not been for his wife, Anne, a granddaughter of Gouverneur Morris of American Revolutionary War fame, whom he met during a visit to California. She co-authored with him one of those anecdotal Victorian travel books which can only be described, rather pallidly, as delightful. In *A Glimpse at Guatemala* Anne persuaded him to write with expansive understatement about the work at Copán. He was hindered by an epidemic of smallpox which emptied the villages around Copán and the outbreak of a war between Guatemala and Honduras on one side and Nicaragua and Salvador on the other. Most of his labourers were conscripted and he was left with cripples and old men. Very shortly there was another problem: he was unable to obtain silver coin to pay his cripples. However, his ally in the village, the matriarchal Nina Chica, came to his aid and collected enough money from her neighbours. Everyone knew Don Alfredo well enough to accept that he would return the money once the troubles were over.

The war swirled to within thirty miles of Copán and delayed Maudslay's work by preventing him from sending the casts to Isabal for shipment to the British Museum. Finally the war ended and it was possible to dispatch the paper and plaster moulds. The paper moulds were made of a flimsy tissue like orange wrappings and so were light enough to be carried on the backs of men. The heavier plaster moulds were loaded on mules. There were about 1,400 pieces and each had to be carefully wrapped and protected with canvas and waterproof cloth. The porters' loads were packed in light crates made of a local hibiscus that had been specially cut and dried in advance, but the plaster moulds required wooden crates. When these ran out new ones had to be cut from cedar stumps with a small blunt saw an inch wide which Giuntini had brought with him for cutting plaster.

It was in every way a thoroughly bedevilled expedition, with the steam age turning a cold shoulder on the beneficiary of a steam-age fortune. Giuntini had been delayed for a month on his way from England when his ship broke her propeller shaft. Now on the way back, he and Maudslay were once again victims of a broken shaft. They drifted several days in the Gulf of Mexico until their anchor was able to find a hold on the Bank of Yucatán, where they stayed surrounded by a jettisoned cargo of over-ripe bananas until sighted by another steamer and towed into New Orleans.

Maudslay returned to Copán again in 1894 (this time with his wife Anne) at the request of the Peabody Museum, which had entered into a ten-year contract with the Honduras government to manage and explore the ruins. The Museum had carried out two years' work when John Owens, the leader of the expedition died of fever. After that tragedy the Museum was unwilling to mount another expedition and Maudslay was commissioned to take over and ensure that the contract, which stipulated a certain amount of work must be done every year, was not broken.

Anne's contributions to *A Glimpse at Guatemala* are delicate and modestly eloquent, like Victorian water colour painting. She was not very interested in ruins but she was fascinated by the scenery and the birds and animal life. Her duties at the ruins were housewifely and she has left a far better description than her husband would ever have provided of the details of daily life there. Maudslay breakfasted on a bowl of hot coffee, pan-dulce and bananas and by seven o'clock was on his way to work carrying note-books, tape-measures and drawing board. Anne attended to airing the blankets and sweeping scorpions and insects from their hut, which had a thatch of sugar cane leaves and a carpet of sweet-smelling pine-needles. The birds were her greatest delight and she would sit watching them from her 'dining room' in the shade of a spreading fig tree. There were parrots, toucans, grey jays, trogons and oropendolas, a handsome species of oriole with burnt-cinnamon plumage whose bubbling cry is the signature tune of the forest sites. There were other diversions such as the leaf-cutting ants who hold their burdens above them like green sails as they make their way back to the nest where the leaves form a humus on which the ants grow a fungus which serves as their food. Then there was a family of turkeys which she fed on gingerbread, nuts and sardine oil, but most loved of all was a squirrel, Chico, who slept in a grass saddle-bag under her mosquito net at night and by day brightened her solitude by running round the hut. Chico returned to England where he nearly perished when some louts landed from a boat at his new Thames-side home in Maidenhead and knocked him off a branch with an oar. He was revived with brandy and ammonia and a vet repaired a broken leg. Before long he was sufficiently recovered to enjoy his usual hot breakfast roll and cake with his tea.

Maudslay never worked in the field again after the Copán trip with Anne. Domesticity may have got the better of him, but on the whole it is more likely that he realized he had nothing much more to add in that direction. His intellectual overview of the work done by himself and others is interesting because of its Darwinian relationship between archaeology and anthropology and the importance he places on the inscriptions. Questions about 'relevance' were clearly as frequently posed in Maudslay's day as they are now. What did so much pioneering effort add up to in the end? Had he done more than reveal the beauties of Maya art and architecture and their natural context? What did the inscriptions add to our knowledge of history and the development of civilization? In

Maudslay's view such questions implied a narrow view of anthropology and history. He wrote in *A Glimpse at Guatemala*:

'If the study of Egyptology and Assyriology possesses a special interest to us through its connection with our ideas of religion, philosophy and art, filtered through Palestine, Greece and Rome, surely it has as well and more value, which American Archaeology shares with it, in showing the evolution of human intelligence? The civilizations of the East are known to have acted and reacted on one another, so that it is often difficult to trace things to their original source, whereas in the civilization of America the culture must to a great extent have arisen and developed in the soil, free from extraneous influence, and on this account may furnish facts of the greatest importance which the East cannot supply.'

America was the natural laboratory of anthropology, free from cultural contagions. And that, of course, has made the work on the inscriptions immensely more difficult and more challenging. They are still the challenge that keeps Maya studies alive and safe from becoming a glorified vacation exercise, a mere churning over of the well-known. There were, as I have said, two major discoveries in the nineteenth century. One was Tikal. The other took place in Madrid in 1863.

14
The Epigraphers

The first man to announce he would decipher the Maya hieroglyphs (and the first of a long line to fail) was a Franco-German from Constantinople with the improbable name of Constantine Raffinesque-Schmalz. In a letter sent from Philadelphia in 1832 to Champollion he informed the French scholar that he intended to emulate his achievements in Egyptology. But there was no Rosetta Stone of any sort at that time that would have enabled an epigrapher to even make a start on decipherment. The discovery that opened the way for a study of what remains one of archaeology's great conundrums did not come until 1863, when the Abbé Brasseur de Bourbourg found in the archives of the Royal Academy of History, in Madrid, Bishop Landa's long-forgotten *Relación de las Cosas de Yucatán*. It contained a description of the Maya calendar, drawings of the glyphs for the days and the twenty-day months and an 'alphabet' of hieroglyphic writing.

Brasseur, who was already an acknowledged authority on Central American antiquity, was understandably ecstatic. He published an edition of Landa's document in the following year and proceeded with tremendous energy and enthusiasm to write a key to the inscriptions. It was published in 1869 with the assistance of the French government. 'It is not without reason I have proclaimed my eureka,' he wrote to his sceptical fellow-countryman, the philologist Léon de Rosny, 'I am master of all the inscriptions.' Hyacinthe de Charencey dismissed such claims: the 'translations' were essentially 'fantasies'.

Brasseur's perspectives were undoubtedly affected by his conviction that the Maya came from Egypt, a belief which led him to attribute to them a far greater depth of civilization than they ever possessed. What was far worse was a fundamental error: he read the glyphs from bottom to top instead of the correct way, from top to bottom.

The glyphs are among the most beautiful works of art produced by the Maya, disciplined and yet imaginative, with the artists permitted considerable licence within the frame imposed by convention and legibility. Eric Thompson has described them as poetry, and so they are, whether or not one can read them (and so far only about 30 per cent of the glyphs have been read). It helps to understand the Maya concepts of time, but one doesn't need to know the finer points of their astronomy or the synodical revolutions of Venus to enjoy them as sculptural writing. They give pleasure in the same way as an illuminated medieval book or carved misericords, portraying forgotten allegories, beneath the choir seats in a church. And that is why I offer no apology for plunging into the calendar system now instead of relegating it to an appendix, where like most appendixes it would be noted but probably not read. The glyphs, as I have said before, are the central enigma of the Maya, and the decipherment of those concerned with the calendar ranks among the greatest archaeological achievements anywhere.

The calendrical inscription below is from the back of Stela D at Copán and the glyphs are perhaps the most expressive and beautiful produced by Maya craftsmen. The burden of time is carried by the gods who show a very human fatigue. The faces in this case signify numbers, with powers according to their position. B1 for instance, is nine bakhtuns, or nine times 400 tuns, the tun being the 360-day year the Maya used in their dates. A2 has the head of five, with a jawbone representing ten added to the face, to make fifteen. The position is that of the katun, so it represents fifteen times twenty tuns. The date falls in 736 A.D. The calendrical inscriptions used as examples are from the Classic Period when the long count extending over thousands – and sometimes millions – of years was used. By the time of the Spanish conquest that method of measuring time had disappeared and the short count of 260 tuns, or 360-day years, the katun cycle was in use.

A 1. Introductory glyph with the moon goddess, patroness of the month Ch'en in which the date falls.

B 1. 9 bakhtuns.

A 2. 15 katuns.

B 2. 5 tuns.

A 3. A barely discernible mark on the face is a hand signifying nil: no uinals (20-day months).

B 3. No kins (days).

A 4. The day of the stela's dedication in the 260-day ritual year calendar, 10 Ahau.

B 4. The sun as lord of the night rising to bear the night sky, represented by a jaguar pelt.

A 5. The day and month of dedication in the 360-day year calendar, 8 Ch'en.

B 5. Not understood.

Calendrical inscription from Stela D, Copán, from *Maya Hieroglyphs Without Tears*, by J. Eric Thompson, published by the Trustees of the British Museum.

The photograph is of a reproduction made from a cast taken by Maudslay's Mr Giuntini. The condition of the stone has deteriorated since those days.

Like other early civilizations, the Maya had difficulty relating the lunar year to the solar year. The former consists of 12 lunar months of just over $29\frac{1}{2}$ days each, making a total of $354\frac{1}{3}$ days; the latter works out to $365\frac{1}{4}$ days. Both the Maya and the Egyptians arrived at a compromise which avoided offence to either system by ending the year at 360 days and following it with 5 extra days (the Uayeb or unlucky month in the case of the Maya) to keep their solar measurements more or less straight. But whereas the Egyptians made up the deficiency in the solar year with leap years, the Maya used a complicated method of calendar correction. How they did it was finally established in 1929 by an American chemical engineer John Teeple who used the glyphs rather as lesser men use crossword puzzles, to pass the time on train journeys.

Venus – and possibly Mars and Mercury – was also the subject of centuries of observation by Maya astrologers seeking to find order in the universe to govern the arbitrary ways of men and nature. The length of the Venus synodical revolution in the heavens varies between 580 and 588 days over a span of 5 revolutions, giving an average length of 583·92 days. The Maya made it 584 so that 5 Venus 'years' equated with 8 solar years of 365 days. The discrepancy between 584 and the actual length of the Venus revolution was made up by corrections amounting to 24 days in the course of 301 revolutions, which reduced the error to one day in 6,000 years. What at first appears to be a clumsy method of keeping the calendar in step was in fact necessary to synchronize it with the ritual year (260 days) calendar. Each cycle of time had its special day in the ritual year on which it completed its revolution. For instance, the ritual and solar year calendars met together on exactly the same days at the end of a 52-year cycle of solar years. Perhaps the easiest way of visualizing the Maya time system is to imagine it as a collection of clocks, all varying in size and all synchronized with the smallest of the lot, the ritual year or tzolkin. The ritual year, incidentally, did not have months. It had 13 (from 1 to 13) numbers and 20 day names, which if you care to multiply them comes to 260 days. The numbers and the days would be used in sequence, so that you would have 1 Ik, 2 Akbal, 3 Kan, 4 Chichan and so on up to 13 when the numbers would start again and number one would attach itself to the fourteenth day name, I Men, and so on. In the second time round Ik would become 8 Ik. By the end of the year each day name would have been attached to each number. The 20-day months of the solar year were dated from 0 to 19, the Maya quite logically regarding the first day as uncompleted until it was ended and therefore not entitled to be called one. All Maya inscriptions had to carry both the ritual year day and the day of the solar year month, which is why at the end of a Maya date you will find something like 1 Ahau 3 Zip, the first being the ritual year date, the second that of the solar year. The Maya calendars are a subject in themselves and the above is simply intended to put the research on them into some sort of context, so I shall move on to the method of counting.

The Maya used a vigesimal system, that is they counted in 20s like the Anglo-Saxons. A man had 10 fingers and 10 toes. In the 360-day year calendar system there was only one exception to this, the uinal or 20-day month of which there were 18 in the year. As in our system, position gave power to numbers. For example, take the figure 1863. We work from right to left: three ones, six tens, eight hundreds, one thousand. In the Maya system the lowest power was at the bottom, the highest at the top, thus in a calendrical inscription the order came out like this:

bakhtun = 20 katuns or 144,000 days
katun   = 20 tuns (or 7,200 days)
tun   = 18 uinals (the 20-day month) or 360 days
uinal   = 20 kins or days
kin   = days

Figures up to and including 19 could be written with bars and dots as well as with faces. This is 12: ⌒⌒ The bars are worth five each, the dots one each. Zero, of which unlike the Romans, they had a knowledge, was shown like this, as a shell ⊂⫘

This door jamb from Palenque (pieced together by Alberto Ruz Lhuillier, the Mexican archaeologist) shows the two sets of symbols together:

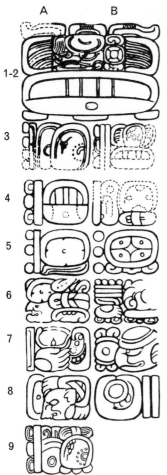

A 1–B 2. Introductory glyph to the initial series or count of the tuns. The head in the centre facing to the left of the page (the so-called variable element) is that of the patron of the month in which the date falls, Zac, the long-nosed god.

A 3. 9 bakhtuns

B 3. 12 katuns (the centre dot is ornamental and is not counted).

A 4. 6 tuns

B 4. 5 uinals

A 5. 8 kins

B 5. The day on which the date falls, 3 lamat, the day of Venus (note the star and the dots which probably denote its 4 phases).

A 6. The old sun god as Lord of the Night (Maya days began at dusk).

B 6. Lunar count showing that on 3 lamat the moon was 19 days old.

A 7. The fifth lunation of the series had been completed or was current.

B 7. Probably stellar information.

A 8. Probably more stellar information.

B 8. The moon sign indicating completion of a lunation. The 2 bars add up to 10. Maya lunar months were alternately 29 and 30 months. This one was 30.

A 9. The month position, 6 Zac. On the door jamb this glyph was separated from those given here by other glyphs. It has been moved up for the sake of simplicity.

Text with numerical bars and dots and symbolic forms of period glyphs (from *Maya Hieroglyphs without Tears*)

The date reads 9.12.6.5.8. 3 Lamat 6 Zac, which correlates with our date of 14 September 678 A.D. For those who want to work out their own correlations it may be useful to remember that most of the dates on stelae and other monuments of the Classic Period fall within 9 bakhtun, which according to the correlation I am using began on 9 December 435 A.D. It simplifies things to begin counting from there. How that correlation was arrived at I will leave for a bit later.

Brasseur never realized the difficulty of the task on which he had embarked when he tried to interpret the glyphs. In addition, he was misled by the 'alphabet' given in Landa's *Relacion*. What Landa's Maya informant did was to draw the sounds of the Spanish alphabet. Thus, the first B (Bay in Spanish) shows a footprint: *be*, pronounced bay, is the Maya word for road or journey, symbolized in this case by a footprint. X (Shay) is a man vomiting; the Maya word *xe*, pronounced shay, means vomit. Here is Landa's 'alphabet':

Landa's alphabet

The Maya script was never meant to be a means of general communication; it was used for priestly records and predictions, and, since mystery is the essence of the divine world, there was little desire and almost no compulsion to simplify it. It did evolve or change, as the codices, or books, from the post-Classic (900 A.D. to the Conquest) Period show, but it never worked on a unified principle. It seems to have elements of every stage of development in writing: pictograms, ideograms and phonetics. In addition, it may have been mnemonic, the glyphs serving to jog the memories of priests who perhaps knew from position, context and tradition what they represented. The phonetic element has received a great deal of attention recently because it can be related, despite the considerable mutations caused by time, to current Maya dialects. The Maya often used phonetics in the form of homonyms, words that sound the same but have different meanings, like 'reed' (the plant) and 'read' (the verb). To take an example unravelled by Eric Thompson: the word *xoc* in Maya means both 'fish' and 'to count', so a representation of a fish is an instruction to the reader to begin counting.

One extract – part of a medical almanac – from the Dresden Codex illustrates one form of the 'punning' method. It shows the moon goddess, who was also goddess of medicine, carrying a burden in the form of sinister birds. The word in play is *koch*. It can mean disease or fate ordained by the gods; it can also mean a burden.

To return to Brasseur: he may have been an imperfect scholar but his discoveries in the libraries were as important as those made in the field. Landa's *Relacion*, as I have said, made possible a start on decipherment. Moreover, Brasseur found the first part of the Tro-Cortesianus Codex (the Tro part belonged to a Señor Juan de Tro y Ortolano; the second part was discovered in Estramadura and called Cortesianus because its purchaser believed it had been brought there by Cortés); saved innumerable manuscripts from destruction when he was in Chiapas at the time of the suppression of the

Church by the Mexican government; was the first person to link Landa's illustrations with the Dresden and Paris codices and the Palenque and Copán inscriptions and he was the simultaneous discoverer of one of the most important Maya documents, the Popol Vuh, the sacred book of the Quiché Indians of the Guatemala highlands.

The Popol Vuh has been described by Sylvanus Morley as 'beyond any shadow of doubt, the most distinguished example of native American literature that has survived the passing centuries'. It recounts the creation myth of the Quiché. I must admit that I find it rather heavy going and not to be compared in enjoyment with the incoherent but poetic prophecies of the books of Chilam Balam. Still the Popol Vuh does give a fairly polished account of what the Maya believed about their origins. The earth was created from water by two gods and provided with animals and plants. After unsuccessful attempts to make men from mud and wood and the creation of a race so wicked it had to be destroyed by a flood, the gods finally produced the Quiché with men made from maize dough.

At the time of the Conquest the Quiché were the most powerful people in the highlands and, as a tribe, at their zenith. In 1524 Pedro de Alvarado (known as 'Alvarado the Cruel') routed the Quiché in a ferocious battle in which the Spanish commander killed the Indian captain Tecum Umam in hand to hand combat. As a result the citizens of Utatlán, the Quiché capital, sued for peace and invited Alvarado to enter. One can still see the remains of the city; in those days it was walled, as well as guarded by a deep ravine. Alvarado noted that there were only two narrow approaches, one over a causeway, the other by a flight of steps. In the town the streets were narrow and the houses lofty. An exploration revealed that the women and children had vanished and the houses were filled with combustible materials. The Quiché planned to trap the Spaniards in Utatlán and burn them alive. Alvarado withdrew quickly without revealing his knowledge of their intentions to the Quiché, whose king and leaders he lured to the plain beyond the walls. There they were executed. Another dreadful battle erupted and the Quiché were finally destroyed. But as with the Maya in the Yucatán, the old traditions made a genuflexion to Christianity and survived secretly. The authors of the Popul Vuh wrote: 'This we shall write now within the Law of God and Christianity. We shall bring it to light because now the Popol Vuh as it was called cannot be seen any more, in which was clearly seen the coming from the other side of the sea, and the narration of our obscurity, and our life was clearly seen. The original book written long ago existed; but its sight is hidden from the searcher and the thinker.'

One theory is that there was an original book written in Maya hieroglyphs that was saved from the wreckage of Utatlán and taken to the nearby village of Chichicastenango, which was later to become a Maya cultural centre. There it was re-written (with accommodations to the Book of Genesis) in Latin script before the secrecy surrounding it was broken towards the end of the seventeenth century by an inquiring, sympathetic priest Father Francisco Ximenez, a Dominican, who either heard rumours of or suspected the existence of the manuscript while he was parish priest of Chichicastenango. 'I found that it was the doctrine which they first imbibed with their mother's milk, and that all of them knew it almost by heart, and I found that they had many of these books among them . . .'

Father Ximenez's translation of the Popol Vuh into Spanish lay unnoticed in the library of the University of San Carlos, in Guatemala City, until Carl Scherzer, a Viennese doctor, visited Guatemala in 1853–4. He took a copy back to Vienna and published it there under the auspices of the Imperial Academy of Sciences in 1857. Brasseur also read the Ximenez text and published the Quiché text with a French translation (for which he relied heavily on the Dominican's Spanish translation) in 1861, in Paris, where it attracted considerably more notice than Scherzer's edition.

There are only four hieroglyphic Maya books in existence: the Dresden Codex, the Tro-Cortesianus, the Peresianus and the Grolier Codex. The Peresianus was found in a basket of old papers in a chimney corner at the Bibliotèque Nationale in Paris in 1860. Wrapped around it was a piece of torn paper with the word 'Peres' on it, and that is all that is known about its presence in Paris. The most recent discovery is the Grolier Codex. The circumstances in which it migrated from Central America to its present home in New York are almost as mysterious as those of the other three codices, but for different reasons. The Grolier Codex is a prime piece of loot found in a cave in Chiapas with several funerary objects including a mosaic mask now in the Dumbarton Oaks Collection. It went on display at a Grolier Club (hence its name) exhibition in New York in 1971 and that was the first and last time the public saw it. Since it was taken out of the country in contravention of Mexican law, the Mexican government could, and undoubtedly would, oblige the United States government to take legal action against the owner under an agreement between the two countries, if it knew who he is. So, the owner will preserve his anonymity and enjoy the codex in the privacy of his own home until it is safe to let it surface for good. It is an eleven-page fragment in fairly good condition which has not added much to the knowledge of the Maya beyond revealing that there were sixteen hitherto-unknown gods ruling the sub-phases of Venus. It has been carbon-dated to about 1250 A.D., which makes it 100 years younger than the most famous codex of the lot, the Dresden.

In 1739 the Royal Librarian of Dresden, Johann Christian Gotze, was on a foray into Italy in search of rare books and manuscripts and either on his way there or on his return he stopped in Vienna, where he was presented with the codex by 'a private person, for nothing, as being an unknown thing'. Gotze, who obviously had more discernment than the donor, marvelled at the beauty of the book and perhaps was awed by the thought of the secrets contained in the hieroglyphs. He gave it first place in a catalogue of the library's contents and stated proudly: 'Our royal library has this superiority over all

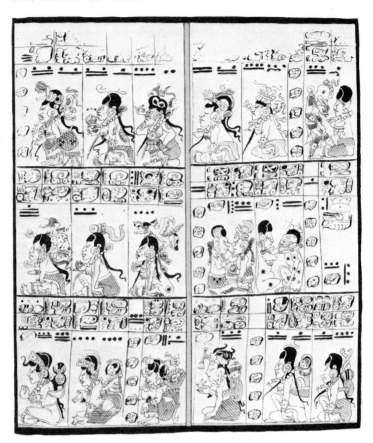

Pages from the Dresden Codex, as copied by Aglio for Lord Kingsborough's *Antiquities of Mexico*

others, that is possesses this rare treasure.' Like all the Maya books it is a long strip of fig-bark paper that can be pulled out and folded back concertina-wise like a screen. The length is eleven and three-quarter feet, the height eight inches and the page width three and a half inches. There are thirty-nine leaves, or sections, all except four of which are painted on both sides, making a total of seventy-four pages of manuscript. Its contents are best described as a combination of astronomical treatise and astrologer's almanac. Alexander von Humboldt, the geographer, published a few pages of it in the early nineteenth century and Augustine Aglio, Lord Kingsborough's Italian artist, copied it for the *Antiquities of Mexico*. On the whole, though, little attention was paid to it until the last quarter of the century when the Director of the Royal Library, Dr Ernst Förstemann, decided he needed a hobby. The son of a Danzig mathematician, he seems to have inherited his father's capacity for abstract reasoning. By the end of the century he had fathomed and pieced together the principles of the long count calendar, interpreted the extremely complicated Venus tables and discovered the base date for the lunar count. An impressed monarch rewarded him with a privy councillorship. Förstemann was the possessor of the best mind that ever applied itself to Maya studies, and like so many men of considerable intellect, he was alert and active at an age when most people have accepted dotage. He was fifty-eight when he took up his 'hobby' and he was still pursuing it actively in 1906, in which year he died at the age of eighty-four; in fact, he published no less than five papers in the last two years of his life.

To explain the principles of the calendar was a marvellous achievement, but if there had been no advance beyond that, the calendrical system would have remained dead, unrelated to our own experience of time. It was an American newspaperman, Joseph Thompson Goodman, who eventually breathed life into the calendars by correlating them with our calendar. If the long count had continued into the days of the Spanish conquest, correlation would have been simple, but as it was, the decay of the system into the short count of the katun cycle meant that the clues to the stelae dates were often misleading. Correlation still is a controversial subject; at one stage there were two rival schools of thought differing by as much as 256 years (a katun cycle expressed in solar years). The clues were found in documents, Landa's *Relación* and in sentences such as this from the Books of Chilam Balam: 'In the 13th Ahau Ah Pula died; for six years the count of the 13th Ahau will not be ended; the count of the year was towards the east, the month Pop began with (the day) fourth Kan; the 18th day of the month Zip (that is) 9 Imix was the day on which Ah Pula died; and that the count may be known in numbers and years, it was the year 1536.' Some of the clues had to be disregarded as misleading, others, such as a mention by Bishop Landa that a certain Maya date fell on 26 July 1553, were of crucial importance.

Goodman ranks second only to Förstemann among the interpreters of the calendar but he would have been deeply insulted if anyone had called him a scholar. He described himself as an 'illiterate *proletaire*' whose authority in the field was derived from years of servitude to the glyphs. A self-made man who began life as a typesetter, his character was prickly, vainglorious and not particularly attractive. He was editing a literary journal *The San Franciscan* when he was encouraged to study the glyphs; before that he had owned and edited *The Territorial Enterprise* of Virginia, Nevada, where he gave Mark Twain a start on the road to fame and formed a lasting friendship with him. Goodman was only twenty-three when he and a friend bought the *Enterprise* and he looked back on that part of his life with nostalgia: as a campaigning editor he had managed to unseat an entire Nevada supreme court bench. He also had a brisk way with rival editors. One who offended him was challenged to a duel and wounded. His staff, including Twain, had the intense cameraderie that goes with youth on small successful newspapers and dubbed themselves 'The Old Enterprise Gang'. Goodman wrote a poem about those days:

> If when we've done with earthly strife
> There be a paradise or sheol,
> Or any other named abode
> Which we may gain through love or pity
> Grant me a heavenly Comstock Lode,
> A spiritual Virginia City.

His attitude towards the academic establishment always smacked rather of a small-town editor fulminating against plots and vested interests in far away centres of power. The academics either tried to keep the glyphs sealed from the outside world like a 'hieratic mystery' or they indulged in fatuous nit-picking. As an example of the latter, he referred to the case of a 'distinguished professor' of the National Museum, in Washington, who had demanded from Maudslay a public explanation of why there was a discrepancy in the position of a sandal-string between a photograph of a stela and a drawing of it. Such people, said Goodman, had made him lose confidence in the ability of learning to solve the 'momentous enigma' of the glyphs; by contrast, he had retained faith in 'the genius of ignorance'.

The overwhelming desire of the self-made scholar to prove himself better than those with orthodox credentials was no doubt responsible for Goodman's sneers and bombast. It seems also to have led to him plagiarizing Förstemann's work and claiming several of the German's findings as his own. Goodman's correlation was largely rejected for twenty years following his announcement of it in 1906 but in time, as amended and tested by Eric Thompson, it has come to be generally accepted. The dates produced by carbon-dating wooden lintels fell within an acceptable radius of the dates produced by his calculations, while those produced by his chief rival, Herbert Spinden, another American, were a very long way out. The Maya began their calendar count from a date which in our chronology would be 10 August 3113 B.C., which was probably the beginning of a huge cycle of time consisting of thirteen bakhtuns, 1,872,000 days – a cycle in which incidentally, we are still living now and which will end if the Maya priests are correct, with the destruction of the world on 24 December 2011.

Time of their own shaping still retains its grip on the Maya. At the beginning of the 1940s, a young American anthropologist, Jackson Lincoln, discovered in the province of Quiché, where Alvarado destroyed Utatlán, that the Ixil Indians had kept the ritual and solar calendars without error since the conquest 400 years earlier. The calendars were at the centre of their existence and no less than twenty-five calendar priests were concerned with maintaining them and the ancient religion, which, although it had many Christian aspects, required sacrifices of fowls, pigs and occasionally bulls. Curiously, the Ixil, unlike their forefathers, had no conception of zero. The area was – and probably still is – a gloomy place, dominated by its semi-pagan shrines and ceremonies and the grim reflections of the past. In an ancient parish register, Lincoln came across a note by a nineteenth-century Catholic priest, Father Baltasar Baldivia, in which he lamented the strength of a native religion that regressed towards 'the old barbarism mixed with the vices and irreligion of other races'. Because of the unexplained disappearance of certain individuals, Lincoln began to suspect that the Ixil were sacrificing rather more than pigs and bulls on the days celebrating the Maya new years. However, the evidence was inconclusive and he left speculation on those lines out of the final report he wrote for the Peabody Museum. Naturally, it was not easy for an outsider to enter the world of the taciturn Ixil, but Lincoln's whole-hearted commitment to their way of life and his detailed knowledge of the calendars won him their respect. The calendar priests often consulted him as a fellow diviner and gifts were brought to him of chicken, eggs, bananas and even money. Penetrating as far as he could into every aspect of their lives, Lincoln in the spring of 1941 celebrated a festival so intrepidly that he became drunk, fell unconscious in the street, caught pneumonia (it was a chilly night) and died. After his death four Indians set out on the considerable journey to Guatemala City to inquire about the well-being of his wife and daughter, whom they had met. They did not know the address but they reasoned that one day Mrs Jackson would be bound to turn up at the central market, near the cathedral. So they posted themselves at the four main entrances and waited. Eventually she appeared on a shopping errand; the Indians assured themselves she was well looked after, and then they went home.

15

Lords of the Jaguar Mat

Time was to become almost as much an obsession with the Mayanists as it was presumed to have been with the Maya. They believed the inscriptions were, in Jacques Soustelle's phrase 'anthems to time', and little else. Goodman, in his down-to-earth American way made his calendrical reckonings in a sales ledger, rather as if the Maya had been the book-keepers of time, jotting down bakhtuns, calabtuns, kinchiltuns and the rest like the commerce of passing aeons. Time was clearly the intellectual foundation of their religion, and it was under-standable that the stelae should be regarded as monuments to chronological abstractions, even if in retrospect the idea does not seem very plausible. That idea was not thoroughly shaken until the late fifties and early sixties. In 1958 Heinrich Berlin, a Mexico City wholesale grocer, announced that he had found in the inscriptions 'emblem glyphs' which appeared to belong to specific sites. It is as if Tikal, Yaxchilán, Copán, Palenque and four other major sites of the Classic Period had run up their own flags in stone. The significance of that finding was

Yaxchilán emblem glyph

that it planted the seed of a line of thought: since the emblem glyphs might be either the names of ruling families or of the ceremonial centres themselves, there was a local significance to the stelae which indicated that they carried historical information – which was what John Lloyd Stephens had suggested 120 years earlier.

Fifteen years before Berlin presented his historical theory, Eric Thompson had amended a date on Stela 14 at Piedras Negras, which is thirty or forty miles down the Usumacinta from Yaxchilán. He changed it from Morley's dating of 800 A.D. to 761 A.D., which was not of great moment to anyone at the time, not even to epigraphers. Thompson, who was a strong advocate of a purely religious purpose for the stelae, noted that Stela 14 was the first to be erected in front of the temple where it was found and described it and similar stelae in front of other temples as showing gods seated in niches formed by the bodies of celestial dragons. Carved beneath the niches were ladders with footsteps ascending them. The apparently insignificant redating became important when several years later Tatiana Proskouriakoff, of the Peabody Museum, realized that the new reading made all the 'niche' stelae the first to be erected in front of their temples.

As Miss Proskouriakoff wrote later:

'My first thought was that the "niche" motif represented the dedication of a new temple, and that the ladder marked with footsteps ascending to the niche symbolised the rise to the sky of the victim of sacrifice, whose body was sometimes shown at the foot of the ladder. It occurred to me that if I searched the inscriptions for a hieroglyph peculiar to those stelae, I might find the glyphic expression for human sacrifice. What I found instead started an entirely new train of thought and led to surprising conclusions.'

In the books of Chilam Balam there is a reference to the enthronement of Hunac Ceel, who seized power in Mayapan after plunging intrepidly into the Well of Sacrifice at Chichén

Itzá to bring back the message from the gods. It reads in part: 'Then they began to take the prophecy of this ruler after it was declared. Then they began to set aloft the house on high for the ruler. Then they began the construction of the stairway. Then he was set in the house on high in 13 Ahau, the sixth region.' The books of Chilam Balam contain references to the 'jaguar mat' or seat of authority (the word jaguar – *Balam* in Maya – having a range of meanings that covers priests and officials as well as the animal). The figures in the niches are seated on cushions marked like a jaguar pelt. So by the time Miss Proskouriakoff was ready to develop the historical theory in a 1963 paper which was to be the heart of what Michael Coe has called 'one of the most exciting chapters in the story of New World archaeology', there was the following combination of events: a new dating, discovery of the emblem glyphs and a new light cast on a reference to the method of enthronement culled from the books of Chilam Balam. The figures in the niches were not gods but human beings, the rulers of the Maya clans and their confederations.

There were two important glyphs on the stelae which that cheerful scholar Eric Thompson (his initials appropriately spell J.E.S.T.) had named 'the toothache glyph' and 'the upturned frog glyph'.

'Toothache' or accession glyph   'Upended frog' or birthday glyph

Miss Proskouriakoff at first thought the toothache glyph was the symbol for human sacrifice, but then she discovered that the date attached to it was not the earliest on the stela. It was anything from twelve to thirty-five years later than the upturned frog glyph's date. The latter, she observed, was not such a significant date that it had to be recorded at the time; it was only thought worthy of inscribing after the toothache glyph date had been recorded. So it was a reasonable assumption that the upturned frog marked the birth or baptismal ceremonies of a ruler and the toothache glyph his accession. The years between the dates bore out the theory: the rulers had ascended to the jaguar mat in four cases at the ages of twelve, twenty-two, twenty-eight and thirty-one.

After the niche stela had been erected, new stelae were put up at intervals of five years until the ruler died or was superseded and a new series of stelae started before another temple. By comparing sets of dates, Miss Proskouriakoff found that in several cases the reigns were surprisingly long for such presumably bloodthirsty and disease-ridden times. The twelve-year-old had reigned for more than forty-seven years and the twenty-two-year-old for more than forty-two, which is considerably better than the average English monarch. Further examination of three of the stelae in one ruler's series convinced Miss Proskouriakoff that the robed figures on the backs (which others had thought were priests) were a woman, presumably the ruler's queen. The birth date in these cases was followed by the same glyphs in each case – presumably her name – with the profile of a woman's face with a lock of hair on the forehead as a prefix. On the third stela there was a small figure seated beside the robed woman and the text contained another birth date which indicated that a daughter was born to the queen when she was thirty-three years old.

Thompson was reluctant and slow in accepting the change in thinking the Berlin–Proskouriakoff findings introduced; his conception of the Maya had always tended towards the abstract. The down-to-earth Coe, on the other hand, was later to welcome the change as having swept away the 'mumbo-jumbo' surrounding the Maya. The 'chronological hypothesis' – of which Thompson was the main upholder – could not be further entertained. Yet in the next breath Coe had to admit that puzzles remained. Berlin and David Kelley had shown separately in 1965 that at Palenque the texts fell into three groups. The latest dealt with contemporary rulers; the next with ancestral kings who may have been historical; and the earliest group fell at the end of the last creation when gods emerged. So, perhaps the truth lies somewhere between the two extremes of opinion: the Maya set their kings, their marriages and their deeds on the causeway of time, the handiwork of the gods ever since a beginning that was almost beyond the grasp of man.

The Berlin–Proskouriakoff findings were taken a little further in 1973 by Joyce Marcus, of the University of Michigan, who theorized* that the Classic Maya world was more formally arranged than generally supposed. On the evidence of emblem glyphs found at Copán and Seibal combined with 'locational analysis', she proposed that Tikal was the grand ceremonial centre, or 'capital', and possibly had dynastic links with other major sites which were geometrically positioned to correspond with the *bacabs*, the divine brothers who bore the sky in the north, east, south and west. The evidence is flimsy, but the theory is an interesting one.

A few years before Berlin had announced his discovery of the emblem glyphs, a young specialist in the evolution of language had published a paper which was to be of equal importance in understanding the glyphs. His 'eureka' was made with acknowledgments to the inspiration of Marxist–Leninism (a point which irked some established Mayanists, who considered it unprofessional, or, at the least, unnecessary) and it came from Russia, a country which had never before contributed anything worthy of note in the annals of Maya studies. Yuri Knorosov decided that while Landa's 'alphabet' regarded as a simple ABC was indeed misleading it might make more sense if approached as a syllabary, perhaps with similarities

* In *Science* (Magazine of American Association for Advancement of Science), 1 June 1973.

to an oriental script combining ideographic and phonetic elements. In 1952 he put forward the proposition that the Maya used two and sometimes three phonetic syllable signs joined together to make one word. This combination reads *tzul*, dog, according to Knorosov.

Tzul – dog glyph

The first part, which represents a slaughtered dog (the Maya, like other Central American Indians, sacrificed and ate dogs) is pronounced *tzu*, and the second part represents a freshwater fish called *lu* in Yucatec Maya. Knorosov also identifies it as the second 'l' sign (pronounced *ele* in Spanish) in Landa's 'alphabet'. Together that makes *tzu-lu*, with one vowel too many. The Maya, whose words are often monosyllabic, merely dropped the last vowel sound to make *tzul*. The same principle, says Knorosov, applies to all their phonetic signs.

Knorosov's chief critic has been Eric Thompson, who was considerably incensed by the Russian's claim to have found the key to decipherment. Using the *tzul* sign for his counter-argument, he pointed out that *tzul* was a word introduced after the Spanish conquest to describe new breeds of dogs never seen before by the Maya. The common Maya names for dog were *pek*, in Yucatec, and *tz'i* in most other dialects. Knorosov also allowed himself too much latitude on sound values, said Thompson, who has accused him of 'playing poker with deuces wild' (Coe, on the other hand, has hailed Knorosov's work as a 'breakthrough'). Knorosov, for his part, has said that the opponents of phonetic readings succeeded in nullifying all the achievement of 'the French school of decipherment', with the result that the few correct readings were almost entirely ignored.

Despite the critics, many of Knorosov's readings have won

acceptance. This one is a compound of three syllable signs which he reads as *chucah*, capture.

Chucah – capture glyph

It can be seen on one of the Yaxchilán lintels where two warriors are depicted in the act of capturing their defeated enemies. The glyph is followed by another which appears to be the name of one of the prisoners, Jewelled Skull. Elsewhere there is another glyph which is probably the name or emblem of one of the victors, a bird crouched on top of a jaguar's head.

As absolutely nothing is known about the history of the Classic Period (apart from the brief legend about Copán being founded by a ruler from the Yucatán) anything that throws some light on events then is grasped at. The jaguar clan's glyphs appear in Piedras Negras, suggesting that Yaxchilán ruled there or commanded its neighbour's allegiance. What may have been the symbol of their dominance, a huge jaguar on its hind legs with one paw extended protectively over the head of a seated figure, occurs in eighth-century carvings both in Piedras Negras and Tikal. Did they carve out an empire for themselves? Certainly at that period there was a considerable uniformity of artistic style. Another question emerges: was their militarism a factor in the decay of the Classic civilization during the ninth century?

In relation to achievement, the work done on the glyphs has been excessive. There is no open sesame to their secrets although there remains a hope that some day someone will feed the right formula into a computer and the right readings will come tumbling out. The Russians tried computers at the Novosibirsk Research Centre with Knorosov's interpretations and had to admit defeat; at the present time the University of Mexico's Centre for Maya Studies is compiling a computer catalogue of glyphs found in the Dresden and Madrid codices and on pottery. Other approaches are based on reconstructions of the Maya dialects spoken at the time of the Spanish conquest. And, of course, there is the Peabody Museum which has taken on the stewardship of the Guttman Foundation's project for a Corpus of Maya Inscriptions as a stepping stone for deciphering them.

Intriguing though they are, Maya inscriptions remain an arcane subject. No feat of epigraphy by Miss Proskouriakoff or Eric Thompson has managed to capture the imagination of this century in the same way as the plumbing of the Well of Sacrifice or the discovery of a rich tomb deep within the Temple of the Inscriptions at Palenque. Only an American would have had the engineering resource and the impiety in the 1900s to think of exploring the well with a dredge and diving suit, which is what Edward Thompson did. He followed in the footsteps of Stephens by taking on a consulship as a means to the end of exploring the Yucatán ruins. An article by him in *Popular Science Monthly* in 1879 entitled 'Atlantis Not a Myth' attracted the attention of Stephen Salisbury, Vice-President of the American Antiquarian Society, who decided that his enthusiastic, energetic temperament was what was needed for a new post he had in mind – Investigator of Ruins in the Yucatán. Charles Bowditch, of the Peabody, agreed to join in the venture and a friendly senator made sure that Thompson would have a reasonable income and diplomatic protection by persuading President Cleveland to make him consul in Progreso. Probably no man suffered more in the service of archaeology than Edward Thompson: his eardrums were damaged by diving into the Well of Sacrifice, recurrent bouts of 'jungle fever' rendered him prematurely bald, he was lamed by one of those Maya traps armed with a poisoned thorn from a fox's body and his toes were crushed by a falling idol. A letter from him to Bowditch in 1904 mentions that his hands were swollen and cracked from constant immersion.

However, the findings in the mud of the cenote were almost worth any kind of suffering; trunkloads of treasures were sneaked out to the Peabody past the Mexican customs by what he called 'my underground railroad'. A disgruntled Maler managed to halt his work at one stage and the Mexican government grew increasingly suspicious of what they regarded as looting.

Thompson spent forty-two years in the Yucatán. After exploring the country thoroughly, he decided to buy the hacienda, or plantation, of Chichén Itzá, whose land included the ruins. He had come across Landa's reference to the Well of Sacrifice and from the moment he read the Bishop's 'quaint old Spanish' in that 'musty old volume' the thought of that 'grim old water pit' and the treasures concealed in its depths became an obsession. As Thompson was to write in *Popular Science Monthly*-style prose in his book *The People of the Serpent*:

'... in times of drought, pestilence, or disaster, solemn processions of priests, devotees with rich offerings, and victims for the sacrifice wound down the steep stairway of the Temple of Kukil Can, the Sacred Serpent, and along the Sacred Way to the Well of Sacrifice. There, amid the droning boom of the *tunkul*, the shrill pipings of the whistle and the plaintive notes of the flute, beautiful maidens and captive warriors of renown, as well as rich treasures, were thrown into the dark waters of the Sacred Well to propitiate the angry god who, it was believed, lived in the deeps of the pool.'

Thompson was a 'frequent worshipper' at the shrine on the brink of the pool. He made measurements and soundings and established that the pool was almost 200 feet across, sixty feet from the rim to the water, and forty feet from the surface to a ten-foot-thick layer of mud on the bottom. His announcement at a scientific conference in the United States that he intended to dredge the well brought protests that he could not expect to descend into its depths and emerge alive. Undeterred, Thompson with typical thoroughness underwent a course in deep-sea diving at the hands of Captain Ephraim Nickerson, of Boston. He had already estimated where a beautiful maiden or warrior of renown was likely to have hit the water by cutting logs to their approximate sizes and weights and having them hurled in from the edge. Apparently assuming that they would sink like stones, he termed the area below where they fell the 'fertile zone'. It was in that area that his dredge, suspended by cables spanning the pool, took its first mouthful of mud.

'I doubt if anybody can realise the thrill I felt when, with four men at the winch handles and one at the brake, the dredge, with its steel jaw agape, swung from the platform, hung poised for a brief moment in mid-air over the dark pit and then, with a long swift glide downward, entered the still, dark waters and sank smoothly on its quest. A few moments of waiting to allow the sharp-pointed teeth to bite into the deposit, and then the forms of the workmen bent over the winch handles and muscles under the dark brown skin began to play like quicksilver as the steel cables tautened under the strain of the upcoming burden. The waters, until then still as an obsidian mirror, began to surge and boil around the cable and continued to do so long after the bucket, its tightly closed jaws dripping water, had risen, slowly but steadily, up to the rim of the pit.'

For days nothing was brought to the surface beyond sherds of pottery, mud, the debris of fallen trees and the bones of deer and jaguar. Thompson began to wonder if this was indeed the Well of Sacrifice. Perhaps he was squandering the money put up by the backers like the Peabody. And then one grey morning after a sleepless night he walked through the misty damp to the well's edge where the men were already working the dredge. There, sheltering under a palm-thatch lean-to, he noticed on top of the bucket as it swung to the shore two yellowish nodules. Examining them, he thought at first they were bog butter and then remembered that, unlike the ancient inhabitants of Europe, the Maya kept no cattle. He tasted a fragment and found the material was resinous, so he put a larger piece in the embers of a fire and instantly a rich odour of incense rose up. 'Like a ray of bright sunlight breaking through a dense fog came to me the words of the old *H'Men*, the Wise Man of Ebtun: "In ancient times our fathers burned the sacred resin – *pom* – and by the fragrant smoke their prayers were wafted to their god whose home was in the sun".' That night Thompson slept long and soundly, assured that he was dredging the right cenote.

The next stage of exploration entailed descending into the muddy depths accompanied by Nicholas, a Greek sponge diver from the Bahamas. Torch in hand and with submarine telephone attached, Thompson shook hands all round as he took the first plunge from a pontoon that had been lowered into the cenote. Feeling only slightly more secure than the sacrificial victims who had preceded them, they explored the bottom, acutely aware of the pressure waves from several huge rocks that fell from the walls. One of their first discoveries was the skeletons of 'three poor women' in a place which a local *H'Men*, or priest, had pointed out to him as the palace of the rain god. Once Thompson floated up to the surface by accident and without warning, striking the bottom of the pontoon with a loud thump and terrifying the workmen who were certain it was the rain god himself.

All Thompson's finds went to the Peabody: gold discs showing Toltec warriors in action, jade, axes, copper and gold jewellery, carved stone, pottery, engraved bones and shells and fragments of cotton. But success was followed by disaster. His hacienda was burned down, his crops destroyed and his cattle driven off by left-wing rebels during one of Mexico's frequent revolutions. 'Much of the fruit of my long life of studies and economics went up in a whirlwind of smoke and ashes,' he wrote. The worst loss was his library, with a vast store of material on the Maya.

That senseless destruction was followed by a long period of depression in which Thompson suffered great mental anguish. He recovered and rebuilt the hacienda which he hoped eventually to turn into a hotel (an idea realized later by others), with part of the plantation as a tropical plant research station. However, the odds were against him. According to his account, the Mexican government listened to rumours that gold worth half a million dollars lay hidden at the bottom of the cenote and as a result attached his property for the sum of 1,300,000 pesos. Eventually an arrangement was worked out whereby the Carnegie Institution took over the hacienda and continued Thompson's research work. The disheartened explorer of the Well of Sacrifice left the home and the ruins he had cherished and returned to the United States to live in retirement at West Falmouth, Massachusetts.

I suppose one can associate Edward Thompson in his diving suit with Hunac Ceel, one diving into the Well of Sacrifice in search of the gods, the other hoping to find the treasure left for them. Alberto Ruz Lhuillier, too, delved downwards in the trail of a Maya celebrity, although in Ruz's case he was not sure what he was looking for when he started and his course took him through the core of the pyramid of the Temple of the Inscriptions at Palenque. It was a very laborious excavation he undertook; from 1949 until mid-1952 he and his fellow-workers bored downwards along a rubble-filled stairway towards one of the richest and most remarkable finds in the history of Maya archaeology. Maya pyramids are often a series of superimpositions, one generation adding to the work of another. Buildings grew by accretion, as in the case of the Nunnery at Chichén Itzá, where Dr Augustin Le Plongeon (an American 'archaeologist' of the nineteenth century who believed Christ's last words on the Cross were spoken in Maya and, on the evidence of some lines he saw on an inscription, that the Maya had invented the electric telegraph) employed dynamite to blow down a wall and found himself face to face with another even more solid wall. Ruz began his excavation as a search for an inner pyramid and temple. The Temple of the Inscriptions had never been explored before. It is named after a text in the temple of 620 glyphs, one of the longest examples of Maya writing and one which, if it could be read, might explain a great deal about those who created such a strangely distinctive culture there in the first millennium A.D.

Ruz had been struck by the fact that the floor of the temple, seventy feet above ground level, was composed of large well-fitted stone slabs instead of the usual stucco surface. While examining the floor he noticed that one of the slabs in the central chamber had a double row of holes carefully filled with stone plugs. He came to the conclusion that the holes were there so the slab could be lowered into place. Presumably it hid an entrance. The stone was raised and revealed a vault and the beginning of a stairway which had been filled in with earth and heavy rocks. Clearing it was to take Ruz and his assistants four periods of two and a half to three months. It was monotonous work as they moved down the first forty-five steps to a U-bend which took them into yet another flight of twenty-one steps. At the top of the staircase they found an offering of two jade ear-plugs and at the bottom, where they were more or less on the same level as the temple plaza, they found another offering consisting of a pearl, shells filled with red paint, jade beads and pottery. They had reached the end of the stairway and now the excavators were confronted by a fresh series of obstacles. A wall that sealed off the stairs from a passageway was demolished, revealing another barrier of heavy stones and cement. Beyond that, at the end of the passageway was a great triangular slab with the skeletons of six youths at its foot. Their heads were deformed in the ancient manner and traces of decorative fillings in their teeth suggested they were the children of Palenque's nobility, not their slaves. Ruz wrote:

'On June 15th, 1952 we were able to make the stone turn and we entered the mysterious chamber we had been so eagerly seeking since 1949. The crossing of the threshold was, of course, a moment of indescribable emotion. I was in a spacious crypt that seemed to be carved in ice since its walls were covered with a shiny calcareous layer and numerous stalactites hung down from the vaults like curtains and thick stalagmites gave the impression of huge candles. These calcareous formations were produced by rainwater filtering through the pyramid for over a thousand years. The crypt was nearly nine metres long by four metres wide and its vault almost seven metres high, reinforced by enormous polished black stone beams with yellow veins which looked like wood. The construction of the chamber was so perfect that its stability remained completely unaffected by the course of the centuries even though it also supported the weight of the pyramid and the temple. The stones of the walls and vault were cut with such care that none had moved from its original position.'

Around the walls of the tomb were the stucco reliefs of the nine lords of darkness, all slightly larger than a life-sized Maya and all dressed identically, with headdresses of quetzal feathers, capes of feathers and jade plaques, jewellery and short skirts with belts decorated with three small human heads. Each held a manikin sceptre, with the face of the rain god and the foot in the shape of a serpent, and a round shield with the features of the sun god. Ruz was not sure at first what he had found. Occupying most of the floor of the chamber was a magnificently carved slab, measuring twelve and a half feet by seven and a quarter. Was it an altar or the lid of a sarcophagus? He tended to think it was the former. One way of making sure would have been to raise it and reveal what, if anything, was beneath it, but that presented problems and dangers he did not want to face unnecessarily. It rested on an almost equally large slab which in turn was held up by six stone supports. Ruz decided to determine whether the bottom slab, which was about three feet seven inches thick, was hollow. A workman drilled downwards from places where there were no carvings and on the second attempt broke through into an inner space. A wire was inserted through the hole and was withdrawn with traces of red paint adhering to it. Ruz knew he had found a tomb, not an altar. Red is the colour of the east in Maya cosmogony, the colour of the rising sun which is the symbol of immortality. The lid had to be raised, a formidable task because of its five-ton weight and the impossibility of introducing machinery into the chamber.

The sarcophagus lid is one of the most remarkable and certainly the best-preserved of the large Maya carvings. It is not in my opinion in the same artistic league as the Copán stelae or the magnificent stucco heads found inside the tomb, but it is very beautiful and intriguing. Ruz is of the opinion that the central figure represents not an individual but a symbol of humanity or perhaps the corn god, but Miss Proskouriakoff's revelations about the Piedras Negras stelae seem to me to throw that view open to doubt. The curiously limp figure which leans back at the foot of the cross gazes upward in what appears to be devotion at the sacred quetzal bird who, perched on top, wears the mask of the rain god, with whose worship the cross is associated. The posture is unusual; the man appears to be young, reclining awkwardly on the head of an earth monster, part of which resembles the tomb with its overlapping lid imposed on the thicker slab beneath. The hands are limp and half closed and the head lolls back on one of the prongs that enclose the seat. It brings to mind a foetus, which supports Ruz's view that the carving represents rebirth and the cycle of life, with the man, like the cross – which is either a maize plant or a tree – being born out of a germinating seed.

While they moved slowly down the rubble-filled stairway towards the tomb, Ruz and his workers had noticed a hollow stucco pipe that followed the treads from beneath the slab in the temple floor to the triangular stone which blocked the entrance to the chamber. On the other side it led to the great carved sarcophagus that occupied most of the floor of the chamber, a hollow serpent through which the spirit of the

Bas-relief on tomb, Temple of the Inscriptions, Palenque (drawing by Augustin Villagra)

god-king could breathe and communicate with the priests in the temple when the time came for them to deliver their oracular messages.

The thought of the contents of the hollow beneath the lid stirred Ruz almost as much as the discovery of the chamber itself. He spent twenty-four hours without leaving the site or sleeping while the lid was raised with lorry jacks set on tree trunks at the four corners. As it rose there came into view a shallow omega-shaped cavity in the lower slab; it was the second lid of the sarcophagus and like the great flagstone on the temple seventy feet above the chamber there were stone-plugged holes – four in this case – by which it could be lifted. As soon as there was sufficient space, Ruz slipped between the slabs and removed two of the plugs. Shining his torch through one of them while he looked through the other he saw, a few inches from his eye, the jade-covered skull of the occupant. The inner lid was lifted off and there was the skeleton of a man about five feet eight inches who had died – according to the evidence provided by an examination of his bones – when he was between forty and fifty. This then must have been the great lord of Palenque, the man who ruled at the zenith of its fortunes, a Maya Pope Julius buried in a pyramid with a jade mask over his face. What a pity that Waldeck, Del Rio, Dupaix, Charnay and a host of others never knew as they clambered, vibrant with speculations, among the ruins of the treasure beneath their boots, of the cryptful of myth-making possibilities within the pyramid of the Temple of the Inscriptions. But perhaps it is just as well it was discovered by a twentieth-century Mexican. Otherwise, by now a Stephens or a Maudslay might have slimmed the sarcophagus lid with saws and axes and arranged for it to be carried away in pieces by ox-cart, bongo and poles borne on the shoulders of Indians for transportation to New York or the British Museum. As it is, one can see it where it was placed more than 1,200 years ago, and that is very much better than seeing it in a museum.

16

A Foot-soldier of Anthropology

If Teobert Maler has an heir in the Petén jungles he is Ian Graham, a tall, rather solitary Englishman who is perhaps the last of the explorer-archaeologists. He works, like Maler, under the aegis of the Peabody, of which he is a research fellow and, again like Maler, he finds great pleasure in the beauty of the jungle, where he spends about half the year. The other half finds him at the Peabody, but eventually he plans to live most of the time in the Petén, making his home a house on a rock overlooking Lake Petén-Itzá. It was Graham's catalogue to an exhibition of Maya hieroglyphic writing in New York which first interested me in the Maya, not so much because of a sudden response to their art, but through his brief history of their archaeology. At this point I should emphasize that in other respects Graham is completely unlike Maler. He is hospitable and generous in his view of humanity; and really, I suppose, when one looks beyond the actual circumstances of his work, he is in most ways more like Maudslay than Maler. I doubt whether Maler would have welcomed me to his camp-site in as kindly a fashion as Graham did one February at Yaxchilán; and I doubt whether he would have been quite as co-operative as Maudslay if I had been a twentieth-century Charnay burdened with massive amounts of equipment and a determination to rename the place after my patron.

The best way to reach Yaxchilán is by canoe but if one is pressed for time one can charter a light aircraft in Villa Hermosa or Tenosique and fly in to the bumpy grass landing strip, dipping over the forested hills streaming with mist, low over the cocoa-brown Usumacinta and then down into a narrow gully of trees and rocks. Graham had a champa on the banks of the river in which he kept his belongings and slung his hammock alongside those of his Ladino crew. A champa is an open-sided hut, thatched with palm and very airy. At night the forest seems to breathe over you and its sounds amble or skitter gratingly by; sometimes the denizens do that as well. The word *champa* is so like the Swahili word used in East Africa for a hut, *shamba*, that I wondered if it had been brought to Central America by slaves imported into Belize. That is not such a far-fetched derivation as it might seem at first glance, since I had come across a reference in a book of reminiscences by a nineteenth-century doctor to a Negro greeting him in the Yucatán with the Swahili salutation *jambo*, but it seems to be as Maya, or Central American, as a tamale.

Graham was close to fifty when I met him at Yaxchilán, but the jungle and bachelorhood must be preservative, for he looks forty, a lean good-looking man who has not accumulated much fat. The elastic step and fair looks which made Maudslay instantly recognizable to Charnay as an Englishman are also denominators applicable to Graham – although strictly speaking he is a Scot, not an Englishman. His father is Lord Alastair Graham and his grandfather was the Duke of Montrose. However, Graham was born and bred in England and regards himself as an Englishman, dismissing as 'a bit spurious' any attempt to call him a Scot. No doubt a study of Galindo, whom he has written about, taught him the dangers of importing a romantic background into the jungle. It is best to be a bit prosaic and not to attempt to match the exotic with the exotic. Otherwise, I imagine, delusions of one sort or another begin to grow during the long nights under a palm thatch.

Yaxchilán has changed a little since Maudslay's and Charnay's days there but not too much. There is the airstrip, of course, and a large patch of ground cleared for the chief custodian to build his huts, grow fruit trees and fatten a few pigs who snuffle among the shale and around a huge ceiba tree, but otherwise the forest still cloaks the ruins. While I was watching the pigs with that sort of calming interest which pigs more than any other domestic animal produce in the observer, I noticed that the round stones scattered about their territory which I had assumed in a vague way without thought were old millstones were in fact Maya altar stones. Yaxchilán is like that: casually rich. It has never been excavated and its virginity is so carefully preserved by the Mexican government that the custodians have not been permitted to dig latrines. Graham was hoping to combine latrine-digging with a supervised excavation but the Mexican government was unwilling to give its sanction. Graham's record is impeccable enough, but one cannot altogether blame the Mexicans, I suppose, in these days of looters. All sorts of bogus latrine-diggers might arrive once a precedent had been established. Well, perhaps not, but that is the way the mind of bureaucratic nationalism works when it begins to think about the dangers to its patrimony.

Graham was working there, when I arrived, on drawing and photographing the carvings and inscriptions on the stelae and lintels. It is the same sort of work he has been doing ever since he came to the Maya area in 1959 as a private archaeologist (he has his own money), was 'bitten' by the place, as he puts it, and stayed on. There has been a steady progression from amateur, gentleman-archaeologist into today's horny-handed professional with the status of Director of the Maya Hieroglyphic Inscription Study. It seems a far cry from what he once considered becoming: a fashion photographer. It took Graham longer than it takes most men to decide where he was going, but now, there he is, more contented than the majority of fifty-year-olds, among his ruins and carved stones. Life, however, is hardly idyllic and the hazards include armed site robbers, the famous *esteleros* of Central America who cut up the stelae and ship them in pieces for sale abroad to museums

Daily Telegraph Magazine

Ian Graham

and private collectors. This makes Graham's life not only dangerous at times but professionally difficult, since the inscriptions can be so damaged that it is impossible to record them accurately, even if the stones are found later; and it is also very hard to trace their provenance and exact position, both of which are important, as Miss Proskouriakoff's studies at Piedras Negras demonstrated. So Graham's role has become that of guardian as well as recorder. Two years or so ago his detective work led to two stelae stolen from Machaquila in the Petén being recovered by the Federal Bureau of Investigation, one from a dealer in Santa Fé Springs, California, the other from Little Rock, Arkansas. They had been taken from their site to Belize and then shipped from a remote bay by an American fishing-boat captain to a Texas port.

There are 180 known Maya sites and, at the last count, 1,322 inscribed stones, some of them in museums and private collections. Graham's work is funded by the Stella and Charles Guttman Foundation (which I mentioned in the last chapter) of New York, whose involvement in hieroglyphics is largely due to one of its directors, Edgar Brenner, an energetic Washington lawyer whose enthusiasm for things Central American runs to having shirts patterned with pre-Columbian designs. Brenner's great ambition is to see the hieroglyphs deciphered and he was the prime mover behind the concentrated effort which began in 1967 with a meeting in New York of scholars and interested organizations. The meeting's chief immediate result was a decision to reproduce all the available material in a Corpus of Maya Inscriptions (named in the tradition of the nineteenth-century Corpus Inscriptionum Graecarum and the Corpus Inscriptionum Latinarum). When he completed the preliminary study in 1969, Graham estimated the work would take him sixteen years. He now thinks that was an underestimate. 'I'll carry on as long as my legs do,' he said one evening. After all, Maler was well into his sixties when he was working for the Peabody. And Waldeck? How old was he? Secure in that tradition, Graham looked quite content at the thought of an old age spent among the rattlesnakes and *esteleros* of Central America.

The site robbers could have put an end to that prospect in 1971 when one of his guides, a forest guard from Tikal, Pedro Arturo Sierra, was murdered with two pistol bullets in the chest near La Naya, in the Petén. It was evening and they were making camp at the time. No one saw the murderer but it was evident that Graham and his guides had run into a gang of looters. Something similar had occurred at the same place two years earlier when a man was shot by a police party. Poor Sierra died almost at once and Graham spent the night hiding in the forest with his other guide, 'full of gloomy thoughts, as you can imagine'.

Graham's protective attitude towards the sites has earned him hostility in some unexpected quarters too. A Washington chest surgeon described to me his reactions after he had been run off several sites by custodians acting on the instructions of Graham who objected to the materials he used in making moulds of stelae. The surgeon, who always carries a gun in the Petén, found himself in the same hotel as Graham at Flores. It is a pleasant hotel by the lake, with the rooms in thatched cottages perched on stilts. In one of them Graham could be heard typing a report, so the surgeon stood immediately below and said in a loud voice, 'I wouldn't mind putting a bullet through the floor of that bastard Graham's room.' That, according to the surgeon, brought Graham down in a hurry for an inconclusive argument about the surgeon's moulding methods.

Perhaps violence is contagious in the Petén, affecting even Washington chest surgeons. Most archaeologists have been confronted with it at some time. A new dimension to the region's hazards has been added recently by Communist guerrillas who see the stelae as a source of revenue. A Californian lady arrived at the Itzimte site to find it occupied by a guerrilla gang dressed in police uniforms and armed with automatics. They abandoned work on the stela they were sawing off and left after she informed them she had told the genuine police in the near-by town of La Libertad where she was going.

The devastation of the sites has caused what Karl Meyer, an American writer, has called the 'Maya crisis'. Pre-Columbian art sells in the United States and Western Europe for prices that make the risks profitable for the *esteleros*. A stela is not exactly in the Rubens or Gauguin class but a good specimen will fetch £30,000. Some are destroyed by clumsy robbers, others have been lost overboard from canoes, but in general it is in the *esteleros'* interest to take care. Usually the stelae are sawn off at the base and slimmed before the inch-thick slab of inscriptions and carving is cut with a saw into square pieces, rather like a bar of chocolate but without indentations between the segments. That makes it more transportable (and easier to hide when it is being taken across country or through customs) and it can easily be stuck together later with epoxy resin. The marks are not easily discernible. 'I tell you, you wouldn't know the difference,' a New York dealer told me once.

I admit to mixed feelings about the looters. It is pleasant to be able to stroll round the Dumbarton Oaks collection ('stuffed with loot', I am told by an authority) in Washington, and look at things which otherwise I would have to go to Mexico City or Guatemala City to see. Are such things more appreciated in those last cities? Hardly. Have the citizens of those countries a right to them? Well, in a way, yes, since they are found in their territory, but there seems to be no reason why sales should not be regularized. At the moment nothing leaves Mexico or Guatemala legally. Obviously the wholesale removal of, say, Copán's stelae from their site would be a disaster equivalent to the sale of Stonehenge's megaliths to some distant museum, but there are stelae, carvings, pottery and so on to spare. Why not an exchange system between museums, as was suggested to me by Graham: Greek vases for Olmec masks? But I doubt whether any sane solution based on acceptance of the idea that there is a universal right to enjoy the creations of the past will emerge for some time. The greed of foreign buyers has produced chauvinism, but beyond that there is indifference and corruption. You can still get what you want in Guatemala City, I am told, provided you have the right money.

Graham's champa had a neat, deserted look on the February morning when I arrived. His four Ladino porters and boatman had gone down-river to cut a trail to our destination, a small temple near a place known as La Pasadita, the little passage, where Graham wanted to remove a section of murals from the inner walls. The original trail which led from the opposite bank, the Guatemalan side, was rather long and one had to pass through thickets of bayonette bamboo, an unpleasant thorny plant which grows near rivers. The men came back in the late afternoon, the chugging of the outboard engine and the shouted greetings of the men to the custodians of the ruins audible long before the dugout, pushing its way against the fast current of the swollen river, nosed into the foot of the steep, muddy bank and was tied to an overhanging tree. They had brought back with them five cojolites, black, turkey-sized birds with red throats, which one of them had shot with an elderly ·22 rifle. They slipped and clutched their way up the bank with the birds held clear of the mud, the boatman, tall, fringe-bearded and lame, arriving last of all. Graham congratulated them on their work and the birds and they stood rather shyly in a group looking pleased.

I was to see plenty of cojolites later. They live rather noisily in the treetops where their black silhouettes show up far too clearly for their own good. Two of those the men brought back were kept and plucked – the tail feathers retained by the boatman to fan the fire – and the remainder given to the chief custodian, Don Juan, who had earlier brought a gift of bluish salted wild pork (which some animal stole in the night) and a dish of boiled armadillo, which tasted rather like rabbit. He came off rather badly in the exchange of gifts, it struck me when I tasted the cojolito, which was boiled slowly overnight and ended up tough and almost tasteless except for a slight saltiness.

We were lucky really to have a man with a gun since the authorities on both sides of the river were alarmed by the spread of guerrilla movements and as a result guns were more closely controlled than before and ammunition was hard to get. Graham explained that if there wasn't a gun in your party it meant a rather limited diet since you had to live on what could be carried. With a gun, there might be not only cojolites but faisans (which is the Spanish for pheasant) and tinamoos, a partridge-like bird which Graham said was the best of the lot for eating. Sometimes in the jungle there were brockets and the larger white-tailed deer to be seen and one often heard and saw peccaries, the small wild pigs. They are quite fierce and can be enraged easily if one barks like a dog. A man Graham knew had barked at a herd and then ducked behind a tree with his machete at the ready until a boar rushed past him, whereupon he sliced off its head. Another Ladino had told him how he had been sitting in a tree overhanging the river with his rifle when he saw a jaguar swimming towards him quite unaware of the danger. Jaguars take readily to the water and often swim across rivers in search of game or a mate. The man waited until the jaguar was beneath the tree and then shot it.

The tracks of animals, and sometimes the smell of them, were always noticeable near the *aguadas*, or waterholes. There would be a multitude of delicate prints left by peccaries, the larger tracks of white-tailed deer, the splodged three-toed imprint – more like a bird's than an animal's – of tapirs. Both puma and jaguar tracks, the former with four toe marks, the latter with five, were common. Some time later I met at Flores, the capital of the Petén, a Californian professor who at the request of a wildlife organization was making a jaguar survey. He was surprised to find that in this age of endangered species, they were really holding their own very well. 'They used to be much fiercer than they are now,' said Graham, noting that they rarely attacked anyone. Occasionally one comes across a palm-covered hide ten feet up a tree, the skull of a wild pig at the foot all that remains of the bait a hunter left for a jaguar.

In a mood of zoomorphic transposition, I thought of the swimming jaguar when I went for an evening dip in the river, struggling hard against the current and then drifting down fast to the moored dugout, a hollowed-out cedar trunk thirty feet long and three feet across in the middle. Above was a vine-covered tree entwined with flowers and harbouring orchids and clumps of bromelias in the angles of its branches. Hummingbirds serviced them like the tiny staff of an arboreal hotel, rising slowly with invisible wings parallel to the trunk until they found the right flower, then darting away. A pair of macaws with pointed wings and long tails flew across the river keeping perfect station, one a fraction behind and to one side of the other, and settled in a tree above the chamba where they sat and observed the scene with unexpected silence. The jaguar, I thought: one moment superbly afloat and then nothing, except, perhaps, a future on the back of a tycoon's wife.

In the evening, supper finished and in my hand a glass of rum into which exactly half a packet of whisky-sour mix had been stirred, I said to Graham that I hoped I wouldn't disturb the usual pattern of his life too much. He looked thoughtful and sat back in his collapsible chair.

'No, I won't say it. Oh, well, I might as well. There is a great camaraderie between the men and myself and having another English-speaking person with you does tend to upset it. We work together and share the chores, and there's no question of sitting apart from them and having a drink, as we are now. They're marvellous people. I've never known one who was lazy or unhelpful. Yes, I must say I'm very unwilling to take along another English-speaking person.'

He sat even farther back in his chair, uncomfortable for a moment, some fraction of Maya time away, not a Great Cycle exactly but one of its lesser divisions.

One goes to bed early in the jungle since it is hard to read in comfort and anyway one often feels rather more tired than usual, and around nine o'clock we unrolled our sleeping bags in our hammocks and adjusted the mosquito nets. The hammocks were the Yucatán type, with the nets held in a long box by cross-sticks, the ends of the hammock protruding like the bows of galleys. One sleeps in a curtained palanquin of cotton net, curled a little like a Polish boiling sausage if the ends are badly strung, but on the whole comfortably, with the stars at dead of night faintly visible through a pearly mist of net. Graham played some fifteenth-century French songs on his portable record-player before we went to sleep and the voices

of counter-tenors rose through the forest trees in an unexpected lullaby for the macaws.

Graham, I noticed, lived out of suitcases and Pears' soap
cartons. The latter, he explained, were chosen 'because English
cardboard boxes are stronger than other makes'. In the morning the cartons and a blue case with a gold trelliswork design
were all packed into jute sacks that had been waterproofed
with natural rubber and turned into packs with shoulder straps
made from the bark of a vine. The packs containing our food
and belongings for four days, photographic and mural-
removing equipment and two large pieces of hardboard to
form a protective sandwich for the fragile plaster murals
were stowed in the middle of the dugout under a tarpaulin.
The crew sat sensibly in the stern of the canoe, which they
boarded first, while Graham and I crouched in the bow where
we were drenched by the lukewarm spray as the boat leaned
over the saucer-lips of whirlpools and bumped, lurched and
skidded over submerged rocks and through rapids. The Usumacinta runs very fast through the gorge below Yaxchilán
as it drops down to the plain that stretches all the way to the
marshy shores of the Caribbean. I understood why Charnay
had arrived by land. It is possible to travel up and down the
rapids with an outboard but with paddles it would have been a
very arduous business, perhaps impossible in a heavily laden
canoe.

A walker in the jungle can usually cover a league, a local
measurement of two-and-a-half-miles, in an hour, providing
the trail is reasonably good. The Central American forests can
be extremely boring, but around Yaxchilán the ground is
broken and rocky and the trees are high and varied, sending
out roots like gorged anacondas to trip one up. There are, too,
innumerable thorns and hooks to catch in the flesh and clothes.
One tree which always seems to grow where one has to stretch
out a hand for support at the top or bottom of a slope has a
trunk entirely covered with spines two inches long that break
off near the top. 'Once,' said Graham, as we rested beside an

aguada from which we had without comment or hesitation cleared the green surface slime to drink, 'I met an American clanking through the forest in a green armour of anodised aluminium.' He reflected on the occasion he had taken a girl student with him on an expedition, a clever girl given to abstract thought about unsolved Maya problems but not very good at seeing what was in front of her nose. 'She was always being swept off her mule by branches,' he recalled. 'She said she wasn't really conscious of pain but I noticed she was always going "ooh! ow!" as she fell against thorns and things.' He was mildly contemptuous of over-theoretical people and pointed out that while his mind was often a complete blank as he walked through the forest he could at least see what was in front of him quite clearly when it came to examining a Maya stone. He prides himself on being practical. 'I think I might have been an engineer,' he replied when I asked him whether he had ever thought of taking up some other career. 'I've always liked engineering.'

We camped at La Pasadita in a rickety champa that smelt as musty as an abandoned haystack, but there was compensation in the site, which overlooked a reedy lake in which the porters caught small, bony fish with hooks they had providentially brought along. The bird life was as rich as at Yaxchilán: toucans in the trees above the champa, russet-chested kingfishers and at dusk a strange hawk that swept slowly over the lake crying 'Ahoy!' in the hollow, unhappy tone of an old man talking in his sleep. There was another bird, the puhuyak, a relation of the whip-poor-will, whose call, sounding like 'Who are you?' presented Graham with a philosophical question which he said he always found hard to answer. In the Maya legend, the puhuyak guards the gates of Xibabla, the place where the spirits of the dead gather. Perhaps by the time of arrival one would know the answer to the question. Shortly before dusk and close after dawn the trees were etched in a moist, calm light and it was easy to see why Victorian engravers loved jungle scenes. They were made for one another.

Graham supervised our diet with housekeeperly frugality. When everything has to be carried on someone's back, food is doled out carefully. Graham sliced the salami (handing out the pieces on the end of a knife), made the porridge from instant oats and served it in enamel mugs, and with great care preserved salt, sugar and Fab washing powder in small, soggy packets. We almost ran out of maize flour for making tortillas. There was a noticeable muttering among the men and Graham looked despondent. 'One shouldn't run out of things like that,' he said. But as it happened, one of the men had brought along some supplies of his own which Graham bought from him. Tortillas and frijoles, the black beans that Latin Americans love, were the staples of our diet. There is a nightmare in every frijol for those not used to them, but like the tortillas they are sustaining.

Despite Graham's eulogy at Yaxchilán on the Ladino character, the men were not notably active. Long after 5.30 a.m., the very latest time at which the day starts in rural Central America, they were still dreaming in their hammocks, leaving Graham and me to light the fire. 'Never in all my experience, which is considerable, have I ever before had to light the fire myself,' I heard Graham complaining to Aurelio, the guide. 'It must be these river folk,' he said to me afterwards. 'They seem rather lazier than the others.'

It was a remote place and only one person, an old man with a rifle, a brindled cur at his heels and a large clay pot wrapped in sacking on his back, passed along the trail while we were there. Graham had failed to find the temple when he first searched for it in 1970, but he returned the following year with Aurelio and located it without much trouble. The temple was a cottage-sized building on a rocky acropolis with a low cliff on one side. A sapote tree stood close beside it, the slim trunk cross-hatched with a chiclero's machete slashes like the lacing on a high boot. It was a bright, airy place – a relief to walk up to after the dankness of the champa. Beyond it were the blue-green ridges of the Sierra Lacandón, from which a breeze blew sparkling the leaves of the trees growing on the temple roof, their roots gripping the stones like the talons of hawks.

La Pasadita was an outpost of Yaxchilán, a solitary temple with a small plaza in front of it and a few buildings. The lake was probably the reason for it being there. Lintels – the carvings of which face downward and are protected from the rain – are often the best-preserved sculpture such places possess. Those at La Pasadita had been torn out some years before, carried down to the river in portable pieces, shipped by canoe to an airstrip and then flown to Mexico. Graham had traced one of them to the Museum of Folk Art in Leyden, Holland. In the temple floor and in front of it were the holes dug where the looters had searched for the graves and the treasures of priests and noblemen. One of the porters found a shallow three-legged dish that had been 'sacrificed' before burial with a hole smashed through the middle. Graham shook it and in one of the legs a seed rattled, probably a sapote seed of the sort used in diviners' rattles. One can never see exactly what the Maya saw but at least it is possible to hear exactly what they heard. The temple was a dangerous place to work in. An Arab curtain of adventitious roots from the trees on the roof fringed the entrance and had to be carefully cut away so that we did not dislodge more masonry as we went in and out. There were four rooms and in the temple's ninth-century A.D. heyday all had been limestone plastered and painted with murals of priests and noblemen, gods and sacred animals. Perhaps there had been accounts of actual events, as in the murals found at Bonampak – not far away – in 1946, where power, pain and death are associated so dramatically in a painting of prisoners being judged and sacrificed that one knows that this was the ultimate Maya reality as the painters saw it. Fear is the emotion that comes through, but there is also a horrified sympathy with the victims, and the picture is held together and given an unexpected touch of sorrow amid its harshness by the central figure of a dead prisoner, lounging and almost casual

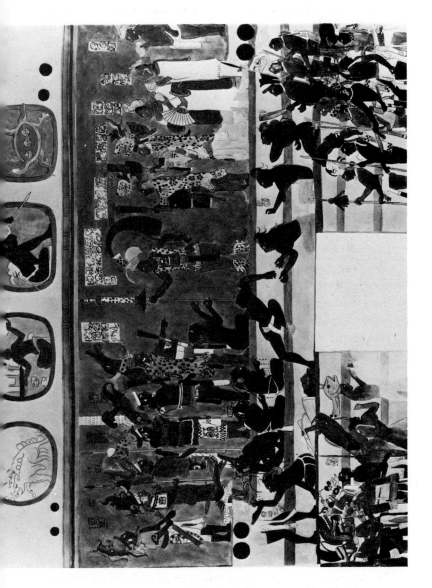

Mural from Bonampak, Chiapas, Mexico, copied by Tejeda

in the looseness of recent death. Nothing like that was to be seen at La Pasadita, but the Guatemala Museum had no murals of any sort and the few hard-to-discern figures on the walls and ceilings had value in scarcity. They were painted in red haematite, indigo and a yellow earth dye and until the doorways crumbled, opening up the front of the temple, must have been visible only by the light of torches. 'Like Ghirlandaio's frescoes, they were painted for the eyes of gods, not men,' said Graham when I asked him why the Maya priesthood had gone to such trouble to paint murals they could never see properly.

It took him three days to remove two small pieces. First he applied five coats of varnish with a spraygun and a brush to provide tensile strength to the surface. After that came two sheets of Japanese mulberry paper applied with hide glue followed by two thicknesses of linen stuck on with more glue. The covering took so long to dry in the humid air that we lit fires in the temple and then worried about dehydration bringing everything down around our ears. Graham's tools were a hacksaw blade without a handle, a serrated knife and a Turkish clasp-knife with a wooden handle that I had brought along. At the end of the three days the murals were pulled away from the wall with only a small piece or two missing. 'The Duke of Devonshire was being shown Syon House,' said Graham, kneeling and examining the linen-covered murals, 'and he was told in great detail about the richness of the stucco, the depth of the ormolu, how much ivory was used and so on. And at the end of it he said "Splendid! Do you know I have always wanted my boy to be a dentist. I do so admire good workmanship".' He was always busy. While the varnish or glue dried he paced the plaza measurements and jotted down notes in a small black notebook. The physical side of the life appeals to him, the sweating over stones, even the cooking. 'Where else today could an archaeologist lead such an adventurous life?' he demanded when I asked whether he had ever considered working elsewhere. 'It's such an active life, too. Always doing

258

something, making maps, taking compass bearings, walking, lifting up stones to see what's on the other side. Not that it's just adventure one's after. I like what the Maya did. I couldn't feel the same way about the Aztecs.'

It is possible to imagine archaeology as a rather saprophytic profession, the living existing on a dead past, but it is surprising how seldom it is. The past is as much a part of our continuum as we are. Graham takes a humble view of his work. 'Someone once described archaeology as the past tense of anthropology, and I think that's true. I regard myself as a foot-soldier of anthropology.'

When the removed murals were ready they were placed in the hardboard sandwich and carried down to the canoe. When I was in Guatemala City a year later I went to the National Museum to see them in their new setting and found that the museum was closed as the roof was falling in. That's a fairly indicative story, really: despite a great deal of angry clamour over the looting of the country's heritage, the government is less than careful of its antiquities and spends a niggardly amount on their preservation. For a country with as much to show to the world as Guatemala, the National Museum is a disgrace.

We spent two days on the Usumacinta and de la Pasión rivers travelling to Sayaxché, a village on a ferry crossing where the murals could be stored until they could be flown to Guatemala City. Occasional passengers, including a speckled hen, joined us from the co-operative farms newly established on the banks. Now that we were beyond the Yaxchilán rapids, Graham and I sat in line ahead near the bows on collapsible chairs that raised us to rather stately eminence, like colonial district commissioners on tour. Unless he is a misanthrope like Maler, an archaeologist working in a poor country becomes involved with the people and their needs. He is looked up to, depended upon. We stopped so that Graham could repair Aurelio's radio and take a photograph of his open-sided farm-house on the Mexican side of the river. He had put a great deal of work into his farm, but was being forced to move because of a government ban on the burning of milpas, a system of agriculture which is perhaps as good as any other in the jungle, but which governments are discouraging because of the smoke caused by vast acreages of burning forests in April and May, and because it is regarded as wasteful.

Farther on we stopped to take another photograph with Graham's Hasselbladt, of a baby this time. Graham hovered around the baby, coaxing it with sweets, moving her several times to find a better light, but she began to cry and the picture session was not very successful. Graham said, 'Once I was asked to take a picture of a dead baby, and that wasn't so pleasant.' He sat bareheaded in the strong sun reading a Mexican novel for most of the time, but broke off now and then to tell anecdotes as vaguely inconclusive as the river itself. Snakes were on our minds rather. One had snapped its teeth into Aurelio's trousers and a *fer-de-lance* had missed me by only two inches.

'When I travelled on the river for the first time, the canoe was paddled by two men. Paddling can be very slow because the current is strong and the dugout heavy, so one keeps close to the river bank where it is usually easier, particularly if you are going upstream. There was a snake curled up on the bank and as we went by quite close to it, it slid into the water and swam straight towards us. They have been known to board boats and I was terrified. But one of the men put down his paddle and raised his rifle and shot it as it swam. A magnificent shot, really, because he had been paddling all day and must have been tired, and the canoe was rocking too.'

As we passed a threadbare hut in a clearing, he remembered:

'I called in there once to see a man whose photograph I had taken nearly 12 years ago when he was lying in his hammock. There he was, still lying in his hammock, looking much older and haggard, and I gave him the photograph and asked if he recognised the face. "Ah, that man is dead," he said. "I knew him once." I thought he was speaking figuratively until he said something about the man having been killed by bandits in Mexico, and then I knew that so much time had passed – and perhaps there was no mirror in the house – that he didn't recognize himself.'

An overgrown settlement came up on our right and cued Graham for a story about an Englishman called Reynolds, who had lived there thirty or forty years ago. He had been a 'rather lowly officer' in the Indian army and when he retired he joined a lumber company and established himself on the banks of the Usumacinta. The company went bankrupt and Reynolds found himself left with little more than his house – built on a Maya hut mound – an Indian wife, several children and a view of the river. He was always talking about 'going home' and he could have borrowed the fare, but 'I suppose he was very honourable really. He had his wife and his children and he didn't want to leave them. So he stayed there and died.' Later I came across an account by Maudslay of an elderly Englishman who lived in much the same area in the 1890s and like Graham's Mr Reynolds had been an officer, or, at least, had given Maudslay 'unavailing hints' (how the Englishness of that phrase reaches out) that he had been commissioned in the British army. He lived there because 'the climate suited him', and he made a little money by taking photographs. Unlike Mr Reynolds, Maudslay's Englishman went – with help from Maudslay – to Guatemala City, where the 'poor old fellow' died in the infirmary.

I thought for a while that Graham's Mr Reynolds must be the same man and that Graham had confused the dates, but, no, there were two rather similar Englishmen in the same neighbourhood. An American writer, Louis Halle, had met John Reynolds in the 1930s while travelling the Usumacinta and tried as best he could to answer his questions on how the Boers were behaving themselves in South Africa. Except for an absence of teeth, Halle thought he might have passed as an

English cabinet minister. His wife served them a meal without speaking or understanding what Reynolds was saying as he poured out the misery he had felt when he realized he was trapped, unable to leave his children. Between him and Guerrero, ignoring Cortés' blandishment four centuries earlier because of his 'three beautiful boys', there was a bond.

Graham, seated behind me, was silent again, deep in his Mexican novel. One can be 'bitten' by a place in many ways: by love, by necessity, through personal failure, by a deep and only partly understood compatibility between the psyche and the place. Mr Reynolds' hut receded and then was lost behind a bend. There was nothing again but the river with its green turtles and herons, as motionless as they had been when the Great Cycle of time began almost 5,000 years ago and no doubt as they will be when it has ended.

BIBLIOGRAPHY

The bibliography of the Maya is dauntingly large. This selection is intended to acknowledge my biggest debts and to assist those who may want to explore further into the background and history of the Maya.

THE MAYA
Michael Coe, *The Maya* (London and New York, 1966).
Michael Coe, *The Maya Scribe and His World* (New York, 1973).
Sylvanus Morley, *The Ancient Maya* (Oxford, 1946; Stanford, 1956).
Alberto Ruz Lhuillier, *The Civilization of the Ancient Maya*, National Institute of Anthropology and History, Mexico City (Mexico, 1970).
Frances V. Scholes and Ralph Roys, *The Maya-Chontal Indians of Acalán-Tixchel* (Oklahoma, 1968).
J. Eric Thompson, *The Rise and Fall of Maya Civilization* (London; Oklahoma, 1956).

MAYA LITERATURE AND HISTORY
The Book of Chilam Balam of Chumayel, translated by Ralph Roys (Oklahoma, 1967).
Popol Vuh, translated by Delia Goetz and Sylvanus Morley from the Spanish of Adrian Recinos (London: Oklahoma, 1950).

EXOTIC THEORIES
Lewis Spence, *Elephants and Ethnologists* (London, 1925).
Sir Grafton Elliot Smith, *Atlantis in America* (London; New York, 1924).

SPANISH SOURCES OF THE SIXTEENTH AND SEVENTEENTH CENTURIES
Bernal Díaz del Castillo, *True History of the Conquest of Mexico.*
Diego Lopèz de Cogolludo, *History of the Yucatán.*
Hernando Cortés, *Letters to Charles V.*
Bishop Diego de Landa, *Relación de las Cosas de Yucatán*, as translated with notes and comments by the Abbé Brasseur de Bourbourg (Paris, 1864) and Alfred Tozzer, The Museum (Cambridge, Mass., 1941).
Bernardo de Lizana, *History of Yucatán.*
Bernardino de Sahagun, *General History of the Things of New Spain.*
Juan de Villagutierre, *History of the Conquest of the Province of the Itzá.*

THE SPANISH CONQUEST
Frans Blom, *The Conquest of Yucatán* (Boston, 1936; reprinted New York, 1971).
Robert Stoner Chamberlain, *The Conquest and Colonisation of Yucatán, 1517–1550* (Carnegie Institution, Washington, 1948).

Charles St John Fancourt, *The History of Yucatán from its Discovery to the Close of the Seventeenth Century* (London, 1854).

Lewis Hanke, *Aristotle and the American Indians* (Indiana, 1970).

Irving Leonard, *Books of the Brave* (New York, 1964).

Philip Ainsworth Means, *History of the Spanish Conquest of the Yucatán and the Itzá* (Cambridge, Mass., 1917).

W. H. Prescott, *History of the Conquest of Mexico.*

L. B. Simpson, *The Encomienda in New Spain* (University of California, 1950).

NINETEENTH- AND TWENTIETH-CENTURY TRAVELLERS, ARCHAEOLOGISTS AND SCHOLARS

Frederick Catherwood	Victor von Hagen, *F. Catherwood, Architect-Explorer of Two Worlds* (Barre, Mass., 1967).
Désiré Charnay	Désiré Charnay, *Les Anciennes Villes du Nouveau Monde* (Paris, 1885; English version, 1887); *Cités et Ruines Americaines* (Paris, 1863).
Juan Galindo	Source material: articles by William Joyce Griffith, *Hispanic-American Historical Review*, Vol. 40, Feb. 1960; and by Ian Graham, *Estudios de Cultura Maya*, Vol. 3, 1963.
Lord Kingsborough	*Antiquities of Mexico*, 9 volumes (1830–48).
Teobert Maler	*Memoirs of the Peabody Museum*, Vol. 4, Nos. 1, 2 and 3 (1908–10).
Anne and Alfred Maudslay	*A Glimpse at Guatemala* (London, 1899); archaeology section of the *Biologia Centrali-Americana* (by Alfred Maudslay) (London 1897).
Sylvanus Morley	*In Search of Maya Glyphs* (Oklahoma, 1971); see also Robert L. Brunhouse, *Sylvanus Morley and the World of the Ancient Maya* (Oklahoma, 1971).
Antonio Del Río	*Description of the Ruins of an Ancient City Discovered Near Palenque, in the Kingdom of Guatemala* (London, 1822).
John Lloyd Stephens	*Incidents of Travel in Central America, Chaipas and Yucatán*, 2 volumes (London, 1841; reprinted New York, 1969); *Incidents of Travel in Yucatán*, 2 volumes (London, 1843; reprinted New York, 1963); Victor von Hagen, *Maya Explorer, John Lloyd*

	Stephens and the Lost Cities of Central America and Yucatán (Oklahoma, 1947) and *Search for the Maya* (London, 1973).
Edward Thompson	*People of the Serpent* (Boston and New York, 1932).
Jean Frederic Maximilien Comte de Waldeck	*Voyage Pittoresque et Archeologique dans la Province de Yucatán* (Paris, 1838); Mary Darby Smith, *Recollections of Two Distinguished Persons: La Marquise de Boissy and the Count de Waldeck* (Philadelphia, 1878); source material: articles by Howard Cline in *Acta Americana*, Los Angeles, Vol. 5, Oct.–Dec. 1947; and by von Hagen in *Natural History*, New York, Dec. 1946.
The Walker–Caddy Expedition	David Prendergast, *Palenque: the Walker–Caddy Expedition to the Ancient Maya City, 1839–40* (Oklahoma, 1967).
Other works	Louis Halle, *River of Ruins* (New York, 1941): Robert Wauchope (ed.), *They Found the Buried Cities: Explorations and Excavations in the American Tropics* (Chicago, 1965).

NINETEENTH-CENTURY HISTORICAL BACKGROUND

R. A. Humphreys, *The Diplomatic History of British Honduras* (Oxford, 1961).

Nelson Reed, *The Caste War of the Yucatán* (Stanford, 1964).

Mario Rodriguez, *A Palmerstonian Diplomat in Central America: Frederick Chatfield, Esq.* (Arizona, 1964).

HIEROGLYPHICS

Charles Brasseur de Bourbourg, Manuscrit Troano. *Études sur le Systéme Graphique et la Langue de Mayas* (Paris, 1869–70).

Joseph T. Goodman, 'The Archaic Maya Inscriptions' published in *Biologia Centrali-Americana* (London, 1897).

Ian Graham, *The Art of Maya Hieroglyphic Writing* (exhibition catalogue with introduction and notes, published by the Peabody Museum and Center for Inter-American Relations, 1971).

Yuri Knorosov, 'The Problem of the Study of Maya Hieroglyphic Writing', *Americam Antiquity*, Vol. 23.

Jackson Lincoln, 'The Maya Calendar of the Ixil of Guatemala', Carnegie Institution, *Contributions to American Anthropology and History*, Vol. 7, Feb. 1942.

Sylvanus Morley, *An Introduction to the Study of Maya Hieroglyphs* (Washington, 1915).

Tatiana Proskouriakoff, 'Historical Implications of a Pattern at Piedras Negras', *American Antiquity*, Vol. 25; 'Lords of the Maya Realm', in *Expedition*, published by University of Pennsylvania, Vol. 4.

John Edgar Teeple, 'Maya Astronomy', Carnegie Institution, *Contributions to American Archaeology*, Vol. 1.

J. Eric Thompson, *Maya Hieroglyphic Writing: an Introduction* (Oklahoma, 1960); *Maya Hieroglyphs without Tears*, British Museum (London, 1972).

INDEX

abstinence, sexual 28–9, 34
Aglio, Agustine 120, 220–1
agriculture 33, 182, 260
Aguilar, Geronimo de 33–5, 47–9
Ahkimpphol 93
Ake, battle of 56–7
Alexander VI, *Pope* 49
Almendariz, Ricardo 108–9, 122
Altar de Sacrificios 19 (map), 185–6
Altun Ha 19 (map)
Alvarado, Pedro de 49, 55, 217–18,
   224
Alvarez, Pedro 66
anahtes, *see* books
animism 24
antiquities: removal of, from sites
   141–2, 153–5, 157, 184, 195, 200,
   219, 234, 236, 245–9, 256, 258–9,
   (Maler's condemnation of) 189–90,
   234; rise of interest in 107–8
architecture 108–9, 113, 159
Aristotle 70
art, Maya 28–9, 42, 61, 107, 165–6,
   210, 232, 256, 258; and religion
   74; at Copán 146, 149–51, 240; at
   Palenque 114–15, 240; destroyed
   by Bp. Landa 73, 77; elephant
   controversy 111–12; Puuc style
   159; sources of 112–13
Avendaño, Andrés de 82, 95–100,
   102–3, 107
Aztecs: civilization of 24, 28, 34, 84;
   'living Aztec children' 143–4

Bacalar 19 (map), 169–70, 173
Baldivia, Baltasar 224
baptism 99
Barnum, P. T. 118, 143
Barrera, José Maria 168
Beanham, William 130

beetles 156
Belize 19 (map), 94, 103, 125–7, 129,
   134, 166, 172–3, 184, 200, 244
Belize R. 19 (map), 125
Berlin, Heinrich 226–7, 229–30
Bernasconi, Antonio 108
Bernouilli, Gustave 184, 189
blood 26, 74, 165–6
boats 128
Boca del Toro 135
Bolonchén 24
Bonampak 19 (map), 256–7
books (anahtes) 37, 73–4, 81–2, 95,
   103, 216–21, 233; destroyed by Bp.
   Landa 73–4
Bowditch, C. 96, 190, 192–3, 233
Brasseur de Bourbourg, C. 192, 209–
   10, 215–18, 265
Brinton, D. G. 13
British: in Belize 94, 125–6, 136,
   166–7; in Mexico and Yucatán 121;
   relations with Cruzob 169–75
Byron, George Gordon, *Lord* 117

Cabot, Samuel 157–9
Cabrera, Felix 109
Caddy, John 128–31, 155, 265
Calderón, José 108
calendrical system 15, 28, 38–40, 43,
   60, 66, 79, 95, 181–2, 209–15,
   221–5
Campeche 19 (map), 47, 62, 66, 94,
   101, 162, 164
Can (*later* Martin Francisco Can) 95,
   98, 101, 103
Canek 82, 86–91, 95–6, 98–103, 163;
   temple of 82
cannibalism 83, 85
Canul, Marcus 172–5
Cape Cotoche 19 (map), 47–8

267